THE IONIAN ISLANDS AND EPIRUS

Landscapes of the Imagination

Landscapes

THE IONIAN ISLANDS AND EPIRUS

A *Cultural History*

JIM POTTS

Signal Books
Oxford

First published in 2010 by
Signal Books Limited
36 Minster Road
Oxford OX4 1LY
www.signalbooks.co.uk

A catalogue record for this book is available from the British Library

ISBN 978-1-904955-65-8 Paper

Cover Design: Devdan Sen
Typesetting: Devdan Sen
Cover images: © Maytree/dreamstime.com; Netfalls/shutterstock.com; Netfalls/dreamstime.com (flaps).
Illustrations: (c) Jim Potts pp. 4, 12, 29, 78, 83, 103, 116, 159, 165, 166, 171, 183, 192, 234; dreamstime.com pp. 1, 26, 41, 55, 177; istockphoto.com pp. i, 43, 91, 125, 128, 139, 144, 207, 210; shutterstock.com pp. 202, 203.

Printed in India

Contents

Preface & Acknowledgements

I first came to Corfu in the summer of 1967, as I had been offered a teaching position on the island. In December 1967 I received a letter from Sir Maurice Bowra, Warden of Wadham College Oxford, my old college, saying "Nobody could blame you for teaching at a school in Greece. What I rather dislike is people going there for a holiday and saying how splendid it all is" (29 December 1967). His comments had a bigger influence on me than I realized in that first year of the Military Dictatorship. I lived and worked in Northern Greece for five years, from 1980 to 1985. I've been resident in Greece again (in Corfu and Zagori) since the end of 2004. When not living in the country, I've been coming almost every year since 1967, so I've seen many changes. My wife is a Corfiot and a true Ionian Islander. Her mother came from Paxos, her father from Zakynthos, but she was born in Corfu. She has written two inspiring and challenging books about Corfu, one in English, one in Greek.

There are in fact 32 Ionian Islands, large and small, of which 13 are inhabited: Othoni, Erikousa, Mathraki, Corfu, Paxos, Antipaxos, Lefkas, Meganisi, Kastos, Kalamos, Ithaca, Kefalonia and Zakynthos. Kythira, although once considered part of the Seven Islands or Eptanisos, is no longer treated as one of the Ionian Islands administratively or geographically.

This book is aimed primarily at a British, North American and Australian readership. I hope it will offer visitors, English-speaking residents and interested tourists from other countries new insights into many aspects of the cultural histories of the Ionian Islands and Epirus. I have tried to adopt an international approach.

The combined populations of the regions of the Ionian Islands and Epirus may only represent just over 5% of the total population of Greece (NSSG, 2008 figures: 580,358 inhabitants out of 11,213,785) but what an impact that 5% has had!

The publication of this book nearly coincides with the 200th anniversary of Byron's visit to Epirus (Prevesa, Nicopolis, Ioannina and Zitsa, 29 September- 3 November 1809) and of the British capture of Zakynthos, Kefalonia, Ithaca and Kythira, which occurred between 2 and 9 October 1809. To adapt the words of Horace, the captive Ionian Islands eventually made their uncouth victors captive. The Ionian Islands became part of the Greek State in 1864, Ioannina and most of Epirus in 1913 (the

Arta district, with Thessaly, had been ceded to Greece in 1881, as a result of the decision of the Great Powers and of the Treaty of Berlin).

⌘

I wish to express my special thanks to the following, amongst many others, who have provided information, insights and inspiration: Maria Strani-Potts, Dr. Kostas Kardamis, John Gill, Brenda Stones, Themis and June Marinos, Demetrius Toteras, Komninos Zervos, Frixos Tziovas, Yannis Pieris, Alexandros Papadatos, Nikos Grigoropoulos, Lena Koronaki, Stephanos Rizikaris, Ian Chessell, Peter Prineas, Paul Cummings, Zoe Kominatos, Raul Scacchi, Gioia Maestro, Pinelopi Mitsi, Demetrios Dallas, the Staff of the Mitchell Library, Sydney, and the Staff of the British Library, London. I also wish to thank all those writers from whose works I have quoted.

A note on the spelling of names

Readers will come across many variant spellings and some inconsistencies in this book. When giving direct quotations, I have retained the spellings used by the writers cited. I have not been systematic in my own usage, preferring Kefalonia to Cephal(l)onia, Ithaca to Ithaki, Cavafy to Kavafy, Capodistrias to Kapodistrias, Nicopolis to Nikopolis, but Komnena to Comnena, Corfu to Kerkyra, Kythira to Kythera or Cyther(e)a, Lefkas to Levkas, Lefkada or Leucadia, Vido to Vidho, Ioannina to Yannina, Janina or Giannena, Prevesa to Preveza, Metsovo to Metzovo, Pasha to Pacha, Epirus to Ipirus or Epiros, Pindus to Pindos, but Dramisios to Dhramisius, Corfiot to Corfiote, Suliot to Souliote, Epirot to Epirote, Chimariot to Chimeriote (but Gardikiote rather than Gardikiot, Parghiote or Parginote rather than Parghiot), Chams to Tsams, Hormovo to Khormova(o), Nekromanteion to Necromanteion, Frosini to Phrosini or Phrosyne, kleft to klepht, Palaiokastritsa to Paleokastritza, Serafis to Seraphis, Aghios to Agios or Ayios.

At times I use alternative or older forms of names for islands (Zante as well as Zakynthos, but not Zacynthus, Cerigo as well as Kythira, Santa Mavra/Maura, as well as Lefkas, Leucas and Lefkada, Corcyra as well as Corfu). Zakynthians are also referred to, interchangeably, as Zakynthiots and Zantiots. It is my hope that the patient reader will not find the many transliteration permutations too confusing or irritating!

This book is dedicated to Jack, Ella and Théo, in the hope
that it will help them to appreciate an important part of
their cultural inheritance.

Introduction

For 42 years I have been trying to develop a deeper understanding of Greek culture. Almost every day I have discovered something new or astonishing.

Greece remains a source of endless fascination. What makes a Western Greek, or an Ionian Islander, different from a Greek from the mainland? What distinguishes a Corfiot from a Kefalonian? With so many Epirots living in Corfu (including the descendants of those who had to flee from Parga and Suli in the nineteenth century), with so many Kythirans living in Australia, it is not even clear what we mean by a Corfiot, a Kythiran or an Epirot. The sea-channel between Corfu and the coast of Epirus is not wide. Lefkas is attached to the mainland. Culturally the islands could have been worlds apart.

To the Corfiot critic and poet Erotokritos Moraitis (in "Solomos"), the identity of the *gigenis Dhitikos Ellinas* (native Western Greek) is self-evident and significant, an identity largely unrecognized in Modern Greece, which has given much greater emphasis to the Anatolian, Oriental, cultural influences. For the Zakynthos-born poet Dionysios Solomos (1798-1857), the National Poet and author of the anthem "Hymn to Liberty", as for many other educated Ionians, Italian was as much a mother-tongue as Greek. Bilingualism, education and music were just some of the elements that seemed to separate the islanders from Turkey-in-Europe, and Greek Epirus, until recent times. For the Ionian Islands belonged, culturally, to Western Europe. Even if Epirus seemed like a foreign country to a Corfiot like Moraitis when he first visited Igoumenitsa, who can deny that Ioannina was also a great centre of education and learning, and that the people of the Zagori villages in Epirus, for instance, enjoyed a high standard of living and a great deal of independence, and that the menfolk, who usually went off to make their living in other parts of Europe or even further afield, brought back with them refined architectural tastes, and that many became enlightened and generous benefactors of their communities?

Erotokritos expressed great sympathy for a poem I had written after attending a conference about *rebetika* music in London, which perhaps sums up this vexed question about Greek identity:

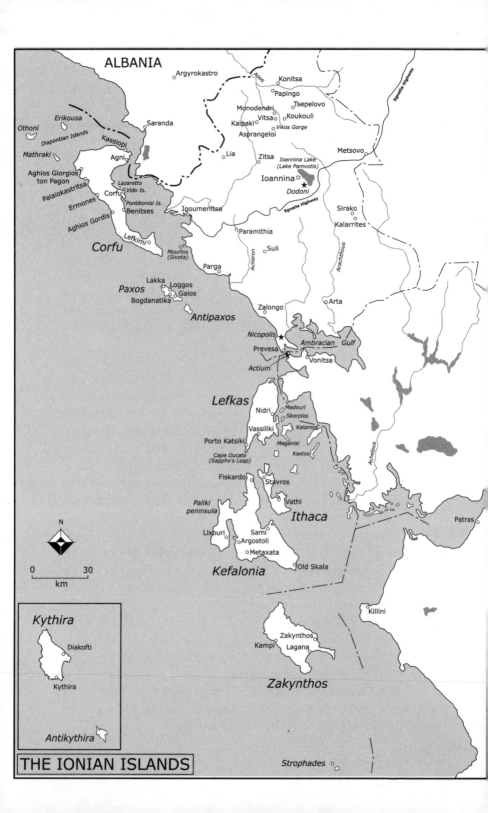

THE IONIAN ISLANDS

GREEK IDENTITY

It was a Conference on Rebetology:
Much talk of Turkish influence,
Oriental modes
And Vamvakaris.
I asked about *Kantades*,
The Ionian Islands, Italian links.
Were they any less Hellenic?
-It wasn't all monophony
And Turkish *"Aman"* wails.
Why had they been *privileged*,
In the histories of the nation?
The Greeks knew how to harmonise,
To use well-tempered scales.
Polyphonic harmonies
Mandolins, guitars,
Preceded *bouzouki, baglama*
In Modern Greece, it seems:
So why were they any *"less Greek"*?
The question was *"too big"*.

(From *Corfu Blues*, 2006)

I love the old *rebetika* songs and Epirot *klarino* improvisations as much as the traditional *kantades* of the Ionian Islands. At the time of writing, I have just spent three days and nights at the Vitsa Panigyri, where the eighty-year-old klarino-player Grigoris Kapsalis from Elafotopos (Tservari) gave his all, and more.

This book takes the reader on journeys through splendid landscapes, on excursions through time, full of adventure and a degree of horror. For those who already know and love the Ionian Islands, the coast of Epirus or the Pindus mountains, I hope they will come to perceive these regions in a new light. This book does not pretend to reveal the "hidden history" of the two regions, but it does throw the spotlight on aspects of history that have been whitewashed or re-imagined, and on overly-nationalistic or revisionist accounts.

Readers will be able to compare their own perceptions with those of the Romans, the Venetians, the Ottoman Turks, the French and the British; they will discover how the mainland Greeks have perceived the Ionian Islands, and how the islanders perceived the Epirots—as well as foreign invaders, occupiers, tourists and visitors.

They may be familiar with the works of Homer, Byron, Lear, the Durrell family, Louis de Bernières and Nicholas Gage, and with stories and legends about Sappho, Odysseus, King Pyrrhus, Ali Pasha, with *My Family and Other Animals*, *Eleni* and *Captain Corelli*, but I feel sure they will find something new to shock, delight or inspire.

For those less familiar with the islands or Epirot mainland, it may be useful to be reminded of the local history. (The book is not chronological, and there are many other books which deal with the history of these islands and regions in a historically chronological way.)

On the mainland, Ioannina fell to the Ottoman Turks in 1430 and was not liberated until 1913. The Turks attempted to besiege Corfu on two occasions, in 1537 and in 1716; while Lefkas endured two periods under Turkish occupation (1362-1479 and 1503-1684).

The Venetians held most of the Ionian Islands for almost four centuries, until 1797. They also held some key mainland ports, such as Parga and Prevesa, so these became effectively part of the Ionian Islands. Then in 1797 the French took Corfu and the other Ionian Islands, to be temporarily driven out in 1799, but they returned in 1807.

The British then invaded the southern Ionian Islands (Zakynthos, Kefalonia, Ithaca and Kythira) two hundred years ago, in 1809, at exactly the same time that Lord Byron and John Cam Hobhouse, in Malta, were persuaded by Spiridion Foresti, former British Minister in Corfu, to visit Epirus and the court of Ali Pasha. It is not clear whether they were co-opted to undertake some sort of secret intelligence mission or whether they were sent unwittingly to help keep Ali onside, as an ally of Britain against the French (or possibly to divert, charm and "sweeten" Ali) while the British invaded islands, which he himself coveted. The Ionians were officially ruled by the British from 1814 to 1864, until the Ionian Islands became part of the Greek state in 1864. The British disgraced themselves by selling Parga to Ali Pasha in 1817; Byron's diversion to Epirus may have been entirely his decision, as from Foresti's stories and descriptions Byron saw it as the sort of exotic landscape and culture he was seeking to stimulate his poetic imagination; this does seem the most likely explanation.

This book deals with that British period at some length, and aims to uncover the true relationships between the British and the islanders.

The Second World War, and the experience of Italian and German occupations, brought an end to the kind of world described by Lawrence Durrell in *Prospero's Cell*. What happened in the years immediately after Lawrence Durrell left Greece forms the backdrop of Louis de Bernières' best-selling *Captain Corelli's Mandolin*, but in Kefalonia rather than in Corfu. Greeks (and others) may dispute the accuracy of that interpretation of history, as they do of Nicholas Gage's *Eleni*, but it cannot be disputed how great an impact these books have had on the popular imagination, worldwide.

Francis King's novel *The Dark Glasses*, which is set in Corfu, where he spent the winter of 1952-3 on unpaid leave from the British Council, Athens (he was one of a handful of English people residing on the island that winter), opens with the comment: "There is something amiss with the younger people here in Corfu, though I find it hard to explain what." The elderly Mrs Nicolidou, one of his Corfiot characters, goes on to explain her point of view: "The old people are very much what they always were, but with the younger people one feels the salt has lost its savour. They have no vitality, no real interest, no resources from which to draw. They're apathetic... Nobody *does* anything. Is it the effect of the war? Or the climate? Or poverty? Or unemployment?"

By the time that Francis King was wintering on Corfu, the Club Méditerranée had opened on the island (he mentions the Club in the novel). Within a decade tourism had taken off, and within two decades poverty and unemployment were no longer so visible. The *effects* of tourism were, sadly, becoming ever more visible by the time that the Colonels fell from power in 1974.

If Byron's Kefalonia and Argostoli have disappeared largely because of the earthquakes the island has suffered, if Lawrence Durrell's and Gerald Durrell's Corfu has disappeared as a result of post-war developments and mass tourism, if Ali Pasha's Ioannina has been destroyed, the kastro and most of the minarets having been levelled, how is it that we can still recognize the veracity and verisimilitude of the drawings and paintings of Edward Lear? The lake and the mountains have not changed so much, nor has the view from Corfu town across to Epirus and Albania. Nature is resilient.

It is hard to decide which periods of history or of foreign domination brought the biggest changes to the islands and the Epirot mainland. The Venetians, with their encouragement to plant olive trees? The construction of fortresses and other defences? The exchange of populations after 1922? The deportation of the Jewish communities during the Second World War? Bombing raids and earthquakes? The advent of international airports, hotels, villas, swimming pools, the dramatic increase in car ownership and mass tourism?

People have also asked me, why the Ionian Islands *and* Epirus? Whether one goes as far back as King Pyrrhus, the Despots of Epirus, the Venetian Republic or Ali Pasha, the close connections between the islands and Epirus (and the mainland ports south of Epirus) have been profound. There has been a greater degree of interdependence than is often appreciated. With the completion of the Egnatia Motorway, the level of contact will greatly increase. To the Corfiot, the hospitals in Ioannina are a literal lifeline. Building materials, *feta* cheese and dairy products (e.g. *Dodoni*) and bottled water (e.g. *Zagori*) also sustain the Corfiot. If the islands have been places of refuge for Epirots and other oppressed Greeks in the past, they now offer employment and opportunities in the tourism industry.

To the Albanian, the region of Ali Pasha's Epirus is accessible again, and Albanians come to find work in large numbers; Ioannina is flourishing as a result of increased trade. The islands, too, have benefited from their skills with stone-masonry.

This book is a mosaic portrait of the islands and special places of interest on the Epirot mainland. It focuses on the landscapes, legends, traditions and historical events that have appealed most strongly to the imaginations of writers, residents and travellers from all parts of the world, including Greece itself.

Chapter One

CLASSIC GROUND

I loved that island home of mine too well,
Too well I loved each cape, each rock, each tree;
Each had become a living nerve of me,
A fibre of my soul, another spell
To fetter me to Ithaca's sweet shore.

That is what Odysseus, still "homesick beyond the grave", felt about Ithaca, as imagined by the botanist and poet Dr. Theodore Stephanides, in his poem "Odysseus" (1965).

Dante imagined Odysseus in hell, explaining his sense of dissatisfaction and undiminished wanderlust after his return home, a restless travelbug which many of us share, however much we may love our native lands. Nothing, says Dante's Odysseus, in Longfellow's version of *The Inferno* (1863), could overcome within him the desire to be experienced of the world, and of "the vice and virtue of mankind".

Perhaps that is why Cavafy, in his much-quoted poem "Ithaca" (1961), considered it better for every Odysseus among us, for all of us, to draw out the journey for as long as possible, to delay the homecoming, as the exploration is more important than the arrival.

Lawrence Durrell and his cronies had a talkative, creative time in Corfu in the 1930s, before the war. Something of the island's inspiring spirit and atmosphere survived into the late 1960s, but it had largely disappeared by the 1980s, when Philip Sherrard wrote a hard-hitting piece, "The New Barbarism", for his *Edward Lear, The Corfu Years* (1988). Edmund Keeley comments on it and makes some qualifications, in *Inventing Paradise* (1999). Sherrard pulls no punches in describing the damage and disfigurement of Corfu and its coastline as a result of greed and mass tourism:

> every stretch of it accessible by road or track has been so butchered and bartered, drawn and quartered, and so immersed and desolated beneath the ferro-concrete hideosity of hotel and boarding-house, discotheque, bar, cafeteria and chop-house ... and the other gimcrackery

and detritus (plastic and mineral) of mass tourism, that one searches in vain, across the wreckage of this dishallowed world, for the virginal loveliness that confronted Lear at virtually every footstep. His beloved Palaiokastritsa, for example, is a total disaster, but it is absolutely no exception.

Many visitors and residents would find that much too harsh a judgement. In the late 1960s this was certainly not the case, and virginal loveliness can *still* be discovered by walking and climbing up and along tracks among the olive groves, or by following the Corfu Trail. Mark Ellingham (creator of the Rough Guides series, and author of the first *Rough Guide to Greece*, 1982) returned to Corfu in 2008 after a thirty-year absence and found it as good as he remembered it in the 1970s. He was particularly impressed by the North-East of the island (Agni and Aghios Stefanos), and the "awesome, jaw-dropping" views and panoramas from Bella Vista, above Palaiokastritsa, and from the thirteenth-century Angelokastro. He was almost as moved as Edward Lear had been. I was happier when the ruins of Angelokastro were in a wilder state, harder to reach but easier to explore, before the excavation and reconstruction work began.

The Stephanides poem represents more or less what Maria, my wife, *used* to feel about Corfu, her native Ionian island, in all the years of our own overseas wanderings, about an island which many have compared in their imaginations to the shape of a sickle or reaping hook, perhaps a bow, a shield, a scimitar, a crescent or half moon, or even a partridge (as in the folk song, "I Perdika")—but which Maria insists looks more like a leg of mutton than any of these.

Edward Lear, looking across at Corfu from a Greek-speaking village on the Albanian mainland, wrote in his journal of 25 October 1848: "The sun is not yet up, and Corfu, like an island of opal, seems to float on the pale grey sea at the cloudless pink horizon." The island must have always fascinated Albanians within sight of it.

Elizabeth Longford, in *Byron's Greece* (1975), thinks that the shape of Kefalonia as seen from the air, or on a map, "looks something like a bullfrog diving headlong to the bottom of a pond, followed by a tiny, two humped fish (Ithaca)". Lawrence Durrell, in *The Greek Islands* (1978), describes Kefalonia as "a large raw-boned island".

It seems appropriate to begin this book concerned with "landscapes of the imagination" with Odysseus, even though it is by no means certain that the island now called Ithaca (one of the so-called *Eptanisa*, Heptanesian, or Seven Islands, also referred to as the "Frank islands") was in fact Homer's Ithaca, or indeed that Corfu was Scheria, the island of Nausicaa (Thucydides, for one, was sure it was). Byron was content to leave the question of the existence of Homer's Ithaca ("not yet admitted") to the "Antiquaries", those gentlemen involved with the arts and tradition.

Did Sappho ever visit Lefkas or did Aphrodite approach the shores of Kythira (Citherea, the "chiefe seate of Venus", according to Fynes Moryson) en route to Cyprus? Did Aphrodite herself dive from the cliffs of Cape Leucata, now known as Cape Ducato, to be freed from her secret love for Adonis, after his death, as Sappho is said to have done for love of Phaon? Did Medea and Jason get married in a cave on Corfu? Was the news of the death of the great god Pan announced in the vicinity of Paxos, as in the legend recorded by Plutarch? Did Othoni have any link with Calypso? Some (Procopius, de Vaudoncourt, Dodwell) suggest it may have been there that Odysseus was kept in a cave by Calypso. The Strophades have been linked with the Harpies. Lefkimi (Corfu) was thought to be the favourite resort of the Nereids. Some have identified Paxos as Circe's island. Kythirans (see Peter Prineas) are in no doubt that Aphrodite was "born in the foaming wave near Kythera and drifted away to Cyprus on the sea breeze in a great sea shell".

So there are plenty of myths to feed our imaginations.

SAPPHO'S LEAP

The story of Sappho's suicide leap from Cape Lefkas is referred to in ancient times by Menander, Anacreon and Strabo. Lord Byron wrote of "dark Sappho" and "burning Sappho" and hailed Leucadia's cape, "the lover's refuge and the Lesbian's grave". Sir Thomas Moore called her "The tender Lesbian"; Waller Rodwell Wright wrote of "Leucate's pale and broken rocks...by Venus doom'd to prove the last sad refuge of despairing love":

Yet shall thy cliffs derive eternal fame
From Sappho's plaintive verse, and hapless flame.

Cape Lefkas

It is perhaps surprising that there is no statue of Sappho on the cape, nor indeed a reconstructed Temple of Apollo (EU regional development funding would surely be available). It is a pity that Napier and Kennedy were never given the opportunity to come up with a design for a neoclassical Apollonian Temple-Lighthouse, in the spirit of the St. Theodore Lighthouse at the cape near Argostoli, capital of Kefalonia. Even a simple information board would be helpful, perhaps with translations of one of Sappho's own surviving poetic fragments and a reproduction of Joseph Cartwright's "Sappho's Leap at Cape Ducato".

Lawrence Durrell seems to have accepted that Sappho did make her leap from the White Cliffs, which "struck the imagination of the world", but asks himself, "Was it accident or intent?" Perhaps he had had a premonition of the later, tragic suicide of his own troubled daughter, Sappho Durrell. Of Sappho the Greek poet, Durrell writes: "The puzzle of Sappho remains—what sort of accident was it?"

Menander had already provided an answer: "They say that Sappho was the first, hunting down the proud Phaon, to throw herself, in her goading desire, from the rock that shines from afar". Here is the full reference, from Strabo's *Geography*:

> Leukatas is a rock of white color jutting out from Leukas into the sea and towards Kephallenia and therefore it took its name from its color. It contains the temple of Apollo Leukatas, and also the Leap, which was believed to put an end to the longings of love. 'Where Sappho is said to have been the first,' as Menandros says, 'when through frantic longing she was chasing the haughty Phaon, to fling herself with a leap from the far-seen rock, calling upon thee in prayer, O lord and master.'

Strabo describes another annual custom that took place at this spot:

> It was an ancestral custom among the Leukadians, every year at the sacrifice performed in honor of Apollon, for some criminal to be flung from this rocky look-out for the sake of averting evil, wings and birds of all kinds being fastened to him, since by their fluttering they could lighten the leap, and also for a number of men, stationed all round below the rock in small fishing-boats, to take the victim in, and, when he had been taken on board, to do all in their power to get him safely outside their borders.

Anacreon (in Menander) put the following words into Sappho's mouth: "One more time taking off in the air, down from the White Rock into the dark waves do I dive, intoxicated with lust."

When I visited Cape Lefcata (also called the Lady's Cape) for the second time, in June 2008, there was total silence in the sacred precinct of the white cliffs, just as Menander had requested of Apollo that there should be. An unprepossessing lighthouse may have replaced the Temple of Apollo (which once "put an end to the longings of love", as Strabo wrote), and there is now a brand new asphalt road in the place of the rough dirt track I drove along on my previous visit twelve years ago, but the disorienting sense of vertigo excited by looking down at the sea and the jagged rocks from the top of the cliffs from which Sappho and others are said to have jumped, willingly or not, had not diminished in the slightest and was still powerful enough to fuel my imagination and to convince me of the essential truth of some of the old Leucadian legends. "The dread height above the eddying deep", Sir Thomas Moore (1826) called the spot that I was visiting once again. At the Cape in Lefkas, there was a woman silently looking down at the same spot, just like one of Moore's maidens of the Cycladian island of Zea (Tzia, Ceos or Kea):

> Among these maidens there was one
> Who to Leucadia late had been—
> Had stood beneath the evening sun
> On its white towering cliffs and seen
> The very spot where Sappho sung
> Her swan-like music, ere she sprung…

The American poet W. A. Percy (1925) has a heterosexual Sappho in a mildly erotic Mills and Boon scenario about to leap to her death in Lefkas for love of the shepherd boy, Phaon:

> Oh, let the anguished crimson of his mouth
> Seek fire from mine, and all his brown, light grace
> Flame into strength to crush my paleness…
> One misty, scarlet kiss within your arms—
> Phaon! Phaon!

Aristotle Valaoritis is less carried away by Sappho's death in his two poems on Cape Lefkas (1993), but is still able to imagine the waves joyfully licking the love-struck bones of the poet. Gounod's operatic homage to Sappho has her leaping from the cliff in its final scene. The poets Christina Rossetti, Mary Robinson and Elizabeth Oakes Smith all produced poems about Sappho contemplating suicide or about to leap to her death. Rossetti wrote her poem "Sappho" (1846) at the age of sixteen; and in 1848, she wrote a poem called "What Sappho would have said had her leap cured instead of killing her." Mary Robinson, in her sonnet sequence *Sappho and Phaon* (1796), imagines Sappho standing on the dizzy precipice before she leaps and then contemplates her dead body:

> OH! Can'st thou bear to see this faded frame,
> Deform'd and mangled by the rocky deep?

Elizabeth Oakes Smith imagines her leaning out over the rock, in her "Ode to Sappho" (1848):

> Over Leucadia's rock thou leanest yet,
> With thy wild song, and all thy locks
> Outspread...

Sappho also provided inspiration for poets like Swinburne and Felicia Hemans (1793-1835). Hemans' "The Last Song of Sappho" was "suggested by a beautiful sketch... Sappho sitting on a rock above the sea...penetrated with the feeling of utter abandonment":

> Alone I come—oh! give me peace, dark sea!

Letitia Elizabeth Landon, or L. E. L. (once almost as renowned a poet as Byron), who herself died in mysterious circumstances—possibly murder or suicide—and whose grave I once visited in Cape Coast Castle, Ghana, wrote in her poem "Sappho" (1824):

> There is a dark rock looks on the blue sea;
> 'Twas there love's last song echoed—
> There she sleeps...

Normally, the Leucadian rock is perceived as white, not "dark". Another of her poems, "Sappho's Song", has Sappho herself anticipating the calm sleep of death in her glorious grave in the deep blue sea.

In Mary Robinson's introduction to her sonnet sequence, she explained how her imagination had felt irresistibly drawn to the story of the "Lesbian Muse", a great mind and talent which had yielded to the destructive control of ungovernable passions: "The sensibility of SAPPHO was extreme! She loved PHAON, who forsook her; after various efforts to bring him back, she took the leap of Leucata, and perished in the waves!"

Swinburne wrote of Sappho's death in the "woman-crown'd" sea, and of her "great green grave" in his poem "On the Cliffs":

> Song's priestess, mad with joy and pain of love,
> Love's priestess, mad with pain and joy of song.

In his controversial poem "Anactoria", he writes:

> I feel thy blood against my blood: my pain
>> Pains thee, and lips bruise lips, and vein stings vein.
>> Let fruit be crushed on fruit, let flower on flower,
>> Breast kindle breast, and either burn one hour.
>> Why wilt thou follow lesser loves?

The poem ends, like so many others composed on the theme:

> … around and over and under me
> Thick darkness and the insuperable sea.

In stanza II of "Ave Atque Vale, In Memory of Charles Baudelaire", Swinburne laments that it is not known "where is that Leucadian grave/ Which hides too deep the supreme head of song… The wild sea winds her and the green gulfs bear/Hither and thither…"

These lines are from Baudelaire's own poem, "Lesbos" (1857):

> Since then I watch on the Leucadian height
> To find out if the sea's heart still is hardened
> And from the sobs that drench the rock with spray
> If it will bring back Sappho…

Those more interested in truth than in legend, or in Sappho the Lesbian rather than in Sappho from the island of Lesbos, have perhaps less interest in the story of her great love for Phaon, the ferryman. They might prefer a poem such as Maureen Duffy's "Sapphic Her Dressing" (Duffy claims to have been Britain's first Lesbian to "come out" in public), or some of the poems by Olga Broumas. John Donne's "Heroicall Epistle, Sapho to Philænis" would also be of interest:

> Thy body is a naturall Paradise…
> why shouldst thou then
> Admit the tillage of a harsh rough man?

Some inhabitants of the island of Lesbos are said to be none too happy about the non-geographical uses of the name of their island, although they welcome tourists of all orientations and claim that they're not homophobic. It was reported in *Athens News* that they told a court on 10 June 2008 that "gay women insult the island's identity by calling themselves lesbians" and that the plaintiffs "are seeking to ban a Greek gay rights group (the Homosexual and Lesbian Community of Greece) from using the word 'lesbian' in its name" because it causes confusion and embarrassment for the women of Lesbos.

Perhaps they would have a better chance of success if they tried to sue the literary estates of Baudelaire, Swinburne or even Maximus of Tyre instead! Maximus of Tyre wrote in his *Orations*: "What else could one call the love of the Lesbian woman than the Socratic art of love? For they seem to have practised love after their own fashion, she the love of women, he of men." In modern times, Sue Blundell argues that the word "lesbian" is "a modern invention: it only began to denote a female homosexual in the late nineteenth century, as the result of the publicity created by a scholarly controversy over Sappho's own sexuality".

C. G. D. Roberts, in his introduction to *Bliss Carman*, writes of the story of Sappho's pursuit of Phaon and her frenzied leap as:

> Nothing more than a poetic myth, reminiscent, perhaps, of the myth of Aphrodite and Adonis—who is, indeed, called Phaon in some versions… It is a myth which has begotten some exquisite literature, both in prose and verse, from Ovid's famous epistle to Addison's gracious fantasy and some impassioned and imperishable dithyrambs of Mr. Swinburne; but one need not accept the story as a fact in order to appreciate the beauties which flowered out from its coloured unreality.

In Ovid's "Heroic Epistle, XV, Sappho to Phaon", Sappho asks: "Why was I born, ye gods, a Lesbian dame?"

> There stands a rock from whose impending steep
> Apollo's fane surveys the rolling deep;
> There injured lovers, leaping from above,
> Their flames extinguish and forget to love...
> Haste, Sappho, haste, from high Leucadia throw
> Thy wretched weight, nor dread the deeps below.

Joseph Addison wrote in *The Spectator* of 15 November 1711:

There was a promontory in Acarnania called Leucate, on the top of which was a little temple dedicated to Apollo. In this temple it was usual for despairing lovers to make their vows in secret, and afterwards to fling themselves from the top of the precipice into the sea, where they were sometimes taken up alive. This place was therefore called the Lover's Leap ... those who had taken this leap were observed never to relapse into that passion. Sappho tried the cure, but perished in the experiment.

Erica Jong's historical novel *Sappho's Leap* (2003) begins with Sappho standing on the cliff about to jump into the sea, but the author says she does not believe in the legend, which she thinks was fabricated by envious male detractors.

For my pains, I lost two hubcaps from my rental car while visiting Cape Lefkas and Sappho's Leap in September 1994, when the road was very rough. Such mundane events do we remember. Durrell calls it "a breathless and bone-cracking excursion". It is no longer a bumpy ride, or as sad and mournful a place as Valaoritis describes it in his poem "Lefkatos", where "now only poor and hungry shepherds in rags roam about it. On its highest rock was once the temple of Apollo; now only leaves and brush exist in the desolate landscape. No one walks there now; none respects the sacred place" (C. Santas, paraphrasing the poem). But my daughter and I recall how dramatic it felt looking down at the sea, leap or no leap, Sappho or no Sappho. I must say that I half-believe the legend.

CORFU/SCHERIA?

Gerald Durrell once said, "I like to think of Corfu as the garden of the gods." If we accept or want to believe that Corfu was the island of the Phaecians, then Homer's description of the orchard, garden and vineyard of King Alcinous has a special meaning. We start with an extract from Pope's translation of *The Odyssey* Book VII:

Close to the gates a spacious garden lies,
From storms defended and inclement skies...
Here the blue fig with luscious juice o'erflows,
With deeper red the full pomegranate glows;

The branch here bends beneath the weighty pear,
And verdant olives flourish round the year...

And, for the sake of variety, a brief extract from William Cowper's translation:

Pears after pears to full dimensions swell,
Figs follow figs, grapes clust'ring grow again
Where clusters grew...

Waller Rodwell Wright (admired by Byron and praised in *English Bards and Scots Reviewers*), in a footnote to his poem "Horae Ionicae" (1809), writes that:

> It is impossible for any one, who traverses the shores of the old harbour with the *Odyssey* in his recollection, to doubt the personal acquaintance of Homer with the scenery of Corfu, or to hesitate in assigning the garden of Alcinous to the spot here described, which lies at the western extremity of the harbour, and is still exclusively devoted to the same sort of culture.

R. Montgomery Martin (1837) accepts that the gardens of Alcinous were situated on the banks of Lake Calichiopoulo. William Miller (1928) says that "Corfu has been blessed with the fruits of the earth and the beauties of nature since the time when Homer placed there the marvellous gardens of Alkinöos, yet in few parts of Greece does such general poverty prevail". Mass tourism has changed that, in many ways.

If Ermones was really the bay and beach that Homer had in mind for the spot where Odysseus was washed ashore (as many writers speculate), and where Nausicaa and her Phaeacian friends used to go and wash their garments in a stream, it is a tragedy what all-round visual pollution and appallingly ugly cement structures have, relatively recently, been allowed to destroy any Homeric associations or atmosphere (and the natural environment, regardless of Odysseus!). Luckily, or sadly, I can remember it as it was in 1967. It was one of the first deserted beaches on Corfu that I ever visited. Ernle Bradford, in *Ulysses Found* (1963), calls Ermones "one of the most enchanting and idyllic places in the Mediterranean and...the only place in Corfu which could correspond with the Homeric description". So it was, in the 1960s. Even more so in 1903, of course, when Lorentzos Mavilis wrote his sonnet "Ermones", which calls to mind our need for the almost sacramental mystery of solitude, for uninhabited, secluded, remote places as Ermones once was, a place for the *Phil-Erimos* ["lover of deserted places"] soul; it still carries that association, alas in name only.

Evangelos Tsimaratos deduces that Nausicaa was washing her clothes in the river at Potamos, a hypothesis also entertained by the Swiss traveller Albert Mousson, who believed that Odysseus came ashore at the beach that once existed at Mandouki. Lawrence Durrell insists that "Odysseus must have met Nausicaa at Paleocastrizza; it is not possible to believe otherwise." Emma Tennant is even more specific about the location, near their house, Rovinia, Liapades, Palaiokastritsa:

> It wasn't long before we discovered that Rovinia ...was very probably just where Homer had placed the famous meeting between the shipwrecked and naked Odysseus and the princess, Nausicaa...The evi-

The beaches at Palaiokastritsa

dence... does appear to conclude that it really was in 'our' bay, on 'our' beach... Rovinia was the scene of the most romantic non-romance of the antique world.

Indeed. As John Julius Norwich writes in Frank Giles' book on Corfu (1994): "Old Corfu hands will argue for hours over the precise point at which Ulysses made his landfall. Fortunately, we shall never know; some mysteries are better left unrevealed."

In 1675, George Wheler visited Corfu's ancient city, Palaiopolis:

On the south-west side of Palæopoli, about two or three miles off, is a plain, well watered with several brooks of fresh water, which make the soil fruitful. It is judged to have been the gardens of Alcinous, King of this place, famous in Homer... here we were full of Homer, especially his relation of the King's daughter Nausica's adventure; who going to bathe her self with her attendants, met with Ulysses cast upon that shore by a storm.

Edward Dodwell, who landed in Corfu at the time that the Septinsular Republic was under the protection of the Russians and the Turks, incidentally witnessing some bloody skirmishes between Greeks and Turks, comments that "Although the *Odyssey* has not the same character of geographical veracity which is so conspicuous in the *Iliad*, yet it cannot be allowed that the Phaecia of Homer is a Laputa, or a Borobdignag."

Lawrence Durrell thought that we still dwell in the shadow of Ulysses. There is a certain irony that the author of *The Alexandria Quartet* and *The Avignon Quintet* seems to have considered *The Odyssey* boring, badly constructed, and marked by self-pity and rhetoric. Yet he considers it an excellent guide to the *modern Greeks*, and he can't find a flaw in the way Homer effectively describes the modern Greeks, especially "the loquacity, the shy cunning, the mendacity, the generosity, the cowardice and the bravery, the almost comical inability of self-analysis".

I am more inclined to echo the note of scepticism to be found in John Murray's *Handbook* (1840) in the entry on Corfu:

The ancients, with a few exceptions, always identified Corcyra with the Homeric Scheria, the dwelling-place of the hospitable Phæcians under their king Alcinous. Many modern travellers have also gratified themselves in tracing points of fancied resemblance between the Homeric description and the present landscape. But, as Mr Bunbury has shown … such identification is wholly imaginary; and "we must, therefore, be content to banish the kindly and hospitable Phæcians, as well as the barbarous Cyclopes and Læstrygones, to that outer zone of the Homeric world, in which everything was still shrouded in a veil of marvel and mystery".

Edward Giffard (1837) had difficulty, which he was unable to solve, in identifying Corfu with the island of Alcinous, because of inconsistencies between the island itself and Homer's Odyssey, i.e. an impossible one-day journey from Euboea to Corfu.

Few Corfiots of the nineteenth century would have entertained such doubts, as the story was a fundamental element in their sense of cultural identity (both Hellenic and European), as is evident in terms of the number of operatic and dramatic works produced on that theme (the tragedy *Ulisse in Corcira* was printed in Italian in vols. 2 and 3 of the *Ionian Anthology*; and Antonio Liberali composed incidental music for the performance of Sajani's tragedy, *Ulisse, re di Itaca in Corcira* in 1834), and even in terms of the "Coming of Ulysses" decor and iconography of the San Giacomo theatre, as the musicologist Dr. Konstantinos Kardamis pointed out to me.

Christopher Wordsworth (1839), nephew of the poet William, whose topographical judgements and deductions I respect, says:

It is not easy to draw a map of the Homeric Phæcia which shall coincide in its details with the localities of Korfou. Nor will the topographer find it a simple task to discover the natural objects connected in the Odyssey with the city of Alcinous. Where are the two fountains which flowed near it?—where is the stream of the River-God whom Ulysses conciliates with his prayers? Is it to be found at the beautiful village of Potamo, or not far from Cape Sideri, to suit the hypothesis, the most prevalent one among the Phæcian antiquaries of the present day, which lands Ulysses in the north-west extremity of the island, because he is brought to it by a northerly wind, and which places the city of Alcinous at Aphiona in that district?

Wordsworth also speculates about the exact location of the Hyllaic harbour which he infers was to the south of the site of the Acropolis and identifies with the "lagune of Calichiopulo", whilst the Agora and its adjacent harbour was to the north of the peninsula of Palæopolis, and toward the modern Kastrades (now known as Garitsa). Wordsworth discusses the Temple of Juno ("near the palace now occupied by an English cannon,— thence called the One-gun battery") and the Temple of Neptune, "the beautiful POSIDEIUM" of Nausicaa.

Professor T. W. Gallant (2002) rightly comments that, while scholars agreed that the Ionian Islands were the site of the Odyssey, there has still been fierce controversy concerning "the precise role played by each island". Although Professor Gallant documents many examples of nineteenth-century British testimonies to the contrary, what cannot be disputed, in my view, is the kind hospitality of the Corfiots and Greeks generally. I agree with William Miller: "The extreme politeness and hospitality of the Greeks in their intercourse with strangers make travel in their country more delightful than anywhere else." That has not changed since the early twentieth century, or indeed from the time of Homer (when describing the Phaecians of Scheria, at least).

One might form the opposite impression from a comment of Dr. John Hennen: "A Corfiot is a very abstemious person, when he eats or drinks at his own expense; but when he feasts at that of a foreigner, he is capable of consuming a vast quantity of food, both animal and vegetable, together with copious libations of wine." The truth is surely the other way round. It is the foreigner who now usually consumes the most food and wine. Viscount Kirkwall was not the only one to say that "the Ionians are naturally an agreeable, generous, quick and hospitable people"

HOMER'S ITHACA

In his poem "On Ithaca Standing" (1937), Lawrence Durrell seems to accept the aura and the traditional claims made for the island of Ithaca as "miracle land".

Bardhyl Londo, the Albanian poet, wrote several poems about Ithaca (1993). Although written before the great political changes in Albania, a verse from his poem "Ithaca" reflects the situation of many more Albanians in Greece nowadays:

Ithaca slumbers under the September sky.
The olive trees are like women awaiting their tardy husbands.
I am filled with a longing for my home far away
For my wife in Tiranë who will not sleep tonight.
Help me, Ulysses!

It seems that Albanians feel a special affinity for Odysseus. Kadaré claims that scientists have explained the name from the Albanian word *udhë*, i.e. Odysseus—Udhësi, wayfarer; Geisthövel points out that the name Odysseus has no Greek stem.

It is a curious phenomenon how the British have always wanted to appropriate the finest elements of the Greek landscape. Many might envy Lord Rothschild's Corfiot estate, even though, in recent years, property owners on the North-East coast of Corfu have had their nights disturbed by the thumping noise of loud discos from across the straits near Albania's fast-developing port of Saranda. The *Daily Telegraph* reported (17 February 1984) that more than 1,000 British people who owned property in Corfu, including Mr Jacob Rothschild, were extremely worried that they might be dispossessed and that their properties could be re-appropriated by the Greek heirs of the original owners, as a result of an old 1927 law designed to prevent foreigners from owning land in frontier areas. Greek justice and fair play were called into question, and court decisions were causing confusion, with uncertainty about possible compensation for buildings and improvements that foreign owners had made to the land. Mrs Thatcher eventually came to the rescue and raised the issue with the Greek Prime Minister.

The desire to acquire property in Greece is not new. Lord Byron thought of buying the island of Ithaca: "I have some idea of purchasing the Island of Ithaca; I suppose you will add me to the Levant lunatics" (letter to J. C. Hobhouse, 4 October 1810). Trelawny recounts a story about Byron's reactions to their brief visit to Ithaca:

> The grey olive-trees, bright green fig, and rampant vine, that grew above our heads, screened us from the sun; the fresh breeze from the sea, with the springs of purest water gushing out of the rocks, soothed the Poet's temper. He turned out of the path to look at a natural grotto, in a grove of forest trees, and said "You will find nothing in Greece or its islands

so pleasant as this. If this isle were mine—I would break my staff and bury my book..."

It seems that Ithaca, rather than Corfu, almost qualified to be christened "Prospero's Cell", as it very nearly became the location of Guilford's Ionian Academy (Count John Capodistrias may in fact have been the first to advocate the establishment of a university, at the Congress of Vienna in 1815, but Guilford supported the proposal). Professor D. T. Ansted was equally confident about Homer's Ithaca: "That Ithaca was really the island intended to be described by Homer, and that he knew it himself perfectly in every nook, there will hardly be much doubt in the mind of the traveller who compares on the spot the poem with the reality."

R. Montgomery Martin (1837) could have been writing today when he says: "Whether this little island were the celebrated Ithaca of Homer is not yet a settled point." When he was writing, "the very name was forgotten until of late".

Martin Young (1977) discusses the "Ithaca Question" and archaeological excavation. As he says, "The Ithaca Question arises from the difficulty of reconciling Homer's account of Ithaca's position with the geographical situation of the island now called by that name... By the outbreak of the Second World War most archaelogists had been forced by the inconclusive or negative evidence of all these Homeric excavations to conclude that the Ithaca Question was a horse which—if not quite dead—was no longer worth flogging." But Young does draw attention to the theories of A. E. H. Goekoop, who believed that Ithaca was part of Kefalonia. Robert Bittlestone has developed his own theories about the location of Homeric Ithaca, but I much prefer the concise account of the history of the idea by D. I. Paizis-Danias, which explores "the 10 principal hypotheses advanced over the past century or so which place Homer's Ithaca on Cephallenia, and to expose the fallacies which they embody". His critique of Bittlestone's book is not without some justification, that "no amount of satellite imagery and creative photographic angles can compensate for the poverty (and immodesty) of the argument". As an Ithacan by birth and a member of the Ithacan Friends of Homer Association, he may be assumed to have a vested interest, and to be representative of what many Ithacans may feel about these theories, but his approach to "the history of the idea" appeals to me. I was told in Argostoli that Kefalonians are "quite relaxed about Bittlestone's theory, but not the Ithacans; at the end of the day it's just another theory. They're all good if they promote the reading of Homer."

Evangelos Tsimaratos, the philologist and high-school teacher from Lixouri, Kefalonia, argues that the area of Paliki in Kefalonia was a separate island (Same/Sami) when Homer wrote the *Odyssey*, that Krani, the larger Kefalonian island, and Same constituted Ithaca—and that modern Ithaca was Doulichium.

I toured the Paliki peninsula, prepared to believe that it might once have been a separate island, but the gods sent no flash of enlightenment or sign of identification, nor did they inspire in me some sixth sense that this was once Homer's Ithaca. The closest I came to that Eureka feeling was when walking on the Acropolis of Sami, facing the southern point of Ithaca. That was the sort of spot I could imagine that Odysseus might have chosen to maintain, for strategic reasons, as a base for his wider island kingdom, even if the existing ruins date from a much later period. But there are enough theories already.

George Wheler, interpreting Strabo's estimates of the size of Homeric Ithaca ("eighty stadia about, which maketh about ten Italian miles"), believed that Homer's Ithaca was "another little island, seven or eight miles from hence, called yet Ithaca; which is much less than this; I believe anciently called Dulichium, because it hath at the east-side a Port, with the ruins of a Town called yet Dolichia, as Strabo observed, it was called in his time; which to me is satisfaction enough".

Ernle Bradford refers to the grave of Wilhelm Dörpfeld, "who endeared himself to the islanders [of Lefkas] by pursuing one of the longest running Ionian hares—the true location of Homer's Ithaka. He was convinced, in the face of what has always seemed reasonable evidence, that the home and palace of Odysseus was here in Levkas. It was one of those *idées fixes*… It ignored Odysseus's own description of Ithaka as lying well away to the west, and as 'rugged and unfit for driving horses', while several places named by Homer can be recognized in Ithaka."

I walked to Dörpfeld's tomb, to commune with him for a while, but he offered no new evidence or insights. Have the archaeologists been flogging a dead horse, or simply chasing after a long-running hare? "Does it matter?" asks Lawrence Durrell in *The Greek Islands*. "Yes, in a profound sense it does, even though we shall never be certain of our ground in this game of classical hide-and-seek."

What are we non-specialists to do when archaeologists allow themselves to be persuaded that, rightly or wrongly, they've discovered the site of Troy, the palace of Odysseus or Alcinous, the tomb of Philip of Macedon or of Alexander the Great, or the Oracle of the Dead (Nekromanteion) referred to in Homer and Herodotus? Should we suspend our scepticism and allow our imaginations or literary associations a free rein? Or should we be cautiously pedantic, and qualify every discovery with an "if" and a "but" in the absence of absolute, conclusive proof to support a theory? Who wants to spoil a good story, or to debunk a treasured myth? Equally, who wants to mislead or misinform visitors? Perhaps competing nationalists or islanders do, or those interested in "the commodification of the past in the race for the tourist dollar", to borrow a phrase of Knapp and Antoniadou (1998).

Lithgow states that "The isle of Cephalonia was formerly called Ithaca, and greatly renowned, because it was the heretable kingdom of the worthy Ulysses, who excelled all other Greeks in eloquence and subtilty of war." Luke Slattery writes that "Ithaca's losses have been great. Without the Odyssey connection…the island would be quite bereft… I'd relished the chance to view myth-drenched Ithaca for myself. But after a week on the island I found myself embroiled in a heated provincial controversy about the Odyssean connection."

The controversy has certainly not subsided, but I'm not sure that the Homeric names given to hotels and restaurants on the island add any special glamour. Slattery is right to ask how "at a historical distance of 2,700 years, can we make any assumptions about Homer's travel itinerary?" But it takes an Australian (and a fan of Patrick Leigh Fermor) to understand the importance of the European dreamtime, and in particular of Homeric dreamings to the Greeks in a place like Ithaca. We tamper with them at our own peril. On the other hand, as Slattery says: "Spend too long with your head in Homer and your feet among ruins and the imagination unseats reason."

OTHONI, ISLAND OF CALYPSO?

At various points, the island of Othoni (Fano or Fanu, in Italian, one of the three Diapontian islands north-west of Corfu; Leake suggests that "Othonus is an ancient name…applied in the plural number to all the

three islands") has been identified, or at least suggested, as the island of
Calypso. Sophie Atkinson writes that "Fano in the north is, so they say, 'the
fair isle,' the 'seagirt island set with trees,' where the bright goddess Calypso
so long held Ulysses in her toils."

The French gave the name "Calypso's Cave" to the large cave (at Aspri
Ammos) at the western end of the island, according to John Davy. Once
a favourite resort of robbers and pirates, Davy thought it better adapted to
their needs than to those of a goddess. Vaudoncourt suggested that Homer
would find it very difficult to accommodate his description of the charming island of Calypso to this spot, but believed that the island was of great
importance as a military station, to observe the navigation of the Adriatic
Sea. Other Mediterranean islands have their claims to be Ogygia,
Calypso's isle, including Gozo, near Malta. Some ancient authorities considered Ogygia as a fantasy island or fairyland in the middle of the At-
lantic. Othoni can hardly be described as "the navel of the sea". You may
disapprove of what Eratosthenes wrote ("You will find the scene of the
wanderings of Odysseus when you find the cobbler who sewed up the bag
of the winds"), but he does have a point. Othoni has about as good a claim
to being the island of Calypso as Paxos does to being Aiaia (or Aeaea), the
island of the enchantress Circe. The Paxos and Othoni theories may sound
attractive to men who have fantasies about Calypso and Circe (until they
read the poem "Circe" by Carol Ann Duffy: they might not want to be
around when she's contemplating her pork recipes in the kitchen).

Kythira and Aphrodite

Kythira is claimed as the first port-of-call and even "chiefe seate" of
Aphrodite, although Cyprus has a stronger claim to being her legendary
birthplace. Lorentzos Mavilis stretches the point by appropriating the
legend, when he claims in his sonnet "Kerkyra" (the island he calls Venus
or Aphrodite of the Isles) that Aphrodite emerged in all her beauty and full
of erotic sweetness from the foaming, frothy seas off Corfu. Ugo Foscolo,
born in Zante in 1778, wrote of his maternal land, in one of his most
beautiful sonnets, "A Zacinto" ("To Zakynthos")"

> The fertile island in the Greek sea
> From which Aphrodite was born,
> And made with her first smile.

Edgar Allan Poe also wrote a sonnet "To Zante", in 1837, and of his "entombed hopes". But in his case, he was not thinking of the goddess Aphrodite so much as someone almost as unreachable, of a broken romance with Elmira Royster, the maiden who was there no more, the woman with whom he was still in love.

Fair isle, that from the fairest of all flowers,
Thy gentlest of all gentle names dost take....
O hyacinthine isle! O purple Zante!
"Isola d'oro! Fior di Levante!"

Andreas Kalvos, in his ode "O Philopatris" (1998), writes seductively that it was the Ionian waves and breezes that were the first to kiss and caress the body of Kythirian Aphrodite, just as the same waves and seabreezes kiss and caress the bodies and breasts of dazzling Zantiot virgins. He must have been homesick whenever he re-read those lines, when living in Lincolnshire, England. Sophie Atkinson writes that "from all the beautiful land of Greece it was Cythera that took to herself the legend of foamborn Aphrodite, and in that island a wonderful shrine long marked the birthplace and favoured haunt of the golden goddess". Maureen Duffy writes in her sequence of three sensuous Lesbian love poems, "Journey to Cythera", of her lover's body as like the island, whose latitudes only she knows intimately: "*Ile des doux secrets et des fêtes du Coeur!*" (a nod to Baudelaire), "Immortal Cythera touch us into eternity..."

Louis de Bernières read one of his poems about Kythira at the "Ionian Inspires" event at the Groucho Club, London, in November 2008. He told me that it is one of his favourite islands. He tutored a creative writing masterclass there in 1999. From his *Observer* article "How I learned to love Greece again", it is evident that Kythira has played an even more important part in his life than Kefalonia, where he feels too easily recognized.

THE IDENTIFICATION OF DODONA

There has been much confusion in the past about the identification of ancient sites in Epirus.

It was two Englishmen who first identified the site of Dramisios (also spelt Dhramisius, etc.) as that of Dodona: T. L. Donaldson, who visited the ruins in 1819 (he published his ideas in 1830), and Christopher

Wordsworth in 1839. Byron visited the site but was not aware that he was looking at the ruins of Dodona: "I do not know that we discovered anything worthy of remark in the Levant, except an Amphitheatre about three hours ride from Yanina in Epirus" (*Letters and Journals*, Vol. 2).

> Oh! where, Dodona! is thine aged grove
> Prophetic fount, and oracle divine?
> What valley echoed the response of Jove?
> What trace remaineth of the Thunderer's shrine?
> All, all forgotten...
> (*Childe Harold's Pilgrimage*, Canto II, st. 53)

Henry Holland also went to Dramasus (*sic*) and in 1815 described

> the remains of an ancient city in the valley, which lies on the eastern side of Olitzka. The ruins are unquestionably more interesting than any other in Epirus, and would be remarkable in any part of Greece, for the magnificent theatre which appears among them; and which in size, as well as in beauty of structure, is perhaps not equalled by any other similar edifice in this country... These ruins have hitherto been almost unknown to the antiquarian; and notwithstanding their magnitude, it is not yet well ascertained what ancient city they represent.

Holland did not guess that he might be looking at Dodona, even though he wrote:

> The question regarding the situation of Dodona, the most ancient of the Greek oracles, has generally been connected, more or less directly, with the country surrounding Ioannina... The modern inquiry respecting the situation of Dodona has been perplexed, by the different position assigned to it in ancient authors; some placing the seat of the oracle in Thesprotia, others in Molossia; others again in the district of Chaonia... The speculations of modern travellers have in general fixed its situation in the country to the north of Ioannina... A careful reference to all the passages in which it is mentioned by ancient writers, has led me to believe, that its real situation was to the south or south-east of Ioannina, and underneath the great mountain of Tzumerka.

Dr. Holland was getting warm, but then cold again.

The Reverend T. S. Hughes also comments on the various theories in 1820:

> Some persons place the site of Dodona upon the Zagoriot mountains on the other side of the lake, others at the village of Protopapas, near Zitsa: others again assert it to have been near the village of Glyki, on the borders of the Acheron, below the Suliot hills; and Dr. Holland…inclines to a situation between the Arachtus and Achelous, under the lofty mountain called Zumerka.

Leake described the site in 1835 and, from the nature of the buildings, conceived them to be an *Ieron*, and place of public assembly, protected by a fortress. "The position is so nearly central in the country of the *Molossi*, that it was probably a place of common sacrifice and political union for the use of all the towns of that division of Epirus."

The Reverend Hughes remarked that "No doubt the reader will be struck, as we ourselves were, with the extraordinary circumstance that a theatre of such vast dimension should have been attached to so diminutive a city. No rational explanation of this suggests itself, unless it be supposed that the theatre in fact did not belong so much to this particular city as to the Epirotian tribes in common." After inspecting the ruins of the theatre, where the rows of seats had been considerably damaged by past earthquakes, he adjourned to the village of Dramisus [sic] to sleep. At the conclusion of Part 1 of his book, he has provided a 16-page "Dissertation on the Oracle of Dodona", which asks his readers: "And if you find a place in the neighbourhood of Ioannina, bearing ruins on a hill, and whose local situation seems to correspond with that I have mentioned, search diligently for inscriptions, in the hope of finding Dodona."

Even at the time of Edward Lear's travels and his visit to see the ruins of Dhramisius (*sic*) on 10 May 1849, he writes that "it was impossible not to be greatly struck with the magnificent size and position of the great theatre". With no apparent inkling that he was looking at the site of ancient Dodona, Lear continues, quoting Leake (and apparently unaware of the published ideas of Donaldson and Wordsworth): "It is supposed that these extensive remains belong to a hierum and place of public meeting of the Molossi: 'a place of common sacrifice and political union, for the use of all the towns of that division of Epirus'." Lear hoped to return to Ioannina "to make drawings to aid at a future day in some poetical illustration of Dodona, for with that ancient city the site of Kastritza is considered by Colonel Leake to be identical; the fortress peninsula of the present city of Yannina he suggests as the position of the Dodonean temple". Lear puts great faith in Leake's topographical suggestions, and believed him to be correct on this matter: "Until I see a more beautiful Dodona I will believe, and it is a harmless even if an ill-founded credulity, that Dodona and the temple did stand at Kastritza and Yannina." Like Byron, Leake and Holland and before him, Lear had already seen the beautiful site of Dodona without knowing it.

George Bowen, who visited the site at around the same period as Lear, rode out to Dramisios in November 1849, "where there is the best preserved theatre in Greece, and other Hellenic remains. The whole are called by the peasants, like all the other ancient buildings, 'the old castle'". No part of the proscenium of the theatre was standing then. Bowen, like others, concluded that the remains were those of a national sanctuary of the Molossians, "very probably of Passaron, where their kings were inaugurated". He lingered in the theatre until after sunset, "repeopling, in imagination, the deserted walls with the thronging crowds of ancient days". Since he had read the work of Christopher Wordsworth, it is surprising that he does not mention the possibility that the theatre was a part of ancient Dodona.

Pouqueville in 1820-22 also identified the site as the ruins of Passaron, but the last time he saw the theatre Greeks were ploughing inside the orchestra and goats were eating whatever little greenery there was between the rows of stone seats.

Another Englishman, Professor N. G. L. Hammond, in 1967 identified the site of Aigai in Macedonia as Vergina, although in both cases it was talented Greek archaeologists who later carried out the excavations which provided hard evidence to support the topographical theories— Konstantinos Karapanos in the case of Dodona, Professor Manolis Andronikos in the case of Vergina—although the latter was initially cautious and refused to accept Hammond's advice to dig there. This is not to overlook the competition and political rivalry between archaeologists and national Schools of Archaeology based in Athens.

I find particularly fascinating the archaeological/topographical detective work of Christopher Wordsworth: "To ascertain the site of DODONA would seem now to require a response from the ORACLE itself. The former dwelling of the spirit, which once guided half the world, is lost... Still, we do not believe that the search for Dodona is hopeless." He goes on to discuss the ruins of the Kastro of Dramisios (Dramisus):

> The consideration of these two facts, the lowness of the situation, and the small extent of the city, seem conclusive objections against the opinion which has ascribed these ruins to Passaron, the metropolitan seat of the house of Pyrrhus. But, though the place which we are now viewing could have possessed no military power, still in a social respect, it seems to have been of considerable importance. Attached to the Acropolis, on the south-east, is the shell of a magnificent Theatre, one of the largest now existing in Greece. It is scooped in the declivity of the hill, with a southern aspect. Now, the existence of a theatre at all, especially in this district, is a very singular circumstance; but the existence of so grand a theatre, in so insignificant a place, is without a parallel in the whole of Greece.
>
> Proceeding eastward from the theatre, we observe another object, very unusual in the remains of Epirot cities. On the north of the theatre, between it and the gate of the lower city, are vestiges of two temples; of the most distant of the two, fourteen columns, or at least the fragments of them, are still standing. There are not, we believe, fourteen other columns remaining together in the whole of Epirus.
>
> Considering the circumstances, and the inferences to be deduced from them, we feel disposed to inquire whether, when contemplating these ruins, we are not treading the soil once hallowed by the presence of DODONA?
>
> The theatre was not designed for the entertainment of citizens only; it served as an attraction for strangers, and provided gratification for those who were brought there by the celebrity of the oracle.

George Bowen repeats the words of Wordsworth in 1852: "The truth is, that to ascertain the real site, would require a response from the oracle itself."

When Hammond first visited Dodona, most of the seating blocks had fallen down the slope, but that was before S. I. Dakaris had excavated and

The site at Dodona

restored the theatre. The extent of excavation can be seen from Hammond's photograph of the unrestored theatre (his Plate I). In terms of "landscape of the imagination", Hammond writes that "The most ancient memories about inland Epirus are concerned with Dodona. The site of Dodona is striking and awe-inspiring, and particularly so if it is approached from the south on the line of the Sacred Way over 'the divine bridge', the natural *theogephyra*." Before Zeus was worshipped there it is likely that Gaia, or "mother earth", was the cult mother-goddess, given that so many aspects of the oracle at Dodona were connected with aspects of nature (oaks, doves, springs, echoes and the wind), suggests Hammond.

This seems highly plausible, although the proximity of the sacred site (4 km) to the new Egnatia motorway from Igoumenitsa to Ioannina (the original Roman Egnatia road ran from Dyrrachium to Thessalonica, connecting the Adriatic with the Aegean), while making a casual visit much more convenient, takes away from the magical sense of remoteness which "cold, wintery" Dodona, the most ancient oracle in Greece, enjoyed in Homer's time and before. It is still a fantastic experience and environment, especially when the wild flowers are in bloom.

I once saw a powerful performance of *Oedipus Rex* in Modern Greek in the ancient theatre; performances are, alas, no longer held in the theatre itself, but on a makeshift stage with wooden seating, which is not quite the same experience. Who can resist giving his or her own impromptu performance for an imagined audience of thousands, or consulting the oracle before the sacred oak-tree?

What I found particularly thought-provoking in Hammond was the observation that "The branch of the Greek-speaking peoples which was particularly associated with Dodona in early tradition was the Hellenic branch proper", the "Hellenes". He mentions writers who place the early habitat of the Hellenes "in the area of Dodoni and the upper Achelous valley". Aristotle defines Ancient Greece as "the area around Dodona and the Achelous...for it was there that the Selloi and those who were then called Graikoi and are now called Hellenes used to live." He even suggests, after discussing evidence from *The Iliad*, that Achilles and the Hellenes came from the area of Dodona.

In terms of my regions and topics, I am happy to be able to mention this possible link of Achilles with Dodona, of Odysseus and Nausicaa with Corfu, and of Odysseus with Bounimae (Voutsa in Zagori). Hammond does not doubt that the earlier names for Corcyra were Scheria and Phaeacia. There is also the later story about Odysseus' links with Thesprotia in Epirus, and of his marriage, after killing Penelope's suitors in Ithaca, with Callidice, Queen of the Thesprotians. He thus became King of the Thesprotians, according to the *Telegony* of Eugammon of Cyrene (written *c.*565 BC). If the original Hellenes did indeed come from the Dodona area, it is perhaps no coincidence that the best Greek spoken in the early nineteenth century was considered to be in Ioannina.

Dodona has continued to exert a fascination for modern poets like Ruth Fainlight (from "The Oracle at Dodona"):

Someone has come to have his fate confirmed.
The stylos bit into the soft lead strip...
'Yes.' All would be as he wished.

ARCHAEOLOGY AND POLITICS
Professor Richard Clogg gave a paper in Athens in 1986 to mark the centenary of the establishment the British School of Archaeology, which he

revised for publication in 2000. He said that "the politics of archaeology in the independent Greek state have as yet been relatively unexplored. Given the importance of the heritage of the ancient Greek world to the formation of the modern Greek identity, this relative neglect is puzzling." He was particularly interested in the sensitive and controversial role of the foreign archaeological schools.

Thanasis Kalpaxis has written on the link between archaeology and hidden political interests, in relation to the excavations of the Temple of Artemis and the discovery of the famous Gorgon pediment in Corfu in 1911. This excavation involved Kaiser Wilhelm II and two archaeologists, the ill-fated Federiko Versakis for the Greek Service and the famous Dr. W. Dörpfeld working for the German Archaeological Institute—and for the German Emperor, who was spending his time on Corfu on political as well as on archaeological issues. The book provides insights into the convoluted diplomatic background in 1911 and the strained relationship between Versakis and Dörpfeld (both of whom saw themselves as the rightful directors of excavations), and not least into the scandal of the suitcase belonging to Dörpfeld which was found to contain antique golden jewellery (including "Penelope's" necklace) and other antiquities which he had sent from Lefkas for safe-keeping.

The superb black and white photographs in the Goethe-Institut's trilingual book on Wilhelm Dörpfeld evoke the landscape of Lefkas at the time. Dörpfeld worked in Lefkas from 1901 until 1913, convinced that he had discovered Homeric Ithaca and the capital of Odyssseus' kingdom. I visited his tomb on Lefkas to pay my respects, but I wonder if that was the appropriate thing to have done. The book makes no mention of his summons from Kaiser Wilhelm to conduct excavations in Corfu, nor of the malicious rumours—which later backfired—and which were possibly circulated by the bitterly disgruntled archaeologist Versakis (as recounted by T. Kalpaxis) concerning the discovery of the ancient ornaments and jewellery from "Homer's Ithaca" (i.e. Lefkas) in the suitcase belonging to Dörpfeld. The distinguished German archaeologist was not officially suspected of any wrongdoing and was considered as being entirely "above suspicion", but mud, once thrown, sometimes sticks. The priceless treasures, which included a gold bracelet and that gold necklace said to be Penelope's, had presumably been kept by Dörpfeld for security and research purposes, but some Greek newspapers were quick to accuse Dörpfeld of theft and of trading in antiquities. The German Embassy became involved and Dörpfeld's name was soon cleared; but it was the beginning of the end for Versakis, who was transferred shortly afterwards.

NEKROMANTEION AND ACHERON

I do not know whether Christopher Wordsworth was also the first person since Pausanias to identify the ruins of a Nekromanteion, or Nekyomanteion (as Hammond and Dakaris call it, using the Ancient Greek form *necys* meaning dead), situated near the north-west shores of the Acherousian Lake, where Acheron and Cocytus, the rivers of Hades, were said to meet, but Wordsworth writes, "We are inclined to believe that this was the oracular shrine where the spirits of the dead were consulted... The banks of the Acheron...were the favourite resort of Necromancy."

Hammond writes, "We know from the Homeric epic that its place was already secure in Greek belief by the time of Homer... Persephone, Hades, and Cerberus may be as old as the identification of the entrance to the underworld at the confluence of the Acheron, the Cocytus, and the Priphlegethon near Likouresi." Pausanius, notes Hammond, "thought that Homer must have seen the district. His description of the entry to Hades

The banks of the Acheron

in the words ascribed to Circe in Odyssey... is very true of the Acheron plain."

Herodotus relates the gruesome but fascinating story concerning Periander, the seventh-century BC tyrant of Corinth, and his wife Melissa, whom he murdered and then raped after her death ("he put his loaf in a cold oven"). Apart from being an alleged necrophiliac, the same Periander, according to Thucydides, sent three hundred sons of the leading men of Corcyra for castration, to be used as eunuchs. Sotirios Dakaris, in his *Nekyomanteion*, plays down the more macabre elements in the story.

The so-called "Nekromanteion", the sanctuary of Hades and the dread Persephone, is, frustratingly, not fully substantiated or universally accepted as such by all archaeologists and scholars, some of whom remain sceptical (among them the American Professor James Wiseman and the Germans D. Baatz and L. Haselberger) and have suggested plausible alternative theories and interpretations of the site, i.e. as a fortified farmstead with a tower. Where Professor Sotirios Dakaris saw evidence of of a bronze windlass and mechanical trickery, Dietwulf Baatz identified third-century BC catapults, without other uses. Whatever the conclusions and findings of different archaeologists, the location of the site near the Acheron and Cocytos rivers, which meet north of Parga on the Epirot seaboard, and the ancient Acherousian Lake, is compelling evidence in itself. Reading Homer and Herodotus in this environment is an extraordinary experience, and such theories should not be allowed to spoil or diminish it. During a visit during the early 1980s, I thought of Shakespeare's *Macbeth* and Hecate's "Get you gone, and at the pit of Acheron meet me I' th' morning; thither he will come to know his destiny." On that visit they led us down to the Hall of Hades, past the maze to Persephone's cave, the dimly-lit pit of Acheron. It seemed as if we had really come to the kingdom of the dead and were surrounded by the shades of shades.

The Reverend Hughes was moved to poetry by the sight of the Acheron River and the craggy hills and rocks of Suli and Kiaffa. He wrote a "Poetical Address to the Acheron":

Hail Acheron! Thou dark mysterious stream!
Hail! Tho' thy terrors like a frightful dream
Be vanish'd: tho' the fearless eagle soar
In circling flight around th' Aornian shore...

At the end of March 2008 I joined a group of Greek professional guides on a short trip on the Acheron, and we saw the hills and mountains of Suli, which we were to visit on the following day, and where we were able to discover for ourselves, as we walked, near the source of the Acheron, the famed river as it rushes down through the gorge, and which, in Hughes' words, "from rock to rock/Bounds with impetuous force and thundering shock". In terms of the landscape of the imagination, the Reverend Hughes seems to have suffered from an overdose of exciting impressions and stimulating associations:

> When I retired to rest, the objects which had employed my waking thoughts still continued to occupy my dreams, and a strange species of pantomimic scenery presented itself to my imagination, wherein Pluto and Proserpine, Hercules, Theseus and Pirithous, Roman conquerors and Greek priests, Ali Pasha [often referred to in histories as Ali Pacha] and San Donato, all played conspicuous characters. These personages, after various evolutions, were collected together, as I thought, upon the steepest crags of Suli, where the rock suddenly opening and vomiting forth a terrible flame, they were all swallowed up in the unfathomable abyss. I awoke with horror.

I hope this book does not give the reader similar dreams and nightmares.

THE IMAGINATIVE LEAP

We need the speculations of romantic (as well as rational) classicists and topographers, and I can think of no more sincere expression of their feelings than these words of Edward Dodwell, when he arrived at Zakynthos, after setting out on his second voyage to Greece, from Messina (which he left on 1 February 1805):

> I cannot describe the sensation which I experienced, on approaching the classic shores of Greece. My mind was agitated by the delights of the present, and the recollections of the past... I beheld the native soil of the great men whom I had so often admired; of the poets, historians, and orators, whose works I had perused with delight, and to whom Europe has been indebted for so much of her high sentiment, and her

intellectual cultivation... The view before me comprehended the most interesting countries in the classic world.

In the more immediate vicinity was Zakunthos [*sic*], with its hills of soft verdure, and its plains of varied wealth; with the town, the fortress, the port and Mount Scopo, the ancient Elatos, towering above with its pointed top... There was ample gratification for the eye and the mind.

I wish I could have felt the same sensation. It has become much harder to experience such a sense of visual and mental gratification in modern Zakynthos.

The Reverend Hughes was asked by Ali Pasha about the motives of Englishmen in undergoing hardships and danger to visit remote places:

I endeavoured to give him some idea of our mode of education and that general cultivation of Greek literature which is apt so strongly to influence the imagination and generate enthusiasm; which impels us to visit the land which nurtured and matured those ancient prodigies of talent, and to contemplate the scenes where so many historical events took place.

In the anonymous *The Ionian Islands under British Protection* (1851) the author exclaims, "Here, —amid the scenery of the Odyssey,—we are transported by a sudden leap over a hundred generations to the...brilliant period of Greek mythology and song; while History, both ancient and modern, supplies us with associations no less striking."

Tertius Kendrick (1822, describing a journey to Zakynthos begun in 1813) initially shared some of the same feelings as Dodwell: "My first landing on the sacred land of Greece can never be effaced from my memory: my heart beat high with veneration and enthusiasm, to find myself on a territory renowned by Homer..." but he was soon complaining of "the almost Hottentot customs of the peasantry", and the "bigotry of the Zantiotes, aided by the prejudice of the priests" which put a check on potential friendships between Englishmen and Greeks "which our own excellent administration of justice should so naturally call forth". It is hardly surprising that the Zantiots were reluctant to show friendship, when Kendrick describes their features as "swarthy and of a villainous cast, corresponding to the vices reigning in their hearts". I have to disagree with him when he writes disparagingly about Corfiot women: "In vain might a person search for a Corfuoite lady, whose mind is chastened by ornamental and useful acquirements—whose charms in discourse would give solidity to virtue, and grace to the common relations of human life."

Thomas Hardy, too, would seem to have had his own highly imaginative vision of what a Corfiot (or half-Corfiot) woman might have been like, if we are to judge by his description of Eustacia Wye in *The Return of the Native*:

> Eustacia Vye was the raw material of a divinity. On Olympus she would have done well with a little preparation... She had pagan eyes, full of nocturnal mysteries... The mouth seemed formed less to speak than to quiver, less to quiver than to kiss. Some might have added, less to kiss than to curl... She was the daughter of the bandmaster of a regiment which had been quartered there—a Corfiote by birth, and a fine musician—who met his future wife during her trip thither with her father the captain, a man of good family... Where did her dignity come from? By a latent vein from Alcinous' line, her father hailing from Phaeacia's isle?

Kostis Palamas wrote, in his poem "Corfu":

> There where Homer's Phaecians still live
> And the East joins the West with a kiss;
> There, where the cypress always grows with the olive,
> Its deep-green costume against the infinite blue;
> There my soul sought to live in harmony,
> With the majestic view of the land of Pyrrhus.

Fynes Moryson made brief visits to Corfu in 1596 and 1597 and observed that "the island is worthily reputed one of the Chief Keys of Christendom".

George Sandys wrote in 1670 that Corfu was "more anciently Phæecia, celebrated by Homer for the shipwreck of Ulysses, and orchards of Alcinous". His description of the island is not altogether accurate: "The South part is mountainous: the North part level." But it rings true when he notes "the whole adorned with groves of oranges, lemons, pomegranates, fig-trees, olives, and the like; enriched with excellent wines and abundance of honey".

William Lithgow (1632) wrote of Corfu, "This isle was much honoured by Homer, for the pleasant gardens of Alcino, which were in his time. This Alcino was that Corcyrian poet, who so benignly received Ulysses after his shipwreck…"

On 15 September 1806, Colonel William Leake noted on entering the Gulf of Molo, Ithaca:

> To the right rises with extreme steepness the great mountain of Anoí, which, being the highest and greatest in the island, we can have no difficulty in identifying with the *Neritum* of the poet… Every peasant is acquainted with the name of Odhyssefs, though few know much of his story, and probably not six persons in the island have ever read Homer… Ithaca, as the poet justly remarks in the Odyssey, is rugged, has no good roads, and is not well adapted to horses; though small, it is not unproductive, but yields good corn and wine, and feeds goats and oxen. So far its modern state resembles that of the time of Homer; but the mountains are no longer shaded with woods, and this may be the reason why the rain and the dew are not so plentiful as the poet represents, and why the island no longer abounds in hogs fattening upon acorns.

Leake also points out that the Greeks never ceased to call the island by its ancient name, although the ordinary people called it "Thiaki" rather than "Ithaki".

FURTHER THEORIES

Some more recent theorists go as far as placing Odysseus' wanderings in the Baltic Sea (Dr. F. Vinci, 2006), or from the Canary Islands and Madeira up to Ireland, Scotland and even Norway (Edward Furlong). Tim Severin developed his own theories, as recounted in *The Ulysses Voyage*, when he sailed from Troy to Ithaca in a replica of a Bronze Age galley; for him the Island of Circe is Paxos. The Vinci theory recently found new support in the form of an extensive article on whether Odysseus set sail in Scandinavia, by Professor W. Mullen. For two summers the classics professor and his students sailed around the Scandinavian part of the Baltic Sea "exploring the strange idea that very early versions of Homer's epics were set there", remapping the story, with its many incongruities, onto a northern setting; as he puts it: "the dirty little secret of classical scholarship is that the eastern Mediterranean has never looked like a good match for Homer's tales". Dr. Vinci is a nuclear engineer by profession, but he has an extensive background in Latin and Greek studies.

Wolfgang Geisthövel (2005) also follows the wanderings of Odysseus, with reference to the theories of Professor John Luce and Professor Armin Wolf and his brother Hans-Helmut Wolf. He points out that since classical antiquity there have been around ninety attempts to locate the places visited by Odysseus. He takes John Luce as his guide in accepting modern Ithaca as Homer's Ithaca, but follows the Wolfs in identifying Calabria as Homer's Scheria, the land of the Phaeacians, and Tiriolo as their city.

There is a persuasive, if browbeating, academic and scientific lobby (R. Bittlestone, J. Diggle and J. Underhill, 2005), and an effective PR machine, which support the latest hypothesis and efforts that seek to prove that Ithaca was actually an island located just to the west of—but now forming part of—Kefalonia. Although their book is richly illustrated and is a source for much valuable information about past theories and the geology of the islands, it is too much of a blockbuster detective story for some tastes. The Greek edition caused a stir when launched in March 2008. Bittlestone, an amateur researcher assisted by distinguished scholars, seems a little too determined to demonstrate that the Paliki peninsula of Kefalonia was once an island itself, separated by a narrow channel that became blocked by rockfalls and landslides, caused by earthquakes and geological changes in the landscape. This landlocked isthmus, he argues, with evidence from boreholes, would make the Paliki peninsula, if and when it was a separate island, accord more closely to Homer's descriptions of Ithaca, as put in the mouth of Odysseus.

Lt. Col. Napier (1825) makes the point that "The Isthmus might easily be cut, and a heavy sea would pour through, during all northerly and southerly winds."

I find the most intelligent commentary on this issue was provided by Christopher Wordsworth: "Is the modern THIAKI, in which we will now suppose ourselves, the ITHACA of the Odyssey or not?" Thanks to a German topographer, says Wordsworth,

> we are called upon to treat the *modern* Ithaca with the same contemptuous usage with which it is said the Sublime Porte once menaced some refractory islanders, when he told them that, if they did not believe the

edict he had sent them, they and their country should be shovelled into the sea; or, if THIAKI is permitted to survive any longer at all, it is ordered to float *away from its present position, and, after a short cruise in the Ionian* sea, to cast anchor on the *western* instead of the *eastern*, side of the island of CEPHALLONIA.

We are assured, that, however we may lament the fact, the sentence of transportation has been passed upon the island of Ithaca, in the lines of the *Odyssey* in which Ulysses gives a history of himself to Alcinous. They occur near the commencement of the ninth book:

"I dwell in sunny ITHACA...
   It stedfast stands, highest above the wave,
   Westward..."

It's alleged that, in these verses, Ithaca is placed to the *west* of the other islands, whereas, in fact, it is to the *east* of them; nor can it be denied that we are here met by a difficulty, in our attempt to identify the geography of Homer with that of our own maps.

Wordsworth believes that the problem of one stubborn passage in a long poem is insufficient ground for such a theory, and he does make a good attempt to explain away the geographical problem.

I keep an open mind. Whether your imagination favours Lefkas (like W. Dörpfeld and E. Mireaux), Ithaca (Sir W. Gell, Sir G. Bowen, D. Paizis-Danias, Professor John Luce and others) or Kefalonia (around ten conflicting theories exist) as the true location of Homer's Ithaca is ultimately as immaterial to me as to whether you think Odysseus came ashore and met Nausicaa at Ermones, Kanoni, Mandouki, Potamos, Afionas, Palaiokastritsa in Corfu—although I am not so keen on Calabria. If Lefkas was Homer's Ithaca (reachable on foot, at various periods) then one has to consider whether Nidri or Vassiliki was the site of Odysseus's palace (www.metrum.org). Dr. Dörpfeld, who is buried at Nidri, believed that Lefkas was the Ithaca of Homer, and that Odysseus' palace was situated close to Nidri.

Since all the islands could have constituted Odysseus' kingdom, all of them have some claim on our imaginations.

Chapter Two
IONIAN HISTORY

Myths, dreams and legends are central to the human imagination; historical and geographical facts can stimulate the imagination but more often they can undermine it. One thinks of the power of the Serbian historical memory and the heroic ballads, epics and songs concerning the Battle of Kosovo Field (the Field of the Blackbirds) in June 1389, when the armies of the Serbian Prince Lazar were defeated by the Turkish forces of the Ottoman Sultan Murad I.

Ismail Kadaré published some of his earlier Communist and national poems in a French language edition in 1981. There is one on "The Defeat of the Balkan Countries by the Turks in the Plain of Kosovo in 1389":

In one day the great European peninsula became Asiatic…
How much blood will be shed to rebuild what has been destroyed!
It's night. A cold and unknown sky spreads out to infinity,
And the Crescent has appeared, all powerful…

The battles of Kosovo never really ceased to haunt the Balkan imagination, and the war of words was taken up by British writers who favoured either the Orthodox Christian Serbs or the Muslim Albanians, like Rebecca West and Edith Durham. More recent writers like Miranda Vickers and James Pettifer seem to continue in this partisan tradition concerning Greek–Albanian issues. They have a different historical and imaginative landscape, perhaps less Philhellenic than some; they seem to see the environment through very different eyes, when they write of the empty interior of Epirus, and the area known to Albanians as Chameria, of the scattered settlements from which Albanians, Slavs and Greeks were driven because of their ethnicity or political beliefs. They describe villages once occupied by ethnic Albanians or Chams, forced towards the end of the Second World War to flee their ruined houses, mosques and other buildings ("The Challenge to Preserve the Cham Heritage"; websites of the Albanian American Civic League, and of the PDI, the European Integration and Justice Albanian Party movement).

Maybe we all find what we are looking for, or what we are encouraged to see. There are many other reasons for the depopulation of Greek mountain villages.

A broader and more balanced view can be found in Bruce Clark's book of 2006, dealing with the impact of the 1923 Lausanne Convention, which resulted in the mass population exchange, 400,000 Muslims being forced to move from Greece to Turkey, and 1.2 million Greek Orthodox Christians "either shifted from Turkey to Greece or, if they had moved already, told they could never return to their old homes". Clark points out the "curious silences" in both countries about the estimated 2,300 Ottoman monuments in Greece which ought to be preserved for aesthetic or historical reasons. Most of them are neglected, ignored and used for unsuitable purposes. Greeks and Turks often pretend these monuments do not exist, yet there are people still alive who can remember when the minarets of Ioannina were still in use. Clark is at his most perceptive when he writes:

> To a condescending visitor from a peaceful and prosperous part of the western world…the remains of a *tekke* or Muslim shrine on the Greek–Albanian border can indeed evoke a charming lost world, far more appealing, on aesthetic grounds, than anything which has been constructed since. What these feelings ignore is the poverty and brutality of the peasant culture in which these buildings may have provided the only solace; and the atmosphere of terror, persisting over several decades, which may have preceded their abandonment.

In terms of preservation of buildings, one might point out the need for better preservation of Venetian structures, too, such as the old boat arsenal at Gouvia in Corfu. Until recently, many of the British Protectorate monuments were in a sorry state of repair, often crumbling and covered with graffiti.

THUCYDIDES AND CLASSICAL HISTORY

For certain periods of history, we are lucky to have historians of the quality of Nicholas Hammond, Anna Komnena (b. 1083, daughter of Emperor Alexios Komneno) and Thucydides, who could present a balanced account and both sides of an argument or dispute (for all the accusations of partisanship or bias that may have been made at one time or another). In terms of the history of Corfu, British readers shouldn't overlook the pioneering volume by Andrea Marmora of 1672.

In *The Peloponnesian War*, Thucydides provides us with the arguments that the Corinthian and Corcyrean representatives or ambassadors made when stating their cases at the assembly to win the support and assistance of Athens.

> *Corcyra:* Apart from all other advantages, Corcyra lies in an excellent position on the coastal route to Italy and Sicily, and is thus able to prevent naval reinforcements coming to the Peloponnese from there, or going from the Peloponnese to those countries.
>
> *Corinth:* The geographical situation of Corcyra gives its inhabitants a certain independence. The ships of other states are forced to put in to their harbours much more often than Corcyrean ships visit the harbours of other states... This neutrality of theirs, which sounds so innocent, was in fact a disguise adopted...in order to give them a perfectly free hand to do wrong themselves...the conduct of Corcyra has been both violent and grasping.

The Corcyreans could be crafty and cruel. Their naval force never made it to Salamis to join the battle against Xerxes' Persian force. Their excuse was the adverse wind, weather conditions and heavy seas. Jervis-White Jervis (1852) dismisses the claims that Corcyra played an influential role in Ancient Greece: "Yet, in what did Corcyra conduce to this influence? In what science or art did she shine? Is it because she afforded Thucydides a melancholy theme for the display of that accuracy of political reasoning which has since become a model to statesmen?" Like Schlegel, Jervis-White Jervis thinks it is a vain effort for a Corfiot to boast of his Ancient Greek ancestry and genealogy, considering the centuries of racial intermingling with barbarian invaders and settlers.

Professor Jeffrey Rusten of Cornell University cites the satirical comments of the comic poet Hermippus (active 430s-410s BC) concerning the Corcyrean claims to be the heirs of the Phaecians, and the poet's prayers that Poseidon will destroy them and their hollow ships, "Since they are of two minds/ So much for that part of the world." Of Corcyra, Rusten writes of "its rich tradition of getting into mythological and historical trouble".

Rex Warner (1972) cites Thucydides' description of the effects of revolution in Corcyra and of the general deterioration of character throughout the Greek world, the first sign of which was that "the simple way of looking at things... so much the mark of a noble nature, was regarded as a ridiculous quality and soon ceased to exist". Words began to change their usual meanings: "any idea of moderation was just an attempt to disguise one's unmanly character; ability to understand a question from all sides meant that one was totally unfitted for action. Fanatical enthusiasm was the mark of a real man". It is perhaps surprising that Jervis-White Jervis does not trace the perceived weaknesses in the nineteenth-century Corfiot character back to the revolution in Corcyra as described by Thucydides, rather than to the usual target of British officials—i.e. the corrupting influence of the Venetians.

Thomas Gallant (2002) does make the point that Sir George Bowen (in an article of 1852) did just that, by tracing the Ionian Islanders' character shortcomings back 23 centuries to antiquity, and to Thucydides' account of the Civil War in Corcyra.

It is a temptation to be resisted, tracing Modern Greek virtues and vices back into the past, whether to the times of Turkish or Venetian domination, or all the way back to classical antiquity. Some are tempted to quote the Greek historian Herodian (AD c.170-240), as if his observations remained valid in Byron's or even more recent times: "an ancient passion of the Greeks was ever to rise against each other desiring to bring down those who aimed at excelling".

Rather earlier, in 229 BC, the island had welcomed Rome's declaration of war on Illyria's Queen Teuta, who had besieged the city of Corcyra; the island was willing enough to be placed under Roman protection. When the Roman galleys came to the rescue and lifted the siege, it was to cost the island five centuries of occupation.

Normans, Venetians and Napoleon

Anna Komnena writes at length of Robert Guiscard, the Norman Duke of Lombardy, and of the hostile actions of his fleet subduing the rebellious island of Corfu. The Byzantine Emperor decided to challenge him, with the help of the Venetians, who at first defeated him near Kassiopi harbour. But "once more he assailed the Venetians. The latter were astounded by the unexpectedness of it, but lost no time in linking their bigger vessels with

Remains of Venetian castle at Parga

iron chains in the port of Corfu, with the smaller ships inside this compact circle (the so-called 'sea harbour')… In the ensuing battle—terrible and more violent than the two previous encounters—both sides fought with an unprecedented passion and neither would give way; indeed they collided head on."

The Venetian ships had no cargo and were floating high in the water, "so that when the men all rushed to one side to oppose the enemy, the boats immediately sank. Up to 13,000 Venetians were drowned. The other vessels were captured, with their crews. Unfortunately Robert behaved in cruel fashion after his famous victory. Many of the prisoners were treated with hideous savagery: some were blinded, others had their noses cut off, others lost hands or feet or both." In a further engagement, the Venetians attacked him off Butrint and won the battle, killing many of Robert's men. Arthur Foss discusses the Normans' interest, under their great leader, the restless warrior Guiscard, in profiting from the decline of the Byzantine Empire at the time of the Crusades. Guiscard is believed to have died in Fiskardo, Kefalonia, c.1085.

Episodes such as I have mentioned, snatched from the historical records and accounts as they stand, give us a vivid glimpse into the changing conditions of the times. The Normans and the Venetians could be no less cruel than the Turks or Ali Pasha. But the Corfiots were quick enough to seek Venetian protection and to vow allegiance to Venice when threatened with invasion in the fourteenth century. The Venetians ruled Corfu from May 1386, for 410 years.

The Corcyreans and Corinthians were as aware of Corcyra's/Corfu's strategic position as the Venetians and Napoleon Bonaparte. Casanova was in Corfu 1744-5, and served as adjutant to the commander of galleasses, the triple-masted galleys then common in naval warfare. Although more interested in pursuing the fair sex, he commented on the naval strategy of the Republic of Venice: "There is one thing that the Republic of Venice will never alter: I mean the galleys, because the Venetians truly require such vessels to ply, in all weathers and in spite of the frequent calms, in a narrow sea, and because they would not know what to do with the men sentenced to hard labour." Writing in 1797, he says that "The convicts of the Republic, however, enjoy many privileges, and are, in every way, better treated than the soldiers... The reason for it is that the Republic has always believed galley-slaves more necessary than soldiers. The Venetians may perhaps now...begin to realize their mistake."

The French fleet arrived in June 1797. Napoleon was to write to Talleyrand, "I think that henceforth the chief maxim of the French Republic should be never to give up Corfu, Zante, etc." This statement, as abbreviated by writers focused on Corfu like Lawrence Durrell and John Forte, is quoted more fully by K. E. Fleming (1999), and continues "In this way we will find resources for our commerce, which would be of great significance to us, and to the future course of events in Europe."

Durrell also quotes an earlier statement, an entry from Napoleon's diary: "With Malta and Corfu we should soon be masters of the Mediterranean." M. Pratt quotes from Napoleon's letter to his brother Joseph, on the throne of Naples: "Corfu is so important to me that its loss would deal a fatal blow to my plans. The Adriatic would be closed, and your kingdom would have on its left flank a port where the enemy could assemble to attack you. You must regard it as more valuable than Sicily. Mark my words: in the current situation in Europe the worst misfortune that can happen to me is to lose Corfu." He wrote to the French Ministry of External Relations that "Corfu and Zante make us masters of the Adriatic, and these islands are of the greatest importance to us." To the Executive Directory he wrote that

Napoleon Bonaparte

"the islands of Corfu, Zante and Cephalonia are more important for us than the whole of Italy together". Napoleon also got rid of all the aristocratic privileges of the Libro d'Oro signori, the "Golden Book" register of noble families (as quoted by Peter Levi from a document in Corfu Archives, "*Touts les fiefs et droits quelconques sont abolis dans cette île. Napoléon*").

J. C. Hobhouse commented that "The friends of universal freedom were, of course, the friends of the Greeks, and long before the cession of the Seven Islands to the tri-coloured flag, the Carmagnole was danced on the shores of the Ionian sea." He quotes a verse from a Greek song, which he offers in translation:

'Tis true the French would have it known
Corfu shall shortly be their own,
Cefalonia too, and Zante
The fairest flower of the Levant.

Once Napoleon had occupied the Ionian Islands, he wrote to the French Directory in 1797, to emphasize how important the islands of Corfu, Zante and Cephalonia were to him. Since the Empire of the Turks was crumbling, the possession of the islands would enable the French to support it as far as that was possible, or to take their share. The time was no longer distant, he wrote, when they would feel that to destroy England truly, they would have to capture Egypt.

Before many years had passed, Konstantinos Stamatis, an agent of the French, "an ardent propagandist for French revolutionary ideas" (Clogg, 1976), would be composing an appeal to the Ionian Islanders, shortly after they had passed from French to joint Russo/Turkish rule in 1798. He tells the Ionian Islanders, "You, first, O eternal shame of my nation, have betrayed your brave defenders, you have trampled under your feet the symbols of their glory, you have run unanimously and with open arms to welcome the chains of tyranny... At this very time, O the ingratitude of it, the Zakynthians, the Kephalonians, the Corfiots themselves, apostasised against their liberators, they have cheered the tyranny..."

Charles James Napier, although convinced of the importance of the Ionian Islands to Great Britain, disputed the strategic importance of Corfu. He favoured Kefalonia. He is still greatly honoured in Argostoli, and the Napier Garden contains his bust, which was defaced by Fascist Italian soldiers in 1943. There is an informative permanent open-air exhibition in the garden which does great honour to his contribution and public works. He believed it was impolitic to give up the Ionian Islands:

> Like the Bermudas, the Ionian Islands possess a *central position*, being surrounded by countries undergoing great political changes, in which changes England, right or wrong, will interfere; with which countries she drives a considerable traffic, and among which she oftentimes has waged and may again wage war. We see that the Ionian islands are midway between England and the Persian Gulf; are two-thirds of the way to the Red Sea: they are conveniently situated to communicate with all parts of the Levant: they block up the mouth of the Adriatic Sea.

CORFU VS. KEFALONIA

Viscount Kirkwall (1864) disagreed: "although Sir Charles Napier, misled by his natural feelings of partiality, would have substituted Cephalonia for Corfu as the military head-quarters of the Islands, such an opinion has never been shared by any other officer of reputation. Corfu is still unrivalled as the strongest and most valuable of eastern fortresses."

Fynes Moryson may have believed that Corfu was worthily reputed as one of the chief keys of Christendom, but Napier did not accept that Corfu was the "key of the Adriatic" or that enormous amounts of money needed to be spent on its fortifications, at the expense of the Southern Islands of Zante or Kefalonia: "the best fortifications for Corfu are British men-of-war". He agreed that Corfu deserved to be called the key of the Adriatic when Venice was a great naval and commercial power, when oared galleys were the ships of war and nautical operations were on a smaller scale. Now that the seas were ruled by fleets, future struggles would take place on the open seas between fleets of heavy ships. The harbour of Corfu was not equal to that of Kefalonia, he argued, as a harbour for large fleets. Kefalonia was best suited for the seat of government. Kefalonia was physically larger; Zante had the larger revenue from trade. Corfu was far away from the other islands, at the northern extremity of the Ionian States. It therefore took no natural lead. "If the idea be entertained, of abandoning all the Ionian islands but one, (and the report seems to gain credit,) then, I think, it should be Cefalonia, not Corfu, which ought to be preserved… Such an island is surely too valuable to give up."

Having recently revisited Kefalonia (May-June 2008) I think he may well have been right. Quite apart from its strategic position, Kefalonia has preserved its natural beauty better than Corfu (in spite of the earthquake of 1953), although both islands have to some extent been 'recolonized' by the British. The population of Kefalonia is much smaller than that of Corfu (37,935 compared to 128,117 in 2008), which accounts in part for its greater cleanliness and lack of rubbish. Kefalonia had a 19.3% increase in tourist numbers in the period January-August 2008; Corfu's numbers fell 3.43% by comparison. But for the period January-July 2009 Kefalonia's figures were down 24% on the previous year, almost certainly a result of the impact of the recession in Northern Europe. Kefalonia has other problems: 3,000 hectares of forest and shrub were burnt recently, and other fires have been started by arsonists, allegedly to create grazing land for sheep. In Napier's time overgrazing of the land by goats was the main problem.

THE BRITISH PROTECTORATE

The idea of giving up all the islands except one was already being discussed before 1833. Much later Sir George Bowen would be arguing the case to Sir John Young (Lord High Commissioner from 1854) and to William Gladstone (Extraordinary High Commissioner, 1858-9) for giving up all the other islands but retaining Corfu and Paxos. Bowen proposed it in 1850: "We wish we could see any method by which England might, with honour and justice, surrender the really Greek islands to Greece, along whose coast they lie, and incorporate with the British Empire like Malta and Gibraltar, the half-Venetian, half-Albanian Corfu... Corfu, if annexed to Greece, must sink at once into a petty provincial town from a seat of Government and head-quarters of a large garrison."

The author would include the small island of Paxos with Corfu, as a dependency. He states that such a plan, if feasible, "would rescue Great Britain from all political embarrassment and would confer a real blessing on the Corfuotes by admitting them to all the privileges of British subjects; while their country would be enriched by the English capitalists and set-tlers who would in such an event make their home on the shores of the Adriatic, in the most beautiful and interesting of islands, by the brightest of seas, and beneath the softest of skies".

The biography of Sir George Bowen edited by Lane-Poole sets out Bowen's position clearly:

Sir George Bowen strongly advocated...that...the proper course for England to pursue would be to give up to the Kingdom of Greece the southern Ionian Islands (Cephalonia, Ithaca, Leucadia, Zante, and Cerigo) which lay along the coasts of that kingdom, and where the population and their sympathies were purely Hellenic; and to incorporate into the British Empire (like Malta and Gibraltar), Corfu, with, of course, its tiny satellite Paxo, which lay off the coast of the Turkish province of Albania, and where all the upper classes and a considerable part of the general population were Italian rather than Hellenic in language, feeling, and customs. Moreover, large sums of money had been spent on the fortifications of Corfu, whereas there were practically no strongholds in the southern islands... He showed that Corfu has always been of supreme importance, both in ancient and modern times, as a commanding naval and military station, controlling the entrance to the Adriatic Sea... The ultimate result of Mr. Gladstone's mission, however, was the surrender of Corfu, together with the southern Ionian Islands.

In a footnote the author explains that much difficulty was created by the premature publication in a London journal of a copy (purloined from the Colonial Office) of a despatch from the Lord High Commissioner, Sir John Young, in which these views were advocated.

According to Kirkwall, "Mr. Gladstone, who had come out such a warm Philhellene, departed thoroughly disgusted with the Greeks in general, and with the Ionians in particular." Tricked by Disraeli into accepting the mission ("in order to indulge his passion for classical scholarship", according to S. Bradford), one wonders how he allowed himself to be manipulated by Benjamin Disraeli, who had entertained pro-Turkish prejudices at least since the time he had conceived the idea of volunteering for the Turkish army, and since being entertained by the Grand Vizir, Reschid Pasha, in Ioannina in 1830. In a letter of 18 November 1830, Disraeli wrote about "the delight of being made much of by a man who was daily decapitating half the Province", adding that "I detest the Greeks more than ever". There were always suspicions in the Ionian Islands that Sir Thomas Maitland, the first Lord High Commissioner, favoured the Turks; his policy of strict neutrality at the time of the Greek War of Independence could hardly have endeared him to the Greeks, who would thereafter often invoke his name when they cursed, "*Skata stin psychi tou*

Metella!" being one nice Kefalonian example from Kavadias' novel, best left untranslated or rendered less offensively as *"Merde à Maitland!"* In another novel, by Kay Cicellis, the teacher of English in Argostoli kept insisting that the correct form of the name was not *Metella*, but *Maitland*.

One wonders how strong Byronic Philhellenic sentiments were in London after Gladstone's failed mission. The Union of the Ionian Islands with Greece may have come as something of a relief to many. In fact, Kirkwall writes, "to grant the cession of the Islands to Greece was the only sensible alternative to the carrying out the plans proposed by Sir John Young." Gardner (1859) was not of that opinion: "By what process of thought could Sir John Young then have concluded that it is to British interests to recede from most of the Ionian islands? They are invaluable to us, and to any power that rules the sea." He had clearly turned against Philhellenism: "Philhellenism was once thought a very great virtue, which Byron did great mischief by encouraging...would that he could rise again, if only to see the land, which turned his head, and visit Mesolonghi, to which he left his heart!...that wretched town...Philhellenism is now a thorough vice, and nuisance, and ought to be discouraged; no good will come out of Greece." Writing in 1858, Gardner recommended that the free press should be at once abolished, as there was no need to fear an insurrection. "The Ionians", he said, "are vociferous, and talk big, and they would, if they dare, shoot from behind rocks and trees, but they have no courage for fighting in the open."

Kirkwall gives details of the 1858 robbery from the Colonial Office of Sir John Young's famous despatch of 10 June 1857, which then appeared in a London journal (*The Daily News*) and subsequently in other papers. In the despatch the Lord High Commissioner had recommended that Corfu and Paxos should, with the probable consent of their inhabitants, "be converted into British colonies... Sir George Bowen is universally believed to have been the adviser of Sir John Young in writing that unfortunate despatch." The Corfiot and Paxiot political representatives naturally protested against this "intrigue against the inhabitants of those islands, who had no other desire than to be united with Greece". Gladstone arrived in Corfu on 24 November 1858, and was soon to recommend the recall of Sir John Young, "especially after publication of the famous despatch".

How much influence did Bowen's wife, Diamantina Roma, exercise on the thinking of her husband (who was President of the Ionian Academy 1847-51)? Diamantina was the daughter of Count Giorgio-Candiano di Roma (President of the Senate of the Ionian Islands 1850-56); her mother was Countess Orsola. It is quite possible that the Count had influenced his future son-in-law's thinking (or vice-versa?). George Bowen and Diamantina Roma were married on 28 April 1856. Bowen was very careful in his book *Ithaca in 1850* to keep the political affairs of the Ionian Islands out of it, "and yet they well deserve inquiry and discussion". He recommended that anyone who might want to discuss the state of Greece could hardly do wrong "in adopting for his observations the same basis as Thucydides", advice which he seems not to have followed himself when he moved from his position at the Ionian Academy to becoming a political servant of the protecting power.

It does seem to be the case, regardless of these political developments, that by the early to mid nineteenth century the nature of naval warfare had changed so much that the strategic importance of Corfu had greatly diminished, partly because Malta provided the main base for the British Mediterranean fleet, although Gladstone would write about Corfu's great strategic importance. Her invulnerable fortifications and ramparts "never prevented our entering the Adriatic", claimed Napier. The ocean was our element, he argued, and the British fleet could range the seas at its pleasure. That was a major change in how the island was imagined and conceived, although not everyone agreed, especially those like Adam and later Bowen who were administering Corfu and the revenues of the Ionian Islands, or those who were arguing for a continuation of the British Protectorate, albeit with concessions and reforms.

C. M. Woodhouse (1968) was clear that by the time the Seven Islands were ceded to Greece in 1864, "The strategic value of the islands, particularly Corfu, which had enticed both Napoleon and Nelson, had become unimportant since they last played a part in the operations leading up to the battle of Navarino. Now they could be safely handed over to the Greeks, provided that the fortification of Corfu was dismantled."

Nikias Lountzis contributed an essay to the Region of the Ionian Islands publication of 2007 in which he argues that Britain abandoned its role as protector of the United States of the Ionian Islands for complex reasons after redesigning its Mediterranean strategy: "the Ionian unifying morale, the new royal family of Greece that secured British influence and, most importantly, the introduction of steam as a power generator. As soon as steamships replaced sailing ships, the Ionian bases lost their military and commercial importance."

ATTITUDES BEFORE AND AFTER UNIFICATION

The desire for Union and freedom was clearly expressed by Aristotle Valaoritis in prose and in poems such as the allegorical and rhetorical "The Rock and the Wave" ("*O Vrachos kai to Kima*"), in which the rock represents the "arrogant, tyrannical British" and the wave symbolizes the "passionate, freedom-loving Greeks" who will crash down and destroy the rock. This popular poem includes lines like "Step aside, rock, and let me pass... the slave's foot will tread upon your neck." Rendered speechless, the hollow rock is destroyed in one fell swoop by the force of the wave; it disintegrates and is obliterated, lost in the abyss, having melted away as if made of snow. The poem must have gone down well with its Corfiot audience and newspaper readers in March 1863.

Would the British have liked it better now if Corfu and Paxos had not been ceded to Greece, if they were British colonies, like Gibraltar, or if we had British military or naval bases on the island, as in Cyprus? I doubt it. What if they were tax havens for the super-rich, or served as bases for the financial and insurance industries, like the Channel Islands or Bermuda? I, for one, prefer Corfu's post-1864 status as an integral part of Greece. It is not certain that all Ionian Islanders felt that way once the longed-for union with Greece had been achieved (or feel that way now, as there are some mutterings about independence, self-rule or autonomy from central government; some "non-stories" were blown up in September 2008 by the Athens correspondents of the BBC and *The Guardian*). The latter carried an article by H. Smith quoting the views of one Corfiot with political aspirations: "The truth is that unification with Greece was the darkest day in our history... It was a huge mistake that we have regretted ever since." She also quoted another Corfiot's observation that "in the coffee shops you hear talk of independence, of people wanting to raise the flag of the Republic of Corfu".

The Kefalonian poet and writer Andreas Laskaratos (1811-1901) has an ambiguous sonnet (easily read as intentionally ironical whether or not we are familiar with his biography) on "The Seven-Islander After Union" ("*O Eftanisios meta tin enosin*"), in which the subject of the poem complains about the new shackles scratching people's skin, and about the misery evident in everyone's existence; the poet's persona (a parody of Kefalonians he had observed, or the voice of the poet himself in "I told you so" mode?) expresses a desire for a return to the beloved "maternal" government of the British, rather than that of the new stepmother Greece, who drinks their blood as if in a taverna. The people are despairing to the extent that they curse the day that "*enosis*" happened: "*Anathema, anathema tin ora...*" ("Curse the hour, curse the day...")

Perhaps Laskaratos was not being in the slightest ironical. According to Kirkwall, Laskaratos' writings were all strongly in favour of the British protectorate. Viscount Kirkwall was George William Hamilton Fitzmaurice Orkney, the 6th Earl of Orkney (1827-89). Laskaratos, "the most honest and the most original, if not the most worldly-wise, gentleman of the Ionian Islands", was brought up by an English stepmother (another source says that it was in fact his wife Penelope who had the English stepmother) and part of his education was at the expense of Lord Guilford; he later spent several periods in England (the second time as a refugee). He became friendly with General Ferdinand Whittingham, Viscount Kirkwall and Sir Henry Storks. According to Kirkwall, he had an open, simple, unimpeachable character and was "a staunch Protectionist, who, if he did not love the English, at all events respected and admired them". In a footnote Kirkwall writes that "Lascarato himself...was strongly against the Union to the last; considering the Protection of England necessary to the well-being and security of the Seven islands."

Reading the section of Laskaratos' *Mysteries of Cefalonia* entitled "The English and the Seven Islands", one wonders just how pro-British he really was, as he is highly critical of the iron rod rule which characterized the Protectorate from 1817 to 1833. He is less than happy that the European Revolutions of 1848 encouraged the British to grant freedom of the press and the free vote, when this was not being demanded at that time by the Heptanesians. These rights had always been refused at other times, when the people were in a more peaceful mood, he says.

Bowen writes of "The monstrous injustice of the writers in the Ionian press... Ever since they were virtually emancipated, in 1849, from all legal restraint, they have been embittering the minds of their fellow-countrymen against the Protecting nation, by the most brutal and groundless calumnies." He condemns Seaton's policies in dealing with "an inflammable Oriental population" and the seditious newspapers which contained such bitter abuse of England and Englishmen, "repudiating British protection and openly advocating annexation to the Kingdom of Greece". He continues, "The present license of the Press in the Ionian Islands is entirely without parallels in the political history."

J. D. Gardner cannot understand why the Ionian Islanders should be dissatisfied: "We have so spoiled and humoured them, that they know not where they are; they cannot bear us;...their newspapers rave, and use language full of sedition, and of every sort of insolence...in short the Ionians want to get rid of us, and to be united to Greece." Gardner blames Lord Seaton for the fact that Corfu and most of the other islands have become "hotbeds of sedition, of insolence to the Mother Country", and that the people are "egged on by the rabid press". The British "have been snarled and barked at, ...hooted, bullied, belied, insulted by the virulent little press, small lawyers, and small men of all descriptions." It "has shown in us a remarkable spirit of forebearance to a race whom we could have crushed in an instant." He recommends government with a firm, strong hand, and he argues that the "Homeric scholar" is not the right sort of person to be selected to manage the islands, as his mind might be bewildered "by a collision of classical associations with British interests". Gardner is opposed to letting our minds be warped by such "humbug" and classical sentimentalism; "Homer, and the Odyssey, and the gardens of Alcinous, are all very fine, but the memory of them stands poor chance in the minds of the great mass of Britons, compared with the delights of cheap currants."

Lord Seaton's liberal policy, following the British tradition of freedom of the press, was surely the right one, in the long-run. Kirkwall writes that "The French revolution, which occurred in February, 1848, and which was imitated in Germany, Italy, and Greece, appears to have been the true cause of the signal change of policy which Lord Seaton in that year adopted in the Ionian Islands. The Tory peer suddenly assumed the character of an extremely liberal agitator." The Colonial Minister, Earl Grey, sanctioned the change of policy.

Laskaratos was not happy that the local journalists and newspapers were preaching revolution and the fall of the Protectorate to the villagers and peasants, without any hindrance or interference by the British who, he says, portrayed the journalists as martyrs of freedom. Laskaratos expresses genuine puzzlement as to the real aims of British policy in the Seven Islands at this time. In a letter of his to his Danish friend Theodor Hansen, of 26 September 1873, he writes about an article he had published in an Athenian newspaper condemning the Union of the Ionian Islands with Greece. His reasons were that two totally different elements had been united. He told the "Old Greeks" that they had been 400 years under the Turkish yoke, which had made them totally Asiatic; whereas the Ionian Islanders had experienced 400 years of *living together* with the Europeans which had perhaps made them European. The two peoples, separated in this way, no longer had the same spirit, habits and customs, or the same character. In a letter of 9 August 1868, he expresses his views about the Greek government and how badly things had gone wrong; he was even predicting catastrophe for the Hellenic nation, as the country was lacking worthy and capable men. "Hellas has no Hellenes", he wrote, "only a bunch of evil egotists, without religion, without morals, without virtue or merit." "Remember my words, you will surely see the Greek nation lose its freedom...the Greeks who are at the centre of things are a crowd of mercenary, self-interested egoists, without any interest in the common good."

Laskaratos and his wife (they had nine children and considerable financial difficulties) operated a school in Kefalonia: "If Greece could but command the services of such instructors of youth as Signor and Signora Lascarato, she would take the first steps towards the realization of her fond hopes of the national restoration to Empire" (Kirkwall). "What good did the granting of Freedom of the Press or the Free Vote bring to our society?" Laskaratos asks in his highly polemical *The Mysteries of Cefalonia*. No good at all, was his conclusion. "We have always used these two precious privileges for bad ends, proclaiming lies and deceit." Even if most of his compatriots disagreed with him, no one doubted his honesty, integrity and bravery.

Although his pro-Protectionist (or rather reformist, anti-Radical, anti-Unionist) sentiments were unusual for a Kefalonian, and strong stuff, even for a much-persecuted social critic and satirical writer once imprisoned for libel, and excommunicated by the Orthodox Church, it is not so unusual even nowadays to hear a few genuinely nostalgic Corfiots imagining that they might have achieved the status of an independent Republic of the Ionian islands. "*Anathema tin ora!*" others would have surely said.

Even a deeply patriotic writer like Aristotle Valaoritis became disgusted with Greek politics and politicians after union with Greece and increasingly retreated to the house he had inherited on the little island of Madouri, to concentrate his efforts on the cultivation of his land and "wild vines" or "*agrambelia*".

Chapter Three

THE CALL OF THE ISLANDS

Return to Corfu

HOMECOMINGS

Many Greeks and foreign visitors have written about the lure of the Ionian Islands, and maybe foremost at springtime.

A poem by Glyn Hughes ("Watercolours, 3", 2005) captures the coming of the Greek Spring; he calls it nature's orgasm, "At its climax in these waves of flowers."

Similarly the Reverend T. S. Hughes in Paramithia, Epirus in May 1815 "felt to the full those ecstatic sensations which a Grecian spring, to which no descriptions can do justice, is capable of inspiring; when a balmy softness and serenity pervade the atmosphere, when the richest tints are painted on the cloudless sky, when every valley and plain is clothed in a deep luxuriant verdure, superior even to that which our island boasts, when every grove is vocal with the melody of feathered songsters, when a

thousand flowers dye the surface of the earth and shed a perfume through
the air, when the bright splendour of the morning sun animates the soul
of man, and the coolest shades of evening refresh him after his daily toil."

I have been fortunate enough to have been able to enjoy many Greek
springs during the course of my 42-year relationship with these areas of
Western Greece. Most of the time I feel a need for the forested mountains
of the mainland as much as for the clear waters of the Ionian Sea. Perhaps
Kefalonians do not need the mainland as much, as they have their Black
Mountain and nearby Ithaca. For me the islands and the Pindus Mountains complement each other, and spring is the ideal time for a visit or a
homecoming to either destination.

My Corfiot wife's family appears to have originated from the North
of the Adriatic and in Venice. The family names took root in islands like
Zakynthos (Strani is first recorded there as a family name in 1519 and as
a place name as early as 1478, in the local land register), Kefalonia, Corfu
and in Paxos, where my wife's ancestors made their homes. Of these four
islands, Corfu and Paxos have been the most important for us. My mother-
in-law was from Bogdanatika, a tiny dot on a tiny island, with a fascinating culture (not so long ago) of fishermen and olive growers.

Travlantonis wrote a story in 1901 which evokes the island atmosphere and islanders' mentality in a convincing but not flattering way. It is
about a Paxiot who went to America for ten or fifteen years, all because of
a beautiful girl called Zacharenia whose father (a priest) did not want him
as a son-in-law. When he eventually returns to Paxos one Christmas, the
whole island comes out to meet the boat bringing him back, even though
it's a cold December day, because the "rich American" had sent dollar notes
home with his letters (Zacharenia's family therefore coming to regret bitterly their decision to reject him as a suitor). Everyone claimed to be a
distant relative or an old friend ("That's what wretched money does, my
Lord!"), and all anticipated that he was probably coming back to find a
wife. What they find at the port of Gaios is a sick, consumptive, dying
man with little time left, already more a corpse than an eligible groom.
Zacharenia and her family thus learn to count their blessings, to appreciate their simple, small island circumstances, the fate she had escaped and
the marriage she had made instead. At the end, Travlantonis has them
getting happily drunk around the table, singing merrily and repeating all
together the old verse:

Paxos and Antipaxos,
Worth at least a dozen Londons!
Gaios and Loggos
Surpass each Paris, a thousand ones!

Paxos, in its natural state, is one of the most beautiful islands in the Mediterranean. Over twenty years ago there were brief threats from an oil company to set up a heliport to facilitate the drilling and extraction of oil from the island. But luckily no exploitable quantity of oil was ever found on Paxos, or rather it was found to lie too deep down in the bowels of the earth; for the time being olive oil remains the only oil the islands have to offer. Hotels came instead, running water (rain water was collected in cisterns in the past), along with roads, swimming pools and villas. There is no comparison between the Paxiots' standard of living now and what it was when they arrived in this world. Is it all good news? The problem with Greek islands is that you never know for sure what may happen to the plots of land right next to yours. The bulldozers arrive when you least expect them.

The Homeric theme of the homecoming, the return to an island (in this case Zakynthos) after a long absence, only to find everything changed, has been explored by Grigorios Xenopoulos (born 1867) in his short autobiographical tale "*Nostimon Imar*" (the title refers to Homer's *Odyssey*, 1, line 168, and that "sweet day" of the return to the homeland, the sweetest dream of those who have been expatriated or forced by circumstances into some form of exile far away). I found a guestbook on the internet where a Kythiran woman from Australia praises the site as "a powerful tool for keeping us in touch with Cerigo; I wish my parents were still alive, to take a deep breath of *Nostimon Imar*".

The story describes Xenopoulos returning to Zakynthos in the summer of 1906, after an absence of fourteen years, with Ugo Foscolo's "To Zante" on his mind. At first, when he has finally landed after a storm, he finds everything changed, with many buildings ruined not only by earthquakes, but even more by "criminals" and "vandals" who have destroyed *his* beloved Zakynthos. He bitterly misses once-familiar church belfries and campaniles, the old colour of the theatre, the characteristic shape of an elegant tower, the pediment and gable bas-relief of a particular building. Like many other Greeks before and since, he addresses his countrymen with great bitterness: "Didn't you respect *anything*?" But he realizes that he too has changed. He has seen more, travelled more, so, for instance, the road seems narrower than it did in the past, the ceilings lower, doors smaller. He left his house when it seemed to him "like a little palace" but he found it no more than a small, modest dwelling, almost a shed, on his return. Nothing is as it was inside his head, as he saw it in his dreams. He thinks he wants to leave again, but gradually he gets accustomed to the changes, to the electric lighting, to the newly-built houses, to the marble plaque that has been placed outside the famed island poet Foscolo's birthplace. He starts to look at things with a fresh eye, finds some things quite attractive. Even his house starts to feel like a little palace once again; and then he bumps into some of his first loves and old flames, who still have the same radiant eyes and harmonious voices... He truly feels he has come back home.

What about a twenty-first century homecoming after a long absence from an island like Corfu? Would environmental degradation and ugly building developments give cause for despair and depression? Grim reality could destroy the green illusion: abandoned, rusting vehicles and air-conditioning units compete with the non-degradable detritus of builders' rubble, illegal fly-tips and landfill sites, which seem to be destroying the sense of natural harmony which prevailed not many years ago. To adapt the words of a long-term foreign resident of Corfu, if the Scots have a sport known as "tossing the cabre", the most famous Greek sport is that of the "Big Throw" or "who can toss the old washing-machine or TV set the furthest down the mountainside".

Corfu was once an earthly paradise. Parts of the island are still relatively unspoiled and unscathed, but the outlook and situation can change at the turn of any corner; even those remote northern parts that James Chatto (2005) has described so well have been subject to substantial or piecemeal development, real-estate speculation and demographic change.

It is a fact of life on the Greek islands that you never know what will be built on the plot next to yours: a taverna blasting out music late into the night, a disco, a dumping ground for builders' rubble, or some commercial development, legal or illegal, finished or unfinished, an eyesore concrete skeleton or an ostentatious villa whose owners borrow elements from both the Taj Mahal and the Parthenon ("in preposterously bad taste", to cite Gerald Durrell). If you are really unlucky, your own plot of land, left unattended, might even become a pumping place for a neighbour's sewage (as John Waller recounts about his property above Aghios Gordis). The journalist Paul Whyles, who owns a house in Rou, Corfu, wrote an article to voice a common complaint about the tipping and dumping of rubbish in beauty spots, gullies and ravines: "Rotting soiled mattresses. The carcases of discarded fridges, their harmful CFC gases long since leaked into the blue skies above. Old car tyres and batteries. Building rubble. An ancient oven. Rusting metal sunbeds and their cushions... and assorted plastic that will take 1,000 years to biodegrade. All dumped without compunction: a stain upon paradise." Even within a short walk of an exclusive development like the Rou Estate, with its spectacular views and stone village houses restored "in harmony with the natural surroundings", in an area of outstanding natural beauty, to quote the developer's prospectus, no one can escape the "befouling of nature on an organised scale", as Paul Whyles describes such systematic dumping, to the irritation of some others who prefer to close their eyes to the problem.

The novelist Spiros Plaskovitis offers a disillusioned late twentieth-century Greek perspective in *The Façade Lady of Corfu*. He has his main character, Dinos Hairetis, returning to his birthplace, Corfu Town, after a ten-year absence. He finds that, from one end to the other, the town "was and was not the same; in the throes of its third successive metamorphosis, both outside and inside". He describes these three periods of great urban change and latter-day 'development' with deft brush-strokes; the impact of tourism finally scatters all memories to the winds.

GREEK LANGUAGE, GREEK VALUES

Australian author Robert Dessaix's novel *Corfu* (2001) is not universally admired by residents of the island, but he puts these telling words into the mouth of his character Celia, who is supposedly based on Fanny Lewis, the widow of the broadcaster, aviator and writer Cecil Lewis, who spent the later years of his extraordinary life on Corfu: "'I'm not an ex-patriate, you know,' said Celia. 'I'm an Englishwoman living in Corfu. There's a huge difference.'"

Ever since the British occupied the Ionian Islands, there's never been a shortage of English men and woman who consider it their right to live on Corfu or the other islands, without necessarily knowing more than a few words of the Greek language. Kirkwall was shocked that so few British officials knew Greek: "Will it be believed by Englishmen, that in 1863, twenty-five years after this sensible and rational order was given, no Resident was ever required to know Greek, nor was his knowing Italian imperative?" In 1837, Douglas had signed a circular to English officials saying that "a knowledge of the Greek language will be required of the British functionaries... and it is...incumbent on them, to make themselves masters of the language."

I found a caption at the Koryialenios Museum at Argostoli that was informative on the official use of the Greek language in the Ionian Islands:

> For 300 years the tuition of the Greek language on a broad scale was not encouraged under Venetian rule. After the fall of the Republic of Venice, the Convention of 1800 between Russia and Turkey...states that "as from the year 1810 no person shall be appointed to the civil service who has not mastered the use of the national Greek language". This is the first official act indicating the fusion of the Greeks as a nation after centuries of foreign dominion.

What is going on in the imaginations of British residents nowadays, as they try to recreate or maintain English gardens, an Anglican Church congregation, an idyllic cemetery, animal protection societies, or pine after British values, administrative procedures and a sense of order in unruly, often chaotic surroundings? Some enjoy the availability of English breakfasts, pubs and restaurants, and the plentiful supply of cheap wine, without understanding the liberating Dionysian spirit which the Greeks have offered to the world, and without caring much about the difference between Robola, Zitsa, Verdea, resinated, or rough local village wines. Alan Bates gave a persuasive interpretation of this profoundly liberating spirit when he finally asks Zorba (played by Anthony Quinn in the film by Cacoyannis) to "teach him to dance". It is not enough to learn to dance in terms of technique and steps; one has to learn to dance with one's soul. It is not an attractive sight to see an ungainly foreigner (such as myself) try to simulate the movements or "steps" of an entranced *zembeikiko* dancer.

For some British expatriates the islands are a kind of Cornwall in the sun, once an inexpensive place to live or retire, now a relatively expensive place to live (especially now that the value of the pound has fallen). Life can be difficult in old age for those who have sold up back home, or for those on modest pensions (though of course it can also be much more re-warding). The editorial of a local newspaper, *Kerkyraiko Vima*, on 29 January 2008, concerned the terrible plight of healthcare on the island; it quoted the public comment of the Deputy Prefect, Christos Skourtis, that to live in Corfu was to live in a state of constant risk and danger of your life, "*vivere pericolosamente*". The Editor went on to enquire what would happen if some of the thousands of permanent British residents of the island were to send these comments and quotations to the English tabloid press, ever-ready to expose any problems or scandals on the island.

THE VIEW FROM THE SEA

Over the centuries the concerns of seafarers, sailors and naval strategists, the issues that haunted their imaginations, were not just the trials of Odysseus or the wrath of Poseidon, but, as for seafarers everywhere, the presence of lighthouses and marker buoys; visible landmarks, such as temples built on promontories; knowledge of shoals and reefs, winds and calms; pirate lairs; safe, convenient harbours and anchorages; access to water supplies, port facilities, docks or arsenals for quickly refitting after storms or battles; information about fortifications and defences; estimates of the effective range of cannons and other weapons; deep enough water and large enough harbours to cope with fleets of increasingly large and heavy boats; the availability of accurate charts, and later the absence of mines; and for sailors with commercial aims, access from the ports to the interior of the country. Obviously some of these factors depended on pre-vailing conditions of peace or war. The Venetians had built an arsenal at Gouvia; the British built many lighthouses, but destroyed some of the for-tifications at Corfu when they ceded the islands to Greece (five forts once protected Vido Island off Corfu Town).

Kirkwall records that "the greatest humiliation inflicted on the Ionians was the destruction of the strong and extensive fortifications of Vido, one mile from the citadel of Corfu. These measures brought to a climax the un-popularity of Great Britain in the Seven Islands; and if the Ionians were furious, a feeling of shame was almost universal amongst the English, whether civil or military…" The sale of Parga to Ali Pasha, and the de-struction of the fortifications on Vido… The British had causes enough for shame as well as for pride in the achievements of the Protectorate. On around 11 February 1864 the demolition works began, and continued until the first part of April; according to Kirkwall there were constant, at first almost daily, explosions; sometimes there were two or more on the same day. They usually took place at five in the afternoon.

Other explosions were to shake the British in their turn. Two British destroyers, the *Saumarez* and the *Volage*, struck mines in Albanian waters in the Corfu Straits on 22 October 1946; as a result 45 officers and sailors died, another 42 were wounded in this famous Corfu Channel Incident. In the 1960s the American Sixth Fleet aircraft carriers would visit Corfu, a "liberty port", and bring marines on R&R visits after action in Vietnam. After the fall of the Greek Junta, in May 1975, the Greek government decided to withdraw permission for the fleet to use the harbour at Elefsis. "The last destroyer landing party to go ashore on Corfu was nearly lynched by hysterical Greek islanders. Even in Athens, American sailors' wives and children from Elefsis have been stoned" (*Time Magazine*, 12 May 1975). The Corfiot shopkeepers lost a lot of business. I have described a visit of the American Sixth Fleet in the 1960s in my collection *Corfu Blues* (2006). At the beginning of the twentieth century, according to William Miller, "Occasional visits from the British Mediterranean Fleet enable contractors and tradesmen to make money."

Nowadays yachtsmen and yachtswomen are more concerned about marinas, moorings and anchorages. There are plenty. In some places new marinas have become both an asset and an eyesore; unfinished ones are the worst, as is the case at Spilia, Corfu. It is certainly not in keeping with the UNESCO World Heritage status of the town and port complex, and has deprived the people of Corfu of one of the main car-parks, which has had an adverse effect on the tradespeople of the lower town. Work on the marina had stopped in July 2008. A reporter for Corfu's *Free News* (December 2008) tried to discover who was responsible for this disaster. Everyone denied responsibility or tried to blame others. The reporter demanded that those reponsible should stop trying to hide or pass the buck, that they should come out and explain to the people of Corfu what in fact was happening with the Spilia Marina, and the money allocated to the project. To add insult to injury, it seemed to many that a mistake in calculating the height of waves meant that the marina was to feature a 3-metre-high wall, which would have destroyed the view of a crucial element of the cherished "urban and port ensemble" which should have been protected, and of Vido Island.

It is not just the foreign visitors and expatriates who complain. Feelings often run high about the state of the pavement in Garitsa Bay, worsened by storm damage. It is a severe blow to the Corfiot psyche to contemplate for long periods unfinished public works.

LANDSCAPE AND PERCEPTION

What is landscape or seascape? What would Romans, Venetians, English officers or private soldiers or Ottoman Turks have *seen* in their mind's eye, as they first approached or finally left the shores of Corfu or mainland ports?

Horace's famous words from his *Epistle* to Augustus (*Epistle* 2.1.157-8), "*Graecia capta ferum victorem cepit et artis intulit agresti Latio*" ("Greece, the captive, made her fierce victor captive and brought the arts into uncultured Latium"), offered little consolation. The Romans may have admired (and plundered) Greek sanctuaries and been captivated and influenced by the sculptures and other booty, at the same time as building some comfortable summer villas, but in the course of 500 years they devastated the trees and natural forests of Corfu.

In the course of 400 years, the Venetians caused many hundreds of thousands of olive trees to be planted. The island was besieged, attacked and laid waste on many occasions, fortifications rose and fell, the town moved from Palaiopolis to the twin peaks where the Old Fortress was built, and then to its present, ever-expanding position.

Edward Giffard, who visited Corfu and Zakynthos in 1836, thought the town of Zante much superior to Corfu town, but considered the island "immeasurably inferior to Corfu in both beauty and grandeur... Here are no dark woods, deep ravines, or craggy mountains—those indispensable ingredients in a picturesque landscape."

Do we all see the same views and perceive the same landscapes when we stand on the same spot under similar conditions?

The dramatic view of the sea at the bottom of the sheer cliffs of Schiza, Kampi, in Zakynthos, takes on a different meaning when one first looks up at the huge cross on the mountainside and discovers that this commemorates the fact that from the very spot where one is standing the Communists hurled non-Communists to their deaths on the rocks below. One could be forgiven for not knowing about this, for the left-wing PASOK government apparently had the explanatory sign removed. People were divided into two categories by the Communists: they were either "Patriots" (i.e. supporters of the Communists) or "Traitors/Collaborators".

What does an Italian feel when standing on the spot near St. Theodore's lighthouse outside Argostoli, Kefalonia, where around 136 officers of the Acqui Division were mercilessly executed as traitors by their former allies on 24 and 25 September 1943, or when looking down at the hole in the ground where their bodies were thrown? Moved by the memorial situated on the hill above this spot, I was able to forgive the malicious defacement of the statue (bust) of Napier in 1943, and of the inscription ("To the Glory of the British Nation 1813") on the stone pyramid or obelisk at the centre of the Drapano (Trapano) causeway, also known as the Devoseto (de Bosset) Bridge. According to the Koryialenios Museum, the inscription (in Greek, English, Italian and Latin) was defaced in 1941 by the Italian Occupying Forces, with the intention of replacing it with a dedication to the poet Foscolo.

The officers were among the many thousand Italian soldiers who were executed in 1943 on Hitler's orders. Louis de Bernières writes about these events in *Captain Corelli's Mandolin*, and the 2005 Italian Rai Uno TV film, *Cefalonia*, directed by Riccardo Milani, dramatizes events following the armistice of 8 September 1943, and most unforgettably reconstructs the Nazi massacre of the officers shot at Casetta Rossa near St. Theodore's Lighthouse. Santi Corvaja's book *Gli Eroi di Cefalonia Settembre 1943* (1984) contains illustrations from the archives and presumably accurate figures for the numbers of Italians killed on Kefalonia: 390 officers out of 525; 9,250 men out of 11,500. More precisely, the number of officers who died: fallen in combat, 65; summarily executed on battlefield, 189; shot near St. Theodore lighthouse, 136: total officers, 390. Figures for the soldiers break down as follows: fallen in combat, 1,250; executed on battlefield, 5,000; lost at sea when three ships were sunk, 3,000; total soldiers, 9,250. In Corfu, 23 officers and 600 soldiers were lost.

Dorrian Lambley, in the succinct *The Mythos History of Corfu* (1984), implies a much higher figure for the Italian dead on Corfu: "After the bomb attack the Germans collected all the survivors and put them in the old fort; then began the massacre of the Italians. Italian officers were taken to the high towers on the north-west side of the old fort and pushed onto the rocks below. Others were hung from Capo Sidaro. More than 2,000 officers and soldiers were drowned in the sea from steam ships. Many had sacks put over their heads and tied around their waists before they were drowned. Other Italians were locked into the holds of old ships which were sunk at sea."

Mark Mazower's authoritative *Inside Hitler's Greece, The Experience of Occupation, 1941-1944* (1993) states that "German punishment was swift and staggeringly ruthless. Some 155 officers and 4,750 men captured on Cefalonia were executed by firing squad after the fighting had finished. An unknown number of Italian officers were shot on Corfu too. Many bodies were dumped at sea, and some were later washed back up on nearby beaches."

Spiros Plaskovitis, in his novel *The Façade Lady of Corfu* (1995), writes that "Everyone believed that the sea below the rocks of the Venetian castle was still stinking from the corpses of the Italian division 'Acqui'. After the Italian surrender, the Germans had emptied the bodies into the sea ..."

Nicholas Enessee, in *Point and Counterpoint* (2005), provides his own estimate of figures: "6,000 soldiers were machine-gunned; 250 officers, along with General Gandin and Staff members, were summarily tried and shot at the Aghion Theodoran area. A further 1,500 prisoners perished as the ship carrying them to mainland Greece hit a mine. The ship sank in minutes with few survivors."

Whatever the Italians' own crimes in Libya or Abyssinia, and the harsh judgement that perhaps they simply got their just deserts for Mussolini's invasion of Greece in October 1940 and for occupying the islands in the first place—and then for changing sides—the fate of the Acqui Division must bring tears to the eyes of any Italian visiting such a beautiful island or the memorial to the fallen, or indeed to any compassionate person capable of appreciating the wonders of nature, the views of the sea and the mountains, and of imagining the last thoughts of those about to be shot down in cold blood, instead of being made prisoners of war.

I should at this point refer to the Italian invasion of Greece in October 1940, and to the annual re-enactment in Kalpaki, Epirus, of the Battle of Kalpaki (28 October-8 November 1940), which brought the battle and the Greek repulsion of the Italian invasion dramatically to life when I watched it in 2006. The well-choreographed simulation of the artillery and tank exchanges of fire, troop movements and falling bombs on the mountainside is impressive. I watched it from the hill on which the monument of the Greek soldier stands, thinking I was in the middle of the real thing. On that evening my sympathies were not with the Italians. Enessee also makes one recall the attitude of the invading and occupying Italians in the spring of 1941, when they pulled down the statue of Maitland to "replace it with the Italian fascist emblem". Enessee cites the inscription which accompanied the emblem: "Here, where Caesar's eagle and the Lion of St. Mark left throughout the centuries an indelible mark of the Latin Civilisation, today return the black shirts of Italy, carriers of (the) light from Rome, to proclaim Duce's will: Peace with Justice amongst people."

Apparently the Italian General made a speech, telling the Kefalonian authorities: "We have conquered you! Therefore from today you are no longer a part of Greece, but of Rome." Enessee states that "During the 29 months that followed, the Italians made no secret of their intention to annex the islands, being the natural successors of Venice. Theirs was not an ordinary occupation force. They were there to arrange for the orderly transition of the Ionian Islands from Greek to Italian territory."

It is perhaps not surprising that at various times Ionian Island poets have bitterly attacked Venetian and Italian occupiers: I think of Aristotle Valaoritis' "Foteinos" (about fourteenth-century Lefkas) and Dionysios Stranis' "To Kerkyra, Enslaved, 28 April 1941- 28 April 1942". Poetry cannot always capture the horrors of occupation. At times a factual, documentary approach is the only adequate response. Mark Mazower writes of the village of Komeno, near Arta, Epirus, where a Wehrmacht massacre of 317 civilian villagers, men, women and children, occurred in August 1943. The troops had been ordered to "leave nothing standing".

A beautiful view for you may be an indifferent or disappointing one for me. Let's say that we're looking at the same trademark picture-postcard view of Kanoni in Corfu, and at the two little islands of Vlacherena and Pontikonisi (Mouse Island) facing Kanoni. A Classics scholar, topographer or archaeologist might think of Homer and see a fleeting vision of Odysseus' "petrified ship". What if, like Edward Dodwell, you translate "Pondikonisi" ("Mouse Island") as "The Island of Rats"? Somewhat less romantic. Nevertheless, Dodwell landed on it and decided it was "probably that alluded to by Homer". A Greek looking at Pontikonisi might be reminded of the popular George Katsaros song "Kerkyra, Kerkyra" about Corfu and Pontikonisi from the Rena Vlachopoulou film *The Countess of Corfu* (1972). Not, as one editor believes, a "traditional song", it was composed at the last minute to fill out the film's credit sequence, and is a simple novelty song making use of the iconic place names of the island: Palaiokastritsa, Benitses, Pontikonisi, the Plateia. It begins with fresh fish and pretty girls: maybe the dominant imaginative landscape of Corfu for the rest of Greece in the 1960s and 1970s?

> The tastiest young girls
> I saw in Palaiokastritsa
> And the freshest fish are found
> Only in Benitsa.

An environmentalist looking at the same view might just see the rubbish on the little beach or the uncontrolled urban sprawl of hotels and buildings that has taken over most of Kanoni, or, when in Zakynthos, worry about the breeding ground of the sea-turtle, *caretta caretta*, on Laganas beach. The *Rough Guide* and other publications pay due attention to the protection and conservation of sea-turtles, but Dimitrios Theodossopoulos studies the issue in a broader anthropological context and in relation to the culture of the people of Vassilikos, Zakynthos, near where the turtles breed.

Pirates and other attackers might have coveted the riches they imagined to be hidden in monasteries such as the fifteenth-century Anaphonitria, Zakynthos, but looking up at the fortified tower guarding the monastery, they might have been deterred by the fighting monks ready to pour boiling oil down on them through the machiolations. The monks of Zakynthos may have been spared from Barbarossa's attacks and sieges, the destruction, plunder and enslavement of young people and rural populations such as Kythira, Kefalonia, Corfu and Paxos experienced in 1537, but this cannot be attributed to Zakynthos' patron saint, St. Dionysios, who lived as an ascetic monk in the monastery, from around 1568. His name was Dionysios Siguro.

An exiled Suliot, driven to seek refuge in Corfu as a result of the hostile campaigns of Ali Pasha, would have looked across at the Epirot Mountains and yearned for Suli and his native country. His assimilated offspring might have felt very differently and over time many of them ceased to be aware of their Suliot roots.

Colonel W. M. Leake would always have Homer, Herodotus, Thucydides, Plutarch, Strabo and Pausanius and the other Ancient Greek and Roman writers in his mind when looking at any Epirot landscape or Ionian

Island harbour, or when speculating about the location of Dodona, the identity of a ruin, a place-name or inscription during his travels in Greece.

A lover of the literature of the Ionian Islands, when looking at the steep, free-standing "Ortholithos" rock-pillar, like an isolated sentry-stone in the sea on the sometimes wild west coast of Corfu, at the southern end of Aghios Gordis, might think of the powerful short story by Iakovos Polylas called "*Ena mikro lathos*" ("A Small Mistake" or "The Error", 1891). In terms of the landscape of the imagination, one could well understand how the natural beauty of the surrounding area on the deserted west coast, before it was developed, could have haunted the imagination of Maria, the unfortunate, poor and long-suffering village wife who is the subject of this story. As a child she had a profound emotional attachment to the mountain-slopes and the green countryside with its vines and old olive trees, and to her father's remote vineyard, as well as to the boundless blue of the choppy, open sea. It is a mystical attachment to the sea and to the land her father had once owned but had been forced to sell. Although she had not revisited the spot for twenty years, that landscape had played on her mind all her life, like a magical piece of music remembered since childhood: especially the sight of a bare craggy rock standing upright in the sea. For her, no place or view in the universe could give her greater joy or inspiration. "The magnificent slope, with its every plant, its every tree, with every patch of land, every terrace, every path and by-way, every passage, had been deeply etched into her youthful spirit... the sea in its turn had opened her mind and had given wings to her imagination... And so her tender young soul had become one with this place."

Maria makes the mistake of secretly lending, without her husband's knowledge, her very modest dowry of inherited gold jewellery to her daughter to deposit and pawn at the store, in order to pay for a doctor and for medicines for a sick granddaughter; but Maria's impoverished husband soon has another urgent need to pawn the trinkets himself, to pay off his debts and to save himself from prison. Because of her small but seemingly tragic mistake, which she feels compelled to confess to the local priest as if a mortal sin, she returns to the beloved landscape and vineyard of her childhood, climbs the Ortholithos rock and commits suicide. Her body is found washed up on the sand at dawn the next day by fishermen.

A Muslim Cham who might manage to revisit an ancestral home in Sivota (Mourtos) or elsewhere in 'Chameria' (Tsamouria, Thesprotia, an area of modern Thesprotia then home to the Cham population) from which his or her family had been expelled, evicted or displaced (either in 1912-14, in 1923, during the 1930s, or in the period 1943-5), would see things very differently from the Greek citizens, refugees and Vlachs who were subsequently settled there. The Cham might imagine old property rights or harbour a sense of loss similar to a German from the Sudetenland or a Greek from Asia Minor. According to William Miller (1928), the Chams were "originally Greeks, who late in the seventeenth century embraced Islam, speak Albanian, but always sided with the Turks. The Chams were exempted from the exchange of populations, and the Albanian government wishes them to remain where they are—at Goumenitsa." The Greeks thought differently.

My mind spins, trying to work out and untangle these complex Balkan issues of identity, ethnicity and belonging, i.e. whether the Chams were really originally Greek, or the Suliots originally Albanian, especially once such people, or their descendants, became fully Hellenized and assimilated, willingly or by means of linguistic and cultural pressure or coercion. In what circumstances was an Albanian in Epirus considered to be an Albanian, a Turk or a Greek? One cannot disagree with Miranda Vickers' opinion (2002) that the Epirus region has historically had a very blurred ethnicity, but I do not plan to touch on this issue in any great depth or to discuss the political arguments and claims about Northern Epirus or Southern Albania in this book.

K. E. Fleming (1999) writes that Ali Pasha was a fluent Greek-speaker and that "despite the fact that he used Greek for all courtly dealings, Ali was regarded first and foremost as an Albanian. His use of Greek did not in any way make him Greek." But Fleming quotes from Dakin (1972) that "His court was Greek and had been the centre of a Greek renaissance." Pettifer and Vickers suggest that "the nature and ethnic background of rulers such as King Pyrrhus is either omitted or grossly distorted" (by Greek historians). Are there not more important things for people to worry about? We are all Greeks, said Shelley (K. E. Fleming even sees this and Philhellenism generally as a surrogate, cultural form of colonization, an attempt to claim and appropriate the Greek past and to possess Greece as an intellectual and ideological satellite of Europe.) The Albanian writer Kadaré admires the Greeks, and would probably subscribe to Shelley's view that "our laws, our literature, our religion, our arts, have their root in

Greece". That does not mean that we have to overlook the Illyrian, Slav, Wallachian or Islamic contributions. Hammond (1967) states that "The Albanians themselves spread into Epirus in the fifteenth and following centuries, and they swept aside some peoples of Slav origin, who at that time occupied most of the country."

Vasso Psimouli (2006) dates the arrival of the Albanians in Thessaly, Attica, the Peloponnese, and then in Epirus, to the fourteenth century. The Slavs, who arrived in the sixth and following centuries, probably spoke Greek by the time of the Albanian invasions, but the Slavonic place-names continued in use until the time of Metaxas. The canton of Ioannina has 334 Slavonic place-names, whereas that of Arta has only 44 and that of Prevesa only 34. Max Vasmer (1941) gives a figure of 412 Slavic place-names for Epirus and 16 for the Ionian Islands (2,123 for the whole of Greece).

The Zagori village of Asprangeloi (now the seat of the municipal administration of the Central Zagori, since being razed by the Germans in July 1943, one of over a thousand Greek villages razed by the time Liberation came, according to Mazower) used to be called Dovra (clearly associated with the Slavonic word *dobro*, meaning "good"). W. Miller (1905) says that "The truth appears to be, that despite the great Slavonic immigration which undoubtedly took place in the dark ages of Greece, the Hellenic race gradually assimilated and Hellenised the immigrants."

Visitors and travellers in the nineteenth century would have been worried about the dangers of catching cholera or malaria in places where nowadays we might only fear the absence of good emergency medical facilities. The prospect or experience of insanitary facilities, the quality of the seawater, food poisoning, unwelcome attentions and harassment can also affect perceptions of place. A person with a tendency to suffer from vertigo would have very different perceptions of landscape from a seasoned mountain-walker, when looking down from one of the high look-out points above the Vikos Gorge or from the highest points of Kefalonia or Ithaca.

We see landscapes through our own eyes, we rediscover them and remake them according to a host of experiences and associations, literary, artistic, historical, professional or purely personal. Road engineers see and "read" things differently from classical topographers, landscape archaeologists, nation-builders intent on defining their *topos,* or semi-nomadic livestock keepers. Hunters, shepherds and goatherds have their particular perspectives about access to vegetation, wooded and open spaces. Scuba divers and marine biologists understand the seabed, reefs, algae and seagrasses in very different ways from holiday-makers. Fishermen have sceptical attitudes to conservationists' proposals to create marine parks, and some wish they could still get away with using dynamite for fishing.

Looking out across the water at the beautiful little islands of Lazaretto or Vido from Corfu Town is very different if one of your relatives or ancestors was incarcerated, evacuated or executed there. The same would once have been true for the island in Ioannina's lake, where one of the monasteries was once used as a state prison and place of secret executions, according to Dr. Pouqueville (1820). Leake states "There are only two or three monks in the island, the monasteries being now used for the lodging of prisoners collected from every part of the Vezir's dominions", although he does not mention executions there.

The Reverend Hughes (1820) says that the seven convents "have frequently been used as places of confinement for state-prisoners, and if their walls could speak, might tell of many a bloody deed perpetrated within them. In one of these receptacles Mustafa Pasha of Delvino was starved to death, and at this very time his two sons were immured in another, cut off from every consolation and from all commerce with mankind." The Muslim *beys* of Gardiki, after the massacre, were also sentenced by Ali Pasha to be kept in close confinement in the island's monasteries, before being strangled to death.

When Hughes visited the island to search the monasteries for manuscripts, he was able to visit six, but not the seventh. It was forbidden, "being at the time the prison of two unfortunate sons of Mustafa Pasha, and the cells of monks occupied by Albanian soldiers". It occurs to me that the severe defacement of the frescoes might be attributable to prisoners and soldiers such as these. Hughes says that "all these religious houses have at various times undergone a similar conversion". Bowen, when visiting a church in Parga (1852), states that "the Turks have amused themselves by disfiguring the frescoes of saints and martyrs on its walls".

Small Greek islands, even in modern times, are not always what they seem, be they in the Ionian or the Aegean seas. Many have been used at one time or another as places of exile, quarantine, isolation, correction, torture, execution, as cruel and primitive asylums for the insane, as political prisons or concentration camps. Apart from Lazaretto, we only have to think of other Greek islands like Leros, Yiaros or Makronisos. Kefalonia witnessed the hangings of 21 islanders by the British authorities after the Skala uprising of 1849. Gallows could apparently be seen in many public places throughout the Seven Islands. Edward Giffard (1837) describes the execution by hanging of a murderer in Corfu: "An eye-witness described it as a peculiarly disgusting sight; the executioner was dressed in a party-coloured suit of red and blue, with a mask of the same colours, with one huge Cyclopean eye in the centre, resembling nothing so much as the clown in a Christmas pantomime."

IMAGES OF KYTHIRA

If we do not know the grim facts about events on such islands, we can turn to Charles Baudelaire's poem "*Un Voyage à Cythère*" ("A Voyage to Kythira") from *Les Fleurs du mal* ("Flowers of Evil", 1857) to see how that great poet imagined one of the most southern Ionian islands. At the start of the poem his heart is happy and free like a bird, and the spirit of Aphrodite hovers over the island, even if it seems to him a sad, gloomy, wretched black island, a barren, rocky desert. Suddenly, as he passes the island, he sees a gallows with three arms, on which the corpse of a hanged man is being eaten by ferocious birds; his eyes and testicles are gone, his intestines are hanging out. Baudelaire identified with the sufferings of the hanged man on the symbolic gallows. The poem may be allegorical, but it is not hard for any of us to identify with the sufferings of the condemned or exiled. Poor Kythira, to be described by one of Europe's great poets as the "Eldorado of aging debauchees" or "old stagers"! "What is this sad black island," he asks, "it's Cythera!" (« *Quelle est cette île triste et noire? – C'est Cythère... Eldorado banal de tous les vieux garçons.* ») No wonder so many Kythirans, or natives of Cerigo, as it was called, escaped from the island to settle in Australia! It is ironic that the John Murray *Handbook* (1840) calls Cerigo the "Botany Bay" of the islands: "convicts are sentenced to different periods of banishment there, in proportion to their crimes". The third verse redeems the reputation of the island, to some extent: «*Ile des doux secrets et des fêtes du cœur!* » or "Isle of sweet secrets and heart-feasting fire!" in Roy Campbell's translation.

Kythira can be, for some, an island of sweet secrets and revels of the heart, where the spirit of Aphrodite (Venus) is like a perfume which fills the soul with love and languor. That may not be the dominant note in the poem, but it is the feeling that surely dominates most visitors to any of the Ionian Islands. Professor Ansted thought that Cerigo, like Corfu and Ithaca, was full of historic and mythological interest. "More than either does it belong to the realms of romantic poetry." He quotes:

'Twas on these shores as ancient poets sing,
What time light zephyrs woo'd the infant spring,
Immortal Venus rose in glowing pride,
Bright as the day-star from the swelling tide.

Ansted does however go on to say that the poet was now justified in saying:

Forsaken isle, around thy barren shore
Wild tempests howl and wintry surges roar.

He admits that Cerigo was very rarely visited and damns it with faint praise by saying that it is chiefly remarkable for its excellent honey.

"Cerigo, celebrated as Cythera, and the birthplace of Helen…was the favourite haunt of Venus. Here was erected to her one of the most magnificent temples she had in Greece. It contained a statue of the goddess arrayed in arms, as Pausanius informs us" (Murray *Handbook*, 1840).

Peter Prineas (2006) mentions the legend that King Menelaos had a summer palace there and that Helen served as a priestess at Kythera's sanctuary to Aphrodite Ourania. He admits that there is no certainty about Helen, but "Aphrodite's temple was real and was well into its second millennium when Pausanias, perhaps the world's first travel writer, went to Kythera in the second century AD to find it."

The Murray *Handbook* also informs us that the island was garrisoned by a company of soldiers, and was a very solitary station, partly because of the "piratical character of the Mainotes" who inhabited the opposite coast of the Morea, and who prevented any free communication with the continent.

Dr. John Davy (1842), when comparing the seven islands and the state of the arts in each, writes of Kythira: "As Zante may be considered the least deficient, Cerigo probably may be pointed out as most so; nor is it surprising, keeping in mind its detached situation, its peculiar position, the poverty of its population, and the manner in which, for centuries, they have been cut off from intercourse with any civilised people." He praises the British administration, but not the population: "When Major Macphail was resident of Cerigo, he exerted himself strenuously to improve the island. He has assured me that the rudeness of the people and their ignorance was almost beyond belief."

Kirkwall (1864) writes about a "most horrible outrage" which occurred in Cerigo in 1821, "upon some Turks, chiefly women, who had taken refuge in the island, and who were all massacred after undergoing the most disgraceful treatment". A detachment of soldiers was attacked, and one of them killed. Five Cerigots were tried, condemned and executed.

George Wheler (1682) describes Cerigo as follows:

> Cerigo hath the Morea north of it, and was called anciently Cithæra, famous for being the native country of Venus and Helen: so that were we to frame an idea of this place from the fame of these beauties, we might imagine it one of the most charming places of the world. But, on the contrary, the greatest part of it is a barren, rocky, and mountainous soil, ill peopled, and can brag of no plenty, neither of corn, wine, nor oyl: which undoubtedly made Venus change her own country for Cyprus; and Helena so willing to be stolen and carried into the pleasant plains of the continent. What beauties it now produceth, I am ignorant of; for I remember not that I saw a woman there.

Tertius Kendrick (1822) remarked that "the people scarcely seem to need the comforts of life, from the barbarous and savage manners they possess." Furthermore, "The inhabitants of Cerigo are much inclined to a savage cast in their character. Their manners and customs are of the rudest and most superstitious order... Cerigo is considered as a place of honourable exilement by the British stationed on it; and well it may be said so, since civilization has entirely fled from the inhabitans. Rude barbarism predominates throughout all classes of the latter, having with it the usual appendages of cruelty, credulity and superstition."

Kythira did not get a very good press in the nineteenth century, so it is fortunate that the Kytherean Association of Australia has done so much to set the record straight, and it is to books such as *Kythera, a History* by Peter Vanges and *Katsehamos and the Great Idea* by Peter Prineas that one can profitably turn to explore the landscape of Kytherian–Australians' imagination concerning their ancestral island home. Prineas is the first to point out how far off the mark most nineteenth-century travellers and administrators were in their assessments, particularly about the island's alleged remoteness and isolation. He talks about the emigration of Kytherians "to Smyrna in Asia Minor, to the Black Sea cities of Russia, and to Egypt and Romania. Some Kytherians even went as far as California and Australia in search of gold".

Thanks, in part, to its negative image of isolation in the nineteenth century, it seems to have remained an island for the discriminating visitor or the returning Greek–Australian.

THE IMPACT OF EVENTS

An imagined or perceived landscape could self-evidently be very different for an emigrant, exile, refugee, expelled or 'exchanged' person; for a man or woman in prison, hospital, or an Old People's home; for a citizen confined to a ghetto; for a happy lover or a bereaved person.

What a different conception of the Esplanade a Corfiot might have had at different times, for instance when it was considered a place of security immediately behind the Old Fortress and now that it is a space for children to play while adults sip their ouzos or coffees on the arcaded Liston promenade. What a different picture a Corfiot might have had concerning the value of land down by the sea or up in the hillside village. In the days when pirates, especially the slave-taking Muslim corsairs like Barbarossa, were a problem (e.g. from 1537) and the most unprotected land down by the sea was considered the poorest inheritance.

Ali Pasha's Castle in Ioannina might not have seemed quite so romantic to an inmate of his harem ("a prison, in which sensuality reigns without love, luxury without taste, and slavery without remission", according to the Reverend Hughes), and the lake was a place where women might be drowned as punishment for infidelity.

To the people of Parga who had to escape to Corfu or Paxos after the British had sold the town to Ali Pasha, the view from Paxos would have had a very different meaning. Turkey-in-Europe was not Greece or the Ionian Islands. The Parginotes had originally requested that they should be taken under British protection, when they sent a message to a British officer on Paxos, Captain Garland, who had taken possession of the island. They were led to understand that if they managed to disarm the French garrison at Parga, they would be granted British protection and be treated just as the Ionian Islands. "And for *whom* did British authorities think proper to expatriate this interesting people, and to rivet the fetters of Greece!" exclaimed Hughes.

Landscapes can change dramatically after the impact of sieges, sellouts, bombings, earthquakes or tourist developments, of course. We only have to think of the case of Barbati in Corfu and the building developments which have devastated the olive groves and once beautiful natural environment beside the sea. Self-destructive human activity *is* avoidable, whereas earthquakes are not. The Northern Ionian Sea and islands (e.g. Corfu) are less subject to seismic activity than the Southern Ionian Sea and islands, a phenomenon also noted by Leake in 1810, when comparing frequency and intensity of earthquakes in Kefalonia (and Prevesa) to Corfu (and Ioannina). There was already a variety of testimony to this at the beginning of the nineteenth century. Tertius Kendrick believed that Paxos "unquestionably formed part of Corfu originally… It is easy enough to conclude that earthquake, assisted by the violence of the sea, effected a separation of this portion of land…"

The essence of a view or a landscape is what it does to your braincells. If you are a Byronist you will see things, to some extent, the way Byron saw them. You may see things the way other artists or writers saw them, like Edward Lear, Joseph Cartwright, Lawrence Durrell, Nicholas or Eleni Gage, James Chatto, Louis de Bernières, to name but a few. Our very concepts of a beautiful view or landscape may have been determined by painters who knew how to frame and compose a sublime or picturesque view, with a carefully positioned olive tree or, in a quasi-Colonial or even Orientalist manner, a peasant in native costume to one side of the canvas.

Perceptions of the "Sublime" in Nature and our perceptions of Ionian Islands are partly determined, if not by our gender, then certainly by our age, or where we have come from. To young Gerald Durrell, as a boy, Corfu was paradise, as it had seemed to the sensitive poetry-writing Sisi of Austria and the sensitive artist–poet Edward Lear, even if it was "a very small tittle-tattle place", as Jan Morris reminds us in *The Venetian Empire*.

If you have just arrived from Australia, Corfu may have little to offer and may seem somewhat Third World. If you have come from Sweden, the climate may make you overlook the more squalid aspects. If you have come from London, Kansas City or Moscow, the colour of the sea may be enough to entrance you, and—for some—the sense of security and the homogeneity of the population may appeal.

People talk of seeing things through rose-tinted spectacles. Many views in the Ionian Islands have been spoilt for me, if not for newcomers, as a result of thoughtless or illegal human activity. Perhaps I too should get my spectacles tinted.

IMAGES OF LEFKAS

Lawrence Durrell is rather unfair about Lefkas in *The Greek Islands*, calling it "a sad little island", complaining about its limitations and claiming, unjustly, that "It cannot vie in natural interest and beauty with the others." Maybe he simply did not have time to explore it properly. Even Arthur Foss (1969) writes that "There is a remote and primitive air which hangs over this least developed of the Ionian Islands" and that the town of Lefkas is "an untidy town, always under repair" with "shambling houses" and "a melancholy reputation". Kendrick thought the inhabitants of Lefkas had more ferocious characters than any of the other Septinsulars, the better classes restlessly pursuing numerous cabals and litigations.

Foss must have visited the island when the port of Vassiliki had never heard of windsurfing and when Nidri's only claim to fame, apart from its popularity with yachtsmen, was its association with Dörpfeld, and its location opposite the small islands belonging to Aristotle Onassis (Skorpios) and the Valaoritis family (Madouri). Ilias Venezis, in his essay on Lefkas, writes with a passion that is similar to Cavafy's feelings about the voyage to Ithaca, that "the journey to Lefkas is a call, a voice that you hear inside but that you do not hurry to answer… You put off as long as you can the journey to Lefkas… Maybe going to the Lefkas of Sikelianos, you will discover the real meaning of Lefkas." Venezis lets the literary and imaginative associations of the island work, as he seeks out the Lefkas of Sikelianos, Valaoritis, Homer and Dörpfeld. Durrell and Foss seem to have missed these dimensions, seeing the reality instead of the ideal that a Venezis could perceive.

I found Lefkada town lively and buzzing at night, and the island has some wonderful beaches. Although Lefkas suffered two long periods under Turkish occupation (1362-1479 and 1503-1684), there is no evidence that I could discover to point to this different cultural influence. Even its major earthquakes occurred at different times from the more southerly islands, and its architectural solutions were different, which gives it a special atmosphere. Many of its old churches are still standing. Valaoritis' greatest, but unfinished, poem, "Foteinos", is set in fourteenth-century Lefkas and deals with an uprising against a Venetian ruler. When Foteinos' son, Mitros, fails to attack the troublesome dogs belonging to their oppressive Venetian master, Foteinos does so himself, killing one and wounding the other, telling his son, "You put me to shame, you are not a *Lefkaditis*."

CRITICISMS AND COMPENSATIONS

However much we love an island or a town, we should not wear blinkers or remain too blissfully unaware of criticism and negative points of view, both past and present.

If you drive up to Corfu's Bella Vista, near Lakones, above Palaiokastritsa, the panoramic view remains as impressive as it ever was, even if it has become something of a cliché. "Nothing can be imagined more exquisite than the broken and indented coast here presented", wrote D. T. Ansted. Mark Ellingham, returning to Corfu after a 30-year absence, was

Shipwreck on Zakynthos

inspired by the "jaw-dropping panorama of the Paleokastritza coast, all wooded islands and outcrops" (*Guardian*, 2008).

Can such breathtaking views become clichés even when experienced on the spot, and not just through photographs, TV programmes or in tourist brochures? Looking down at the "picture-postcard" views of Porto Katsiki beach in Lefkas, at the famous shipwreck bay in Zakynthos, or at the "Ortholithos" rock at Aghios Gordis, Corfu, is (or used to be) a subtly different experience each time, depending on one's mood or state of receptivity. Perhaps only the Greek poets and prose-writers can capture the *essence*, because it is also a question of *a way of seeing* and thinking, a matter of the texture of language, of connotation and association (in the way, for instance, that Seferis' poetry contains echoes and elements of Homer).

But foreign writers have come very close to pinning down the special qualities of the Greek landscape and of places like Corfu Town; usually full of praise for its beauty, there have also been some significant notes of dissent:

> I never got to like the town of Corfu. It has a desultory air which by evening became a quiet, irritating sort of dementia. You are constantly drinking something you don't want to drink or else walking up and down aimlessly feeling desperately like a prisoner... Corfu is a typical place of exile. (Henry Miller, *The Colossus of Maroussi*)

> Corfu marvellous—but for a short time. The mountains, the sea, the colours all splendid, but lacking vital energy, *amolissants* (enervating), sleep-inducing, fatal for a fighting soul. (Nikos Kazantzakis, Letter, 21 October 1926)

Gerald Durrell may have thought that life in Corfu in the 1930s was like living in "one of the more flamboyant and slapstick comic operas", but by 1987 he had changed his mind:

> Going back to Kerkyra recently was like paying a visit to the most beautiful woman in the world suffering from an acute and probably terminal case of leprosy—commonly called tourism... The people of Corfu were blessed with a magnificent, magical inheritance, an island of staggering beauty, probably one of the most beautiful islands in the whole

of the Mediterranean. What they have done with it is vandalism beyond belief. (Gerald Durrell, Sunday Times)

Now that Corfu's Old Town has been inscribed in UNESCO's World Heritage list, people are finally becoming more conscious of the need to preserve its integrity and authenticity and to start (late in the day) protecting the natural and cultural heritage of the Old Town and the island as a whole. The catastrophic forest fires in Greece of August 2007 have perhaps raised the population's awareness about the environment. In the past the Ionian Islands lost many historical buildings because of earthquakes. Corfu has been spared, and UNESCO is right to state: "The urban and port ensemble of Corfu, dominated by its fortresses of Venetian origin, constitutes an architectural example of outstanding universal value in both its authenticity and its integrity." Local politicians still seem incapable of agreeing on a co-ordinated programme to preserve or conserve the integrity of the Old Town or the island as a whole. It is more likely that it will become a kind of "Potemkin Village", subject to a quick make-over, prettification and clean-up whenever the UNESCO World Heritage List assessors hove in sight. At other times any make-over is unbearably slow.

Earthquakes may have spared Corfu's Old Town, unlike Zante's or Argostoli's; the British did not destroy all the town's fortifications when they ceded the island to Greece (what the "law-abiding England" did destroy with explosions was the subject of a highly critical poem, "*Ta Kastra Mas*", by Gerasimos Markoras), but modern-day developers and families' desires to build legal or illegal structures, and to leave half of them unfinished, often covered with graffiti, have done more damage to the integrity of the island.

I prefer to live near town. Forty years ago I would have chosen to live in the north-east, somewhere between Barbati and Kassiopi. It is difficult nowadays to talk of the authenticity or integrity of once idyllic places like Barbati, Kalami or Kassiopi. When we want to go for a swim now, we go as far as Aghios Giorgios ton Pagon, at the Afionas end of the beach, where the water can be icy-cold but where it is still crystal clear and where there is no risk of bacteria from fish farms or of waste discharged from large cruise ships, either of which might cause viral conjunctivitis and middle ear infections. But at the other end of the beach, as ecologist Dirk Stoller has shown, the river carries the contents of the cesspits and the toxic olive waste (*mourga*) into the sea when the tourists are not looking. Locals bulldoze sand over the river's mouth and outlet to the sea to hide the pollution. Closer to town the water at Barbati still seems delightful, provided one closes one's eyes to the ravaged environment and endless building of new houses and holiday homes.

Life in the town can be trying too. The compensations far outweigh the disadvantages, of course. Corfu *is* a vibrant and elegant town, full of colour and activity, a joy to walk around in any season (some overcrowded tourist *kadounia* and other streets with ugly electricity pylons and transformers excepted), and the local cultural activities are sufficiently frequent and varied, since the development of the Ionian University, to keep most residents contented. It may not be a challenging place for "a fighting soul", like Kazantzakis; it may be claustrophobic at times, but good company is easy to find. One need never be lonely in Corfu.

Corfu is usually imagined as an island of sunshine and light, but in the *Argonautica* "sailors beholding it from the sea, all black with its sombre woods, call it Corcyra the Black".

D. T. Ansted referred to the town with its "gloomy recesses…so black in their own darkness, that the Greek or Jew seated within is as invisible as the spider in its web"; he talked of "adjoining houses tumbling down, and not affording shelter enough for an English pig; churches, only differing from stables by bells placed above them"; in short, a town "where there have been no architects, and no idea of taste".

Dr. John Hennen considered Corfu's esplanade as "the harvest-field of the physician", and that "even the very best houses of Corfu are destitute of the comforts usually met with in those of the adjacent continent of Italy; the majority are very bad, and some of them execrable. An appearance of dilapidation runs through the whole town." In some respects, the facilities in the houses of Corfu were very little improved even a century or more after Dr. Hennen was writing his book in 1830. The *calle morto* (the 'stagnant street' enclosure at the back of houses) may have disappeared, but chamberpots were still being emptied straight into the sea in the mid-1950s. As an experienced and travelled medical doctor he was concerned by all the fleas, bugs and other vermin he saw, but "for stationary filth, of the most disgusting nature, I should think no part of the world could produce a parallel to the beds of Corfu".

It is fortunate that the likes of Ansted and Hennen were not on the UNESCO World Heritage List committee. Other writers have seen things far more positively. Dodwell enthused: "I have seen few places so strikingly beautiful as the island of Corfu: almost every point of view is a perfect picture." Lord Carlisle (quoted in the Murray *Handbook*) said "Any one who wishes to condense the attractions of southern scenery, and see it all in the utmost comfort and luxury, need only come to Corfu." Edward Giffard considered that "Corfu is one of the loveliest spots in the world, with the greatest variety of scene that can be conceived in so small a space." René Puaux wrote in 1913: "Yesterday, April 30th, the last of the Epirotes left Corfu for their coast villages, from which they were driven away during the Albanian "fury" last November. Ten thousand of them had then flocked to this blissful isle, whose roses and orange trees make it an earthly paradise at this season of the year."

How differently we all see townscapes!

The Greek Orthodox Church

The Greek Orthodox Church has many colourful and solemn traditions, and it has to be said that the Corfiots manage to balance a laid-back attitude to religion with a relaxed attitude to life generally. Their Patron Saint, the Cypriot St. Spiridion, has been there to help them, whether against famine, the plague or Turkish invasion, at least since his mummified remains were slung over a mule and brought to Corfu from Constantinople around 1456, according to legend.

Lawrence Durrell wrote that the Island is the Saint. Elsewhere in *Prospero's Cell* he describes the relic as a mummy, "a funny little old man like Father Christmas". He says, in *The Greek Islands*, that anyone who has seen the Saint carried in procession around the town is unlikely to forget the monks and priests "like a moving flower-bed with their brilliant gonfalons raised on high".

The Australian writer Kester Berwick, who lived for over twenty years in Gastouri, Corfu, is quoted by Robert Dessaix (2001) as telling him over the phone that he could not abide Easter on Corfu, "The crowds, the priests, all that jiggery-pokery–not to mention the pot-throwing." On the subject of pot-throwing, Kirkwall writes that the Corfiots nurtured a great hatred of Judas Iscariot. It was the supposition that "good Christians are stoning, in imagination, the traitor Jew", Judas Iscariot. "The Greeks will

Aghios Nikolaos church (1612) at Upper Vitsa

not readily confirm this fact to a stranger, yet it is generally believed." The pot-throwing "jiggery-pokery" is now a huge draw and crowd-pleaser at Easter. Peter Bull (1967) found his first Corfu Easter unforgettable, but he didn't enjoy the "near-pagan" aspects and was deeply alarmed by the "mass slaughtering of lambs with the attendant smearing of blood on doorways."

Back in the nineteenth century, Private William Wheeler was *not* impressed by a ceremony he wrote about on 12 August 1823:

> To give you a notion of the misery attending this religious ceremony the church is thronged to suffocation, the glass stands at 92 or more in the shade, the place is full of candles and lamps all in full blaze, a most intolerable smell of incense mixed with stinking breath highly seasoned with garlic. To this add the fumes from about fifteen hundred bodies then you will be able to form some notion of what is passing within the walls of the Church of St. Spero.

Henry Holland was in Zante ten years earlier, in the spring of 1813, for carnival and for the All Saints Festival:

A more pleasing spectacle was the festival of All Saints, in the spring of the same year; celebrated among the olive-groves near the city, where half the population of the place was assembled in their best dresses, some walking, some dancing, others playing on the guitar, or forming a part in the religious processions; and various groups dining under the shade of the olive trees, according to the custom of the day."

Jervis-White Jervis clearly did not enjoy the constant ringing of Corfiot church-bells, which he found intolerable, "a heathenish tom-tom... These engines of auricular torture rattle on Sundays, and on festa days...day or night, there is incessantly some bell twankling violently in the immediate neighbourhood..."

In Corfu the priests in black gowns walk their rounds, not just during the processions for St. Spiridion, but they do not seem too interested in inhibiting or denying people's joys and desires. Neighbourhood gossips are a much bigger threat, it would seem. In Maria Strani-Potts' novel *The Cat of Portovecchio*, set in the 1950s, it is the local priest who has the *morosa* (mistress) and needs to have his desires bound with briars. Nikos Kazantzakis did not have a very high regard for the Greek clergy or the monks either, but most Greeks seem entirely at home with their national faith. Jervis-White Jervis wrote about the "degraded" and corrupted state of religion, and believed that "though the Corfiot Greek Church can boast of many eminent and learned men, yet, taking the Greek clergy as a body, they are particularly slothful and uneducated." He goes on, "The authority of the clergy being thus maintained by imposing on the superstitions of the people, they did not consider it requisite to affect a rigidity of morals."

Tertius Kendrick (1822) had little good to say about the character of any of the islanders, in this case the people of Kefalonia: "The Papas of the island are, for the most part, of low birth, excessively ignorant and illiterate. Superstition holds its dark and frightful reign to a surprising degree over the peasantry, who experience its terrors pretty often..." He describes some of the miracles which "are yearly performed by the church, to keep up the deception...", for instance with the help of Saint Gerasimos, the Patron Saint of the island: "A phile is produced, containing a white liquid: if the prayers of the Lixuriotes are heard, the saint announces it by causing the liquid to change into a red colour. This, of course, is accomplished, and an amnesty of sins given... I suspect the pious Papa who manages the phial, is acquainted with some curious and entertaining experiments in chemistry, and, amongst other secrets, with the transmutation of colours."

Byron was unflattering about the Greek clergy: "Indeed a more abandoned race of miscreants cannot exist than the lower orders of the Greek clergy" (*Childe Harold's Pilgrimage*, Note 11).

When discussing the inhabitants of Parga, Kendrick writes, "The influence which the priests have on the people is excessive, nothing being done without their previous concurrence. Learning they have none, being ignorant and superstitious, yet willing to encourage roguery whenever a due share of plunder is given them, for which absolution is delivered in return!"

Sir George Wheler arrived at the port of Kassiopi on 17 July 1675. He describes the church of Panagia (also mentioned by Casanova):

> This little church is famous for a picture of our Lady, to which they attribute miracles, and whereof I had a mind to try the skill. The way is thus: Strangers, that have a mind to know whether their friends are alive or dead, go to the picture, and clap a piece of money upon it, thinking of some friend. If the person they think of be alive, the piece will stick fast; but if dead, it will drop down into a sack placed underneath: so that, dead or alive, the priest is sure of the money. I applied some farthings, which I had, to try how, and where they would stick; but had no other thought, nor end, being before well satisfied, that it was but a religious juggling. Some of them indeed stuck, but all to one and the same place; those that were clapt on any where else, falling still to the ground. The picture is painted upon the walls, and is very smooth and shining; so that I attribute the sticking to some clamminess of the varnish; which they take care, shall never be wanting in some places of it.

Wheler was not much less sceptical about the miracles attributed to St. Spiridion, in Corfu town. He visited St. Spiridion's church on 18 July 1675: "They attribute to him the doing of a miracle about thirty-five years since, restoring the sight to a blind man, who came, and prayed to him, prostrating himself before his body. And of this they keep an annual remembrance ever since; which happened when we were here."

According to K. Klimis (or C. Climis), when the revolutionary French occupied Corfu in 1797, "being atheists, they hurt the deep local religious feeling by ridiculing the patron Saint". Kirkwall said that the French Republicans had "imprudently made some attempts to shake the supremacy of the Greek religion. They had, indeed, desisted on perceiving the great discontent of the people, but the attempt increased their growing unpopularity." Elsewhere he comments, "The French, whether as infidels or Roman Catholics, were equally hateful to the superstitious masses."

The Protestant British were not much better. Thomas Atchison, "late Captain in the Royal Regiment of Artillery", was tried in a General Court Martial in Malta and found guilty of "direct disobedience of orders" and other charges which resulted in his loss of commission, dismissal and stigmatization because he was opposed, as a Protestant, to British officers and troops being commanded to take part in "the idolatrous ceremonies of the Roman Catholic and Greek Churches at Malta, Corfu and Zante". He wrote a letter to *The Record* newspaper on 13 September 1829 about officers and men being required to take part in the processions of St. Spiridion: "the bones of a dead man worshipped by the Greeks as the Guardian of the Island…for the worst uses of priestcraft and superstition". British officers were ordered to help support the Saint's canopy and to "follow the bones" with lighted candles, while "as many as sixty of the deluded Greeks prostrate themselves before the Relique… The sick and the lame are brought out at the same time to the Relique for cure, and considerable gifts of money and other offerings are made to it immediately the procession is over, to propitiate the favour of the bones, producing a considerable revenue to the proprietors of the Relique (a family or rank named Bulgari), and to the priests, who have a share."

The Government *Gazette* of 29 December 1841 reports on the American missionary who nearly caused a revolution by having a leaflet printed in Greek in Athens, highly critical of the Greek Orthodox Church and its "idolatrous practices", which he distributed at the solemn mass in St. Spiridion's Church on St. Spiridion's Day in December 1841. The church was crowded, inside and out; the wind band of the Philharmonic Society (founded 1840) participated. The missionary took advantage of the crowds to distribute his leaflets, causing confusion in the church, "an imprudent act which irritated the population". There was an uproar; people tore up the leaflets, threatened the missionary's life in words and deeds. He ran away to seek asylum in the house where he was staying. The police were unable to calm the angry crowd, which broke into the building. Four or five people made it up to the first floor, tore up more booklets and threw them from the window onto the street full of people. Luckily for the missionary, he was on the second floor.

The military authorities were called in; people threw stones, threatening the public peace. The garrison soldiers from the fortress tried to quell the riot. One person was killed and several wounded in the fighting between the soldiers and the incensed crowd of citizens. Twenty-seven people were held responsible. The *Gazette* published an official notification, dated 28 December 1841, from the Lord High Commissioner's Office. In view of the events, His Excellency had resolved that immediate steps be taken for "putting a stop to such disgraceful proceedings". It was ordered that all coffee-houses, wine-shops, those in which "spirituous liquors" were sold, taverns and eating-houses should be closed at 4 p.m. and not opened again until 7 a.m. the following morning. If inhabitants should break the public peace, civil laws would be suspended and Martial Law proclaimed. What did the pamphlet contain, that so inflamed the Corfiots? It seems that some or all of the Ten Commandments were included, as well as excerpts from the Gospel of St. Matthew. The missionary must have highlighted God's commandments prohibiting the bowing down to or worshipping of other gods or idols.

John Davy, Inspector-General of Army Hospitals, emphasized the superstitious character of the clergy and people (1842): "The clergy of the Ionian Islands are eminently ignorant… If the priesthood is ignorant, how can the mass of the people be otherwise? They are ignorant in an extraordinary degree, and as superstitious."

Henry Holland complained about the "pompous minuteness of ritual" of the Greek Orthodox Church and of the "seeming puerilities of a superstitious worship", while the Reverend Hughes was not impressed by the priority given to the Lenten fast in Ioannina: "The crime of eating flesh in Lent is that against which the highest price of absolution is fixed: adultery and murder may be compounded for at a much lower rate."

K. E. Fleming points out that both Orthodox Christianity and Islam were criticized as superstitious and backward in the time of Ali Pasha, both religions being denigrated in similar ways: "The Greeks, then, are, like the Muslims, in a position of double jeopardy: they measure up neither to the imagined standard of classical Hellas nor to the 'correct' form of Christianity as practiced in the West." One thinks of Louis Dupré's 1819 double portrait of a Greek priest and a Turk, *Un Prêtre Grec et un Turc.*

Enduring British attitudes towards the Church may perhaps be summed up by an anecdote of Edward Lear's, from a journal entry of 10 January 1858:

> Lady Headfort (with an aide-de-campe) has been doing the sights of Corfu... At the Greek Cathedral a beggar came & importuned the glittering Marchioness, who at the moment was indulging in the natural & pleasant act of sucking an orange. Lady H., after a time, paused & said or implied 'silver & gold have I none' but such as she had (being the half-sucked orange) she politely gave the beggar-woman, who (oranges being any number for half-penny) threw the fruit in her Ladyship's face, & rushed frantically out of the desecrated edifice...

Louis de Bernières' article in *The Observer* on 20 March 2005 expressed his love for Greece at the same time as his hostility to the monopoly of the Greek Orthodox Church "on historical and metaphysical truth". Like any nineteenth-century British visitor, he felt able to write that he found the "priest worship" of the Greeks "positively horrible", and claimed that, as a result, the country was not capable of nurturing original thought. He made an exception for the wonderful poets and musicians that Greece has produced.

Meanwhile the Corfiot Nicander Nucius (Níkandros Noukios, 1841) was very aware of the attitudes of the Protestant and Lutheran churches. He visited Augsburg and wrote of the influence of Luther. He expresses shock that in church "both men and women promiscuously, and of all ages, sit down in rows... But they detest the Roman Pontiff, and heap on him insults without number, both in their writings and their speeches; nor will they in any way submit to the dogmas of the Romish Church... And they consider all other Christians as superstitious, and living under a delusion."

It should be noted that the Greek Orthodox Church itself seldom had very much good to say about the Pope or the practices of the Roman Catholic Church. A Corfiot poet (D. Stranis, 1942) at the time of the Italian Occupation during the Second World War could even write of Rome as "a whore" and of the Pope as "the Antichrist":

Rome, the great prostitute, attacked you,
Rome's armed murderers and Fascists invaded.

Andreas Laskaratos (1811-1901) was a Kefalonian who was excommunicated for the views he expressed in *Mysteries of Cephalonia* (1856), attacking prejudice and superstition: "ikons that shed tears, the ignorance and avarice of the clergy". The excommunication remained in force until 1900, just before his death in 1901. Apart from attacking priests, sycophants and idolatrous practices, some of the stories he tells in this and other works present religion as seen from the point of view of a Holy Relic or a donkey, or they concern an Archbishop who is surprised to find so many priests and saints down in hell. A British acquaintance, Ferdinand Whittingham, the military commander in Kefalonia for a period in 1863, who requested that Laskaratos write his own autobiography, considered that if all the Greeks had been like Laskaratos, a Greek Renaissance and a larger Greek Empire would have been more possible and would have come about more quickly. Laskaratos was a Christian, but he was too rational, liberal, progressive and perhaps puritanical in his interpretation of the faith for most Orthodox Greeks. His countrymen accused him of being an atheist, an Antichrist, a Protestant, a devil and all sorts of other names, but he was first and foremost a truth-teller and an objective analyst of his society's ills.

The other volumes of interest are his brief autobiography, written in Italian, and his correspondence. Reading his letter to Hansen of 27 December 1868, one can see why the Greek Orthodox might see him in such an unfavourable light: "I will reaffirm with a loud voice my criticism and disapproval of the worship of Saints and of icons, of miracles, of Lenten fasting and other similar infamies... I hope that this unprecedented outbreak will be a terrible blow to Orthodox superstition." If the Church saw him then as "an Antichrist", he in turn saw the traditions of the Orthodox Church as "anti-Christian". Perhaps he had been influenced by the Church of England during his first period in London (1851). His newspaper, *O Lichnos* ("The Lamp"), was considered anti-clerical and "Protestant" and his political conservatism and nostalgia for the "good old days" of the esteemed British "Protectorate" did not help his reputation. It is perhaps not surprising that his statue in Lixouri faces towards that town, with his backside facing out towards Argostoli, as some Kefalonians like to relate.

But Laskaratos remains a central figure, an important dissident, and it is high time that his autobiography and correspondence, as well as his other works, were made available in English.

A PLACE OF CONTRADICTIONS

Laskaratos, as a twelve-year-old boy, actually met Byron in Kefalonia; but Byron's letters and the *Journal* he started when he first arrived in Kefalonia in 1823 were not very positive about his experiences. Byron apparently told Dr. Henry Muir, the Health Officer at Argostoli, that he stopped writing the journal "because he could not help abusing the Greeks in it" (Note, Vol. 11). On 28 September 1823 he wrote:

> After all- one should not despair, though all the foreigners I have
> hitherto met with amongst the Greeks are going or gone back disgusted.-
> Whoever goes into Greece at present should do it as Mrs Fry went
> into Newgate – not in expectation of meeting with any especial indica-
> tion of existing probity- but in the hope that time and better treatment
> will reclaim the present burglarious and larcenous tendencies which have
> followed this General Gaol delivery. -When the limbs of the Greeks are
> a little less stiff from the shackles of four centuries – they will not march
> so much "as if they had gyves on their legs."——At present the Chains are
> broken indeed-but the links are still clanking- and the Saturnalia is still
> too recent to have converted the Slave into a sober Citizen- The worst
> of them is- that (to use a coarse but the only expression that will not fall
> short of the truth) they are such d——d liars; -there never was such an
> incapacity for veracity shown since Eve lived in Paradise"......But they
> may be mended by and bye. –

Byron was driven mad by the monks and the abbot at the eigh-teenth-century Kefalonian monastery of Agrilia, dedicated to Saint Cosmas, on Mount Agrilion, above Sami, by the "whining dotard" and "pestilential madman" of an abbot whom Byron just wanted out of his sight. Byron notes in his journal that he went over "to the monastery of Samos on the other side of the bay", but as Elizabeth Longford points out, Trelawny "places the monastery in which Byron had his seizure on Ithaca not Cephalonia", at Kathara Monastery (Moni Katharon); when I visited this Ithacan monastery I initially came to the same conclusion

Lord Byron

as Elizabeth Longford, that the ascent, being "long, precipitous and arduous", was too far and too high for such an excursion, which Trelawny says occurred on 12 August; even by car nowadays, the sensation of vertigo induced, driving endlessly upwards, around the steep, hair-raising bends, is enough to give anyone a seizure, as is the sight of the very overweight monk making the journey up and down the mountain on his old motor-scooter. I chatted to him when he arrived, quite unperturbed, at his little shop selling silver crosses and icons; but I much preferred my conversation with the elderly and more talkative Greek gardener, who has been looking after the monastery for around forty years, living there since a young man in virtual solitude. He was glad of some company. Like many other monasteries, it needs a lot of money for proper restoration. Re-reading Trelawny's account, I begin to wonder whether he might not have been right in placing the monastery on Ithaca. It fits with my own experience and imagination. Their excursion was overnight, using mules and muleteers, and Trelawny's description seems accurate: "On the summit of a high mountain in the island there is an ancient monastery, from which there is a magnificent view of the Ionian Sea, Greece, and many islands... It was late when we started... Following a narrow zigzag path between rocks and precipices in single file, as our mules crept upwards our difficulty increased...it was dusk before we reached the summit of the mountain..."

The only other explanation I can give is that Trelawny may have visited the monastery again, in different company, on another occasion several years after Byron's death. He spent about two years on Kefalonia and the Ionian Islands, with his young Greek wife Tersitza Kamenou, half-sister of controversial independence fighter and hero-brigand Odysseus Androutzos, before returning to England in 1828.

If Byron was ambivalent about the Greeks, he did not doubt the beauty of the environment or of the village in which he settled and wished to linger. In the same month he could write in his journal about the house he had rented in Metaxata (finally destroyed in the 1953 earthquakes; he also experienced one himself in 1823). But in general he felt at peace in this quiet place: "Standing at the window of my apartment in this beautiful village, the calm though cool serenity of a beautiful and transparent Moonlight, showing the Islands, the Mountains, the Sea, with a distant outline of the Morea traced between the double Azure of the waters and skies, has quieted me enough to be able to write."

Elizabeth Longford (1975) gives us her own impressions of the sights that had become familiar to Byron during his five month stay on the island: "Its sparkling girdle of deep-water coves; its stony paths winding up from the sea through deep green valleys of arbutus, olive, orange and lemon;… its rising uplands aromatic with pines, myrtle, lavender and sage; finally, high above Argostoli, its bare indigo and umber plateau of volcanic rock known as the Black mountain and crowned by the Venetian castle of St. George, the capital of the island up till 1757…"

Corfu has always been a place of contradictions which arouses emotions from devoted love to intense despair (like Byron's feelings for Greece and the Greeks). The British have never been shy to talk about the political or religious corruption of other nations, particularly those they have occupied, colonized or "protected". William Gladstone was more respectful, and an exception. The Ionian Assembly was not averse to having a priest purify the building if a Protestant "heretic" should address it, as happened to Sir Henry Storks. Religious insults and snubs could be made in both directions. In 1890, the two original British cemeteries on Corfu were handed back, by agreement between the two governments, to the Corfu Municipality, and the graves were moved to an annex of the (present) San Rocco cemetery in 1903 (this had opened around 1855). "This caused much consternation in the British community" (Justin Corfield, 2000). There were letters to *The Times* in May 1904. Perhaps such incidents helped to focus the mind and to cause a shift in attitudes. Religious stereotyping became less offensive.

We no longer have to make conscious efforts to strike a fair balance, or to state, as Kirkwall did in 1864, how difficult it is for any Englishman to write impartially about the Ionian people, as revealed in many works written during the years of the Protectorate, works which "indiscriminately praised the English, and as indiscriminately abused the Ionians."

Sophie Atkinson (1911) was certainly less supercilious at the turn of the century about the Palm Sunday procession: "It is an open and wholly genuine profession of faith, and I think no Corfiote would venture to discredit either St. Spiridione's great and special protection of Corfu, or even the numberless smaller miracles attributed to him… May Corfu long be happy in such unquestioning faith."

PERCEPTIONS OF THE BRITISH

It is flattering if one comes to be counted among the modern Philhellenes, but to the Greeks the Anglo-Saxons are too often the modern barbarians, when not being incomprehensibly or uncouthly British. We should never forget what the Corfiot Nicander Nucius thought of the British when he visited Britain in 1545 and 1546: "The race of men indeed is fair, inclining to a light colour; in their persons they are tall and erect; the hair of their beard and head is of a golden hue; their eyes blue, for the most part, and their cheeks are ruddy; they are martial and valorous, and generally tall; flesh-eaters, and insatiable of animal food; sottish and unrestrained in their appetites; full of suspicion."

There may no longer be much evidence of more refined British habits and customs in places like Corfu, "the discreet picnics among the olive groves" or of the rock-cakes and chutney mentioned by Lawrence Durrell in *Prospero's Cell*, but, as he says, we will find traces of them if we look deeply enough.

The historian William Miller (1928) wrote that "nearly half a century's experience had made it obvious that the British Protectorate was irksome to most of the inhabitants and a source of no profit but much annoyance to the Protecting Power".

The Reverend Hughes wrote of a dinner party to which he was invited with a party of British officers and countrymen in Zakynthos. The British "are in general more respected than beloved by foreigners, especially by those who are subjected to their authority... The reason lies in that lofty carriage and hauteur which the Englishman generally preserves, and in that distance which he interposes between himself and those who he considers his inferiors: in the contempt he feels for their society, he forgets to make due allowances for their want of those advantages which he has himself enjoyed..."

William Goodisson (1822) also commented on the difficulty of uniting the Greeks with the English. He attributed this, in great measure, to the disposition of the English themselves. A Frenchman, he says, may despise every other nation, but has the policy and good manners to conceal his opinion. "A surly Englishman despises all the world; and what is worse, he makes them know and feel his contempt, having neither the good sense nor politeness to keep his spleen to himself... Whatever the reason, the fact is, that the Greeks and English do not associate together as they ought."

G. F. Bowen suggests that if the Protectors and Protected did not mix much in each other's society, the fault lay with the British rather than with the Greeks: "Those Englishmen alone who speak their language, and have visited them in their own cottages, can fully certify with what respect and even affection they have invariably been treated by the peasants."

Kirkwall also regretted (1864) how little the Greeks and English mixed freely and cordially. "The dinner-table, as we understand it, is not one of the institutions of the Ionian Islands."

Many exceptions can be found to these observations, in terms of Anglo–Corfiot or Anglo–Zakynthian families. One thinks of the Sargint family, which lived on Zakynthos from around 1680. But I wonder if there is not an element of outmoded social snobbery surviving in Zakynthos, illustrated by these comments by Nikos Lountzis in his bilingual book of the Sargints' drawings of the island's most distinguished mansions and churches:

> Generation after generation married into Zakynthos families, thus creating a particularly charming synthesis, or character. We can simply call it Anglozakynthian being the product of the best English and Ionian elements, unblemished by questionable social "mixes". I remember that, when first meeting Richard Sargint in London, he not only impressed me as an English gentleman but also as a Zakynthian aristocrat [*he uses the word* afentis *in the Greek version*]. Surely it is true that nobility, par excellence, and belonging to certain people of charisma, overcomes differences of race and culture, such as the Ionian and the English.

If the local aristocracy was resistant to social change, Henry Holland pointed out how resistant the Greek clergy were to *any* change:

> In Cephalonia, two papas or priests were for some time very active in opposing the schemes of improvement which have lately been carried on there. It is a curious instance of their tendency to resist innovation, that when Major Du Bosset [sic] wished to introduce the culture of the potato, many of the men laboured to convince the peasants, that this was the very apple with which the serpent seduced Adam and Eve in paradise.

Louis de Bernières' *Captain Corelli's Mandolin*, a book bought by as many as a million and a half readers (three million, according to the author, counting all foreign language editions), describes, in a mildly patronising manner, the superstitions associated with religious faith in Kefalonia, including the blossoming of a sacred lily.

PERCEPTIONS THROUGH TIME

The Ancient Romans used Corcyra, Apollonia and Ambracia as their chief ports and points of access to Epirus. Nicopolis, an important city for several centuries, was a titular see and metropolis, founded in 31 BC to commemorate Augustus Caesar's (Octavian's) victory over Antony and Cleopatra at the Battle of Actium. Plutarch, Chaucer, Shakespeare and Byron were all fascinated by the behaviour of Antony and Cleopatra at the Battle of Actium, as was the Cuban-born French poet, José-Maria de Heredia. Christopher Wordsworth and Henry Holland give good accounts of the battle. Byron, in a letter of 12 November 1809, wrote that he had seen the remains of the town of Actium, near which "Antony lost the world in a small bay where two frigates could hardly manoeuvre, a broken wall is the sole remnant. On another part of the gulph stand the ruins of Nicopolis built by Augustus in honour of his victory." In *Childe Harold XLV* he writes:

> Look where the second Caesar's trophies rose:
> Now, like the hands that rear'd them, withering.

Leake observes that Nicopolis was considered the capital of Southern Epirus and Acarnania during the first three centuries of the Roman Empire.

St. Paul intended to spend the winter there. The Reverend Hughes infers that Nicopolis was indeed honoured with his presence. What does Titus 3: 12 actually say? "When I shall send Artemas unto thee, or Tychicus, be diligent to come unto me to Nicopolis: for I have determined there to winter." St. Paul may have *intended* to spend the winter there, but there appears to be no hard evidence that he did so.

The mosaics of the Manius Antoninus house in Nicopolis, used from the second to the fourth centuries AD, provide impressive testimony—as if we did not know—that the Romans knew how to enjoy the good life in a civilized style in some parts, at least, of the Ionian Islands and Epirus. In spite of the harshness of the Roman conquest and occupation of Greece, the Romans can be considered among the first tourists or summer vacationers.

There is ample archaeological evidence of well-appointed Roman villas on Corfu and Kefalonia, such as the ruins of the Roman villa (third century AD) in the village of Skala in Kefalonia with its well-preserved mosaic floors.

The Roman Emperor Nero arrived at Kassiopi (Corfu) in AD 66, but he was more interested in singing and playing the lyre than anything else, according to Suetonius: "Having gained some knowledge of music…as soon as he became emperor he sent for Terpnus, the greatest master of the lyre in those days, and after listening to him sing after dinner… he…began to practise himself… Finally encouraged by his progress, although his voice was weak and husky, he began to long to appear on the stage…"

Nero declared that "the Greeks were the only ones who had an ear for music and that they alone were worthy of his efforts. So he took ship without delay and immediately on arriving at Cassiope made a preliminary appearance as a singer at the altar of Jupiter Cassius, and then went the round of all the contests" (Suetonius, *The Lives of the Twelve Caesars*).

The Romans may have behaved in a civilized way in their summer villas, but the decline and division of the Empire into the Eastern and Western Empires, and the rise of Constantinople, ushered in other forms of oppression in the Byzantine period. Sir Steven Runciman (1975) conceived the Byzantine Empire as a splendid, but not static, civilization, which lasted eleven centuries; George Finlay dates the Empire's three distinct periods as falling between 716 and 1204; Dionysios Zakythinos traces its history over the the period 324-1453; Donald M. Nicol (1994) states that it lasted "for about 1100 years". David Talbot Rice (1935) makes the point that the term Byzantium usually serves to designate "all that was done and produced in the Byzantine Empire as a whole between 330 and the arrival of the Turks at the middle of the fifteenth century". Dorrian Lambley, in his short history of Corfu (1984), writes about "the great Byzantine era, a wonderful and advanced civilisation that was to last 888 years", whose influence "reaches down to us today", but most archaeologists and historians preferred to study the classical period and the glories of Ancient Greece.

Whereas Yeats had visions of hammered gold, starlit and moonlit domes, John Fowles perceived them as dark and oppressive, in his poem "Byzantium". Fowles seems to have loathed Greek churches with their "Clusters of foul mycotic caps/ Enshriners of the worst of night":

> I know Byzantium: Byzantium
> Is anything that tortures light.

In two lines he manages to condemn the civilization responsible for some of the most beautiful churches in Epirus, whether Byzantine or "post-Byzantine". If any period is sometimes considered as the Greek "Dark Ages", it is the period following the Fall of Constantinople in 1453, until around 1800, and yet extraordinarily beautiful churches, monasteries and icons were created in Epirus during these centuries, quite apart from stone bridges and mansions, and Venetian-influenced towns and country houses on the islands. After Crete fell to the Ottomans in 1669, following the twenty-year siege of Candia, Corfu benefited (in terms of both icon-painting and literature) from the influx of Cretan refugees and artists, so it is not helpful to generalize about the "dark ages in Greece". As Ilias Venezis writes in *Lefkas*, "What I find so moving about religious art of the Ionian islands is the conflict, as the spirit of Byzantium is invaded by Western spirituality… How could the Ionian Sea ignore Venice?"

Byzantine landlords allegedly had the right, "the customary obligation", to "deflower the bride before the wedding". This practice of *droit de seigneur* or *ius primae noctis* is not mentioned by Katerina Nikolaou in her Greek-language booklet on *"The Place of Women in Byzantine Society"*, and it sounds as if it might have been an unproven myth or generalization. The age of marriage for women during the Byzantine period was fixed by law at 12 or 13 for girls (Nicol confirms that the "canonical age for marriage was twelve for a girl"); sometimes an anxious father married off a daughter at a younger age, hoping to secure, as early as possible, a better fate for his daughter. Citing the opinion of Professor Cyril Mango, Nikolaou discusses his view that misogyny was a basic dogma of Byzantine thought, and that the Fathers of the Church painted feminine nature in the darkest colours, warning men of the dangers of female influence. The Byzantine author N. Kekaumenos, who wrote a manual of proverbs and advice on household and military affairs in *c.*1078, wrote "Keep your daughters as prisoners, confined and inconspicuous." Athough women were supposed to live restricted, secluded lives within their houses, far from the eyes of other men, the reality, Nikolaou suggests, was otherwise. Perhaps that is so, but there is substantial evidence that unmarried Greek women continued to live under conditions of strict seclusion in nineteenth-century Ioannina and in Zakynthos. Mousson (1859) observes that this was also true in Corfu towards the end of the British Protectorate.

How did the widows or young women of Ioannina and their families feel when they were forcibly wed to Serbians (by order of Thomas, son-in-law of Simeon) or to Ottoman Turks, according to Greek chroniclers? The Greek Christians had to make the best of it, at the end of the fourteenth century when the Turks first arrived, and presumably in the fifteenth century after the Turks had taken Ioannina (1430), as they could do nothing against the *firman* of Sultan Murat, or Amurath, II, as noted by Leake. The Reverend Hughes also relates how the Mahometans wished to become domiciled in Ioannina and to take Greek wives. They would wait outside the doors of the churches until the congregation came out, then "each person seizing upon the damsel that pleased him best, carried her off in defiance of her relatives and friends. The parents, after a short time, seeing no remedy for the evil, consented to the nuptials, and gave the customary dowry to the husbands... After this event the Mahometan population of course increased."

What did the Venetians think of Corfu? Many of them took Greek wives, and the evidence points to the fact that a high proportion was willing enough to embrace the Orthodox faith as well as the women. It seems that they soon made themselves at home in the islands. Whether or not the islanders found their protection and rule as congenial as they had hoped when they first invited them in is a matter of debate (A. Valaoritis' poem "Foteinos" suggests an attitude of profound hostility). British and Italian historians differ significantly in their understanding, and no two Corfiots seem to be able to agree. Perhaps it depends on what benefits and social position one's family had acquired within the feudal system, and a rather backward and decaying system it was towards the end. Those unfortunate Corfiots forced to give their sweat and blood in helping to build the fortresses had suffered immensely, there can be no doubt.

How much did the Venetians care about the fate of ordinary Corfiots, such as the fishermen of Mandouki, when the Mandoukiots had to face the second Turkish siege of July and August 1716? The Turks stormed, assaulted and occupied the area for a time. Fortunately the Corfiots did have the Venetians to help defend them, as well as Field-Marshall Count Matthias Johann von der Schulenburg, various irregular soldiers *and* St. Spiridion. Military strategy and considerations of personal spiritual salvation were kept separate but were mutually reinforcing.

Over on the mainland, what did the people of Parga feel about the actions of the British in 1817? What did the British and the Ionian Islanders think? Ioannina had been lost in 1430 and did not become Greek until 1913 (Arta and district were ceded to Greece in 1881; Arta had been lost to the Turks in 1449). Parga, where the castle was considered by the Venetians as the eye and ear of Corfu, was sold to Ali Pasha by the British in 1817. Napier, in *The Colonies* (1833), says that the people of Parga were extremely ill-used by the British government, and Charles-Philippe de Bosset wrote a damning book about the events.

The Reverend Hughes commented that the French had refused to cede Parga to the tyrant Ali Pasha, but, he asked himself, "Who can reflect without horror that the British flag, which succeeded it, proved the winding-sheet of Parghiot independence?" Parga, he remarked, was a name "at the very mention of which every Englishman must now feel the blush of shame tingle on his cheeks". Hughes thought it unjust that the British should have delivered Parga to Ali Pasha, and that the measures taken were both cruel and impolitic. Like many others he was distressed by the thought of a Christian power giving up the rights of fellow Christians "to an infidel tyrant". For an Englishman, it was painful to dwell upon—an apparent breach of faith and violation of an agreement. He describes the disinterment of the bones of their ancestors, the burying or burning of the remains in secret places to prevent "profanation by the Turks", then the sight of the people kissing the land which had given them birth, taking with them a handful of soil, or the sacred ashes of their ancestors, as they prepared to embark for Corfu and Paxos.

Edward Lear was anxious to leave Parga when he visited it in May 1849: "A dark cloud hangs over the mournful spot. Would that much which has been written concerning it were never read, or that having been written it could be disbelieved!" In spite of the beauty of the spot, the white buildings crowning the rock, the waves below, the whispering olives above him, the convent islets, and the broad bright sea beyond, he wanted to get away quickly. "The picture, false or true, of the 10ᵗʰ of April 1819 was ever before me, and I wished with all my heart that I had left Parga unvisited."

That is not the advice one would give today; it is important that British visitors and others are made aware of that period of history. Even Sir Thomas Maitland, in a private letter of April 1817 to Earl Bathurst (then Colonial Minister), admitted, according to Bowen (1852):

> There was no measure more detrimental to our character than this cession.... Whatever may have been the *diplomatic* justice or policy of the cession of Parga, it is certain that the shock given by that lamentable transaction to every Christian in the East, lessened the influence of England far more seriously than could be compensated for by any gratitude on the part of the Turks... At all events, no Englishman can wander among the ruined houses and deserted gardens of the beautiful spot, without a feeling of shame and regret that *his* country should have abandoned to the infidels a gallant Christian community, which had defended against them for four hundred years its liberty and its religion.

The Reverend Hughes was favourably disposed to the Parghiotes and their character, calling them a very industrious, honest and moral people, in spite of what was being said by those who sought to depreciate their good qualities. He blames Hobhouse for quoting an Albanian song which spread the idea that the Parghiots often indulged in the crime of piracy, claiming that there had never been any known example of a Parghiot pirate on the coast of the Adriatic.

Andreas Kalvos (1792-1867, whose father was from Mandouki in Corfu, and his mother from Zakynthos), in his "Ode to Parga", writes of how the Pargiots left behind their familiar fields in escaping from the yoke of slavery, preferring the bitterness of *xeniteia,* poverty and destitution, in a foreign place. But the hands of a caring Greek fate will bring them back, says Kalvos, to the place where they had burned the remains of their ancestors.

No wonder that Kalvos would also write, Anglophile that he was, at least later in life, a poem called "The Wishes", which was clearly addressed to the British "protectors" (and which Theodorakis set to music, as part of "Songs of Strife"):

Better, much better
For the Greeks to be dispersed
All over the world,
Begging for bread
With outstretched hands
Than for us to have protectors
…The hand you held out
To a foreign people—
As a symbol of protection—
Choked us, and still stifles
The oppressed population…

Kalvos complains that the Greeks fought fearlessly and courageously for the Cross, while "You" (i.e. "We") secretly supported those fighting against the Cross and Truth, and fought against it in Greece. And now, he says, you hold out your hands in order to offer us your protection! "Withdraw them!" he commands, defiantly striking his lyre and giving us still much food for thought.

My Greek edition of Kalvos' *Complete Works* contains a five-page commentary on this poem, "The Wishes". It makes uncomfortable reading for a British person. Greek attitudes of hostility and resentment towards Britain are undisguised in this study of the poem, in which the British are described as "heartless", "devious", "cynical", "murderous", "traitorous", "devils", as "political game-players", full of diabolic plots and machinations; "allies like snakes", with no understanding of friendship or loyalty, but people who mistreated the Greeks in Asia Minor, who offer and offered the terrible, murderous hand of help and protection, which caused such harm, disaster and calamity during the War of Independence of 1821 and throughout the period of the free existence of the Greek nation. The British are accused of digging the graves of the Greeks: in short, dry colonials, from a murderous hornets' nest of an island, who set foot in Greece with the sole aim of occupying and exploiting the oil-reserves of the Middle East.

I am not sure that Kalvos intended all of this, but the critical editor has kindly extrapolated it for the benefit and edification of Greek schoolchildren and readers of the *otherwise Anglophile* Kalvos, who chose to settle and live in England, wrote warmly of London and Albion, where "rays of most sweet freedom nourished me and gave me comfort", and who, like

Solomos, wrote with appreciation of the contribution of Byron, that admirable spirit of Britain and ill-fated friend of the Greeks. One of the students he tutored in Corfu, the equally Anglophile Laskaratos from Kefalonia, describes his second stay in London, a year of exile in 1856, as "monotonous and oppressive". It is as well to be aware of these perceptions, of how other nations imagine the British, and to acknowledge at least some of their foreign policy mistakes.

It seems that Solomos, whom Laskaratos had also met when in Corfu, expressed some of the "prevailing anti-British feeling" when writing his "Hymn to Liberty" on the Hill of Strani, in Zakynthos. Romilly Jenkins states that three verses "were subsequently modified or expunged by the poet at the request of Lord Guilford", but they appear in the standard Greek editions. Jenkins translates the offending verses (two follow):

> To the starry heaven above
> Islands of the Ionian main
> Raise their song of joy and love [i.e. to Liberty],
> Raise their hands—Alas in vain.
>
> They are bound in fetters now
> That no wit can e'er untie;
> Branded every servile brow
> With the words "False Liberty".

Pseftra Eleftheria, "phoney freedom", are the words he uses for the "False Liberty" offered by the constitution imposed by the British Protectorate. But his lyrical poem "On the Death of Lord Byron" (not published

Plaque to Lord Byron, commemorating his visit to Zitsa in October 1809

in his lifetime) reflects the deep shock that Greeks and the world at large felt on hearing of the death of Byron. Solomos calls first on the Suliot heroes to pay their respects (the Suliots, who had stretched out the welcome hand to Childe Harold: "Oh! Who is more brave than a dark Suliote, / In his snowy camese and his shaggy capote?"), but advises the Suliot traitors (sadly there were some) to stay far away.

The Greek folksong, "The Exile of the Parghiots" (Passow, CCXXII), expresses the fate of the people of Parga:

> "Say, do the Turks attack her now, or does the battle burn her?"
> "The Turks have not attacked her now, nor does the battle burn her;
> But all the Pargiots are sold, are sold as goats and cattle."
> (Basil Photos, 1963)

Another version of the song of Parga, "Parga's Lament", a heroic song set to music by Dvořàk, is based on a Czech text by V. B. Nebeský (itself a translation of the Greek folk song) from "Three Modern Greek songs", Op. 50, 1878:

> Three birds took flight from Preveza,
> To Parga made their way…
> O Parga, O Parga,
> The Turks will march on you…
> Jesus Christ was sold for money,
> For money they've given you too.
> Take your children and your mothers,
> And you, priests, now take your saints.
> Lay down your weapons, you young men.
> Wide and deep now dig your graves,
> And from the earth remove
> Your fathers' heroic bones
> So that no Turk may ever walk –
> Walk upon those he never conquered.
> (tr. Joy Kadečkovà)

There are two other moving folksongs about the sale of Parga and the role of the British in P. Aravantinos's *Epirotika Tragoudia*.

Hobhouse thought "the character of the Pargotes is amongst the worst of the Albanians: their connexion with the Christian states has taught them only the vices of civilization, and they are not less ferocious, but are become more refined in their cruelty and violence. Their town is the refuge of many of the robbers whom Ali has driven from the mountains." Perhaps Hobhouse had been influenced by Ali's propaganda: "the Pasha has his attention fixed upon this town, and will probably succeed in his designs."

What did the Greeks really think about the Janissaries and Ottoman harems? I found myself surprised, when re-reading C. M. Woodhouse's *The Story of Modern Greece*, to note some of his views and interpretations of the "Dark Age" of Greece (1453-1800). He thought it likely that the Greek peasant of the fifteenth to seventeenth century was better off than his counterpart in Western Europe and that even the tribute of children, or the Janissary child-tax, was not deeply resented because it offered opportunities for a good career, and was "generally welcomed as such." H. C. Darby (in Heurtley *et al.*, 1967) suggests that membership of the powerful Janissary Corps was at first seen as a curse, but "came to be regarded by many parents as a blessing". Richard Clogg writes that "the levy did afford the opportunity for children from poor backgrounds to rise to the very highest echelons of the Ottoman state structure... Moreover, highly placed janissaries were sometimes able to show favours to relatives or to their native villages." Woodhouse also claims that parents did not generally resent giving their daughters to become odalisques in Ottoman harems, and that "the centuries of foreign oppression are therefore exaggerated, though not wholly mythical".

This stands in contradiction to the accounts of cruelty and oppression recorded by most British travellers and by Greek historians themselves. The relative lack of contemporary evidence of parents' true feelings is hardly justification for a historian to make assumptions either way. Woodhouse points out, more reasonably perhaps, that a Greek primate or an Orthodox bishop "could be as oppressive as a Turkish *pasha*", and that "it was certainly preferable for a Greek peasant to be under the direct control of the Sultan's house than under a Roman Catholic domination or at the mercy of his own fellow-Greeks". He further suggests that Venetian rule in the Ionian Islands and the fortified ports of Epirus was more oppressive than that of the Turks, "The conviction that the turban of the Prophet was preferable to the Cardinal's hat was reinforced by the experience of

Venetian rule, especially where it could be contrasted with Turkish rule in the immediate vicinity." This is a fundamental and perhaps irreconcilable issue of opposing historical imagination and interpretation.

What did the Islanders think of the Venetian Rule? Dr. Flavio Andreis of Verona felt aggravated by the aspersions cast on the University of Padua by British writers of the nineteenth century. John Davy, for example, suggested that the Venetians well understood that knowledge is power, and were determined to keep the Ionians in ignorance. While many Ionian islanders did go to study at Padua, "it was imperative they studied nowhere else... The professors of this University, which was under the influence of Venice, were strictly prohibited from teaching any thing tending to open the eyes of the Ionians to their real condition; and the studies and examinations were so conducted, that in three months, an Ionian could obtain his diploma as a doctor of medicine or law."

Tertius Kendrick was critical of the motives of wealthy Kythirans concerning study in Italy: "The education of those, who are rich, is, like the youths of Cephalonia, obtained in Italy, and acquired more for the purpose of refining their villainy in law and physic, to better them in easing the peasants of their property, than for the general and accepted motives which compel parents to give their children these mental advantages."

The danger of accepting such statements at face value is considerable. Dr. Andreis is convincing that Davy's assertions were improbable, given the high reputation of the University of Padua (founded in 1222 or even earlier), which was renowned for its research, and at different times included in its faculty and student body such illustrious names as Copernicus, Galileo and Tasso, as well as Foscolo, Tertsetis, Vilaras, Capodistrias and Casanova. It seems to have been a fairly free-thinking institution. Brian Dicks points out that the Ionian Academy was beginning to lose students to Italy: "increasingly...the academy was losing students to Pisa and Padua and other Italian centres of learning, as well as to the University of Athens which was founded in 1837". Perhaps John Davy had seen the writing on the wall, and was making some deliberate propaganda against the degrees offered by Italian universities.

Thomas Gallant (2002) discusses the way that both the Ottoman Turks and the Venetians were held responsible by Westerners for the degeneration of Greek culture. On the Ionian Islands, "the Venetians rather than the Ottomans were cast in the role of the corrupting snake responsible for the Greeks' fall from Hellenic Eden".

There is no consensus among Corfiots about Venetian rule, as far as I can tell. They may have been enslaved by the Venetians, but at least the Venetians were "*Europeans*", they were not "*the enemy*". To some extent, this is a view expressed in hindsight, and takes little account of the suffering of those forced to build the fortresses, tend the olive trees or work as galley-slaves.

In spite of the suffering, tragic events and cultural conflicts of history, why do people from many countries still love to visit Greece and Corfu in particular? The Serbs, and particularly descendants of those retreating, starving Serbs who died during the horrific march over the Albanian mountains, or while convalescing on the island of Vido (after the allies had finally evacuated over 150,000 of them to Corfu, Gouvia, from Valona), may come on pilgrimage to visit the Serbian War Museum in Corfu Town or the Serbian monument on Vido (formerly St. Vito; ancient name *Ptychia*). They also come for the beauties of Corfu, which was perceived as a green "island of salvation" by the exhausted soldiers after their heroic exodus of 1915-16, even if many of them died soon after their arrival. Every day bodies were buried at sea just off Vido Island.

Flora Sandes, who fought with the Serbian Army, gives us a first-hand account in her autobiographical book (1916):

> We had been looking forward to Corfu as a sort of land flowing with milk and honey, with a magnificent climate and everything that was good, but our ardour was rather damped when we landed at that hour at a small quay, feet deep in mud, miles away from the town, and about 8 miles away from our camp...
>
> Corfu may be a lovely climate and a health resort and everything else that is delightful at any other time in the year, but it was a bitter blow to us when it rained for about six weeks without stopping after our arrival... There was no hay at first for us to sleep on, and the incessant wet, combined with the effects of bully beef, on men whose stomachs were absolutely destroyed by months of semi-starvation was largely responsible for the terrible amount of sickness and very high mortality among the troops during the first month of our stay there. This was especially the case among the boys and young recruits, who, less hardy than the trained soldiers, were completely broken down by their late

hardships and died by thousands on the hospital island of Vido. They could not be buried in the small island, dying as they were at the rate of 150 a day, and the bodies were taken out to sea.

One would like to see some form of modern memorial to Flora Sandes, one of the most famous women soldiers of the First World War.

ROMANTICS AND LOVERS

However grim the historical record, people keep coming. The Germans and Italians come to Corfu and Epirus in spite of the invasions and occupations during the Second World War, in spite of the destructive bombings, massacres (e.g. the Acqui Division) and the burning of villages. The British may know or remember little about the actions of the more despotic or ruthless Lord High Commissioners during the fifty year *Anglokratia* (English rule), about the impact on Greeks of the Cyprus problems of the 1950s, or about the controversial involvement of British troops in the events of December 1944, and the five week Battle of Athens (33 days of fighting, 250 British dead).

People have a habit of falling in love on Corfu, but primarily *with* Corfu. The Greek–American Eleni Gage wrote in 2004, "But I knew, already…that I would choose Corfu over the vast majority of men. Now, more than a decade later, I have yet to meet the man for whom I would trade the island." Louis de Bernières admitted in an *Observer* article that his relationship with Greece had involved "both love and difficulty, exasperation and pleasure". It began when he was 28. He had gone to Corfu with a woman, who, it turned out, was planning to dump him. They spent a fortnight "in a horrible part of Corfu, infested with horseflies, where the discos thumped all night and the dogs barked along with them". Their Glaswegian neighbours there had discovered that "it was cheaper to be drunk for two weeks in Greece than in Glasgow"—even after paying for their flights. In spite of being given the push by his girlfriend on the last night in Corfu, Louis decided then and there to become a writer. He swore he would never return to Greece, but was back in Corfu before very long, on his own and in a much more attractive part of the island. Since then he has also discovered the delights of Kefalonia and Kythira.

Apart from the many works of popular fiction set on Corfu and other Ionian Islands by British, American and German writers, Ionian Island poets have always sung the praises of the islands—famous poets like Solomos, Kalvos, Mavilis, Valaoritis, Sikelianos, Dendrinou and many lesser poets.

In "Greetings to Corfu", Orestis Alexakis writes of Corfu:

> You taught me the alphabet of Beauty,
> The litany of Love...
> The inner light of flowers...
> I will always be your child.

Lorentzos Mavilis once said that every young Greek should go to Corfu to acquire the noble seed of culture, and in order to cultivate the spirit and genuine, authentic Greek literature; the best path towards Parnassus, he believed, was along Corfu's Spianada Square, because in Corfu the intellectuals and creative artists had built strong foundations. Although those sentiments are still gratifying to contemporary Corfiots, they were truer of the period of the Eptanesian school of writers, from Solomos and Kalvos up to the times of Theotokis (1872-1923) and Mavilis, than they are of today's Corfu. The Corfiot path to Parnassus has, perhaps, become the path for idle pleasure-seekers and students of the Ionian University to find the quickest way to the coffee-shops. Incidentally, the reason why people can enjoy the Spianada, especially young children who play there without a care, owes something to the position of the Old Fortress. The Venetians permitted no buildings to be built within rifle-shot of the Fortress, and they designed a clear, level, open space where cannons could be freely fired, and where people could be gathered in an emergency. Many buildings and dwellings in the area known as Borgo were demolished in order for the Spianada to be created, beginning in the sixteenth century. So the road to Parnassus was built on military foundations and on the need for defence and security. It seems appropriate, since Mavilis himself fell in battle.

Corfu is not just the Liston, the Spianada, St. Spiridion's Church, the fortresses and the Old Town. There are other spots, suburbs like Mandouki and villages such as Karousades, Gastouri, Sinarades and Loutses, that have provided inspiration to writers and poets.

Oscar Wilde visited Greece in March/April 1877, whilst still an undergraduate at Oxford, and wrote a sonnet about the Corfiot village of Santa Decca (Aghioi Dekka or Ten Saints):

...For Pan is dead, and all the wantoning
By secret glade and devious haunt is o'er...
....Great Pan is dead, and Mary's son is King.
And yet- perchance in this sea-trancèd isle,
Chewing the bitter fruit of memory,
Some God lies hidden in the asphodel...

He wrote another sonnet, "Impression de Voyage" at Katakolo (a port south of Patras, near Pyrgos), which seems to sum up what all classically educated Oxbridge students and scholars ever imagined and felt about setting foot for the first time in the Greece of their fantasy:

From the steep prow I marked with quickening eye
Zakynthos, every olive grove and creek,
Ithaca's cliff, Lycaon's snowy peak,
And all the flower-strewn hills of Arcady.

Empress Elizabeth of Austria epitomizes the romantic tendency. "Sisi", as she was affectionately nicknamed, worshipped and made a cult of Achilles and the poetry of Heinrich Heine. She emulated him in her poetic diary and often thought that her poems were dictated to her by the spirit of Heine. She loved the peace and quiet of the orange and olive groves of Corfu, the playful dolphins and seagulls with which she could readily identify. According to Constantine Christomanos, Sisi expressed a desire to be buried in Corfu, with the stars above her and the cypress trees sighing for her.

Doch ker' ich heim in deine Buchten,
Wenn mir des Lebens Sturm missfällt.
Was ich und meine Möven suchten,
Hier find' ich's—Ruhe vor der Welt."
("Abschied und Rückfahrt", 15 November 1887)

In a literal translation, this can be rendered: "But I return home to your bays if life's storm displeases me. What I and my seagulls were seeking, I find here—Peace, away from the world."

She missed the island, her vision of the Garden of Eden, and the Ionian

Sea with a fierce nostalgia when away. In *Sehnsucht nach Corfu*, October 1887, she yearns "for the cypress trees that stand high on the grey rocks, from which, gravely and forgotten by the world, they look dreamily towards Albania... I wish I could go walking and reflect once more in the aromatic orange grove, as I used to do once upon a time, all alone with my solitary dreams." In *Meeresfahrt*, October 1888, she sighs that "Longing will eat one's heart out, it robs one of peace of mind and happiness; and night and day you will dream and think back to the blue seas of the Ionian."

Casanova spent time in Corfu in 1744-5 (from around 12 May 1744 on his first visit and then over a period of about a year, fom mid-September 1744 until late September 1745; he cast anchor in the harbour of Venice on 14 October 1745), as an officer and ensign in the Italian military, and adjutant to the commander of the galleasses, as related in his *Memoirs*. His narrative is of interest for reasons other than his relationships with the hard-to-get Madame F, or La Foscarini, "the lady who was the most eminent for beauty and gallantry", and Melulla, the beautiful Zantiot courtesan resident in Corfu who was "the delight and the rage of all the young men in Corfu".

Casanova died in Bohemia in 1798, shortly after the Venetian Republic had been defeated by Napoleon, in 1797. He appreciated the words of Pliny the Younger: "If you have not done things worthy of being written about, at least write things worthy of being read." And he did. Like Byron, he can even be amusing about catching a dose of gonorrhoea or the clap in Greece (cf. Byron's letter to J. C. Hobhouse of 15 May 1811: "I had a number of Greek and Turkish women, and I believe the rest of the English were equally lucky, for we were all *clapped*. I am nearly well again of that distemper..."). Casanova writes, "On the third day, as I got up in the morning, an awful pricking announced the horrid state into which the wretched Melulla had thrown me. I was thunderstruck!" Casanova's Corfiot sempstress, "who had procured some young needlewomen to sew my shirts, had expected I would fall in love with one and not all, but my amorous zeal overstepped her hopes, and all the pretty ones had their turn; they were well satisfied with me."

Casanova writes about "the primitive ignorance" of some of the inhabitants and about those who sell magic amulets, scraps of cloth against witchcraft and other gewgaws against goblins. At Kassiopi, he learns about "the oracle of the Virgin Mary". Casanova is delighted to hear that the oracles are not yet defunct, to know that "they will endure as long as there are in this world simple-minded men and deceitful, cunning priests". Casanova then discovers that he himself is to be cursed (by the priest who delivered the oracle), that he will die for seducing several young girls whose husbands now refuse to marry them. Casanova goes to the church and threatens the priest, in no uncertain terms. Later he complains to the *Proto-Papa Bulgari* about the priest's threats; the Proto-Papa admits that the Kassiopi oracle is nothing but a cheat, "but it is very difficult to put a stop to it; it is an old custom".

Casanova then relates the story of Melulla:

This Melulla, of fatal memory, was a courtezan from Zante, of rare beauty…although she was very beautiful, I was very far from thinking her as lovely as Madame F——, putting my affection for the latter on one side…

I went upstairs mechanically, and she took me to a voluptuous boudoir; she complained of my being the only one who had never paid her a visit, when I was the man she would have preferred to all others, and I had the infamy to give way… I became the most criminal of men…

Before my adventure with the worthless Melulla, I enjoyed good health, I was rich, lucky at play, liked by everybody, beloved by the most lovely woman of Corfu…After my fatal meeting with the courtezan I rapidly lost my health, my money, my credit…The influence I had over Madame F—— faded away little by little, and, almost without her knowing it, the lovely woman became completely indifferent to me.

I left Corfu without money, although I had sold or pledged every-thing I had of any value. Twice I had reached Corfu rich and happy, twice I left it poor and miserable…

He left Corfu towards the end of September and cast anchor in the harbour of Venice on 14 October 1745, landing on 25 November, after performing quarantine on board ship. There is definitely a down-side to being a Casanova.

CUSTOMS AND MANNERS
Professor D. T. Ansted wrote in 1863 that "The habits of the English at Corfu are somewhat monotonous; and our countrymen do not mix much with the natives."

Thomas Gallant (2002) picks up on this commonly-expressed senti-ment. "The British made constant reference to the fact they were never invited into Greek homes to dine." He also points out that "identity was bound up with eating habits... Englishmen riled against Greek eating habits..." They had little time for anyone who "went native" and "ate when Greeks ate". Going native by marrying a Greek girl was also frowned upon by many; Gallant cites an entry in Edward Lear's diary recording an occasion when one of his typically Anglo-Saxon countrymen grumbled bitterly that a nice young English officer, having married a really nice Greek girl was "ceasing to be English entirely, & becoming Greek alto-gether".

Tertius Kendrick (1822) wrote: "The Corfuoites, from what motive I know not, never think of inviting the English to their houses; and neither will they attempt any kind of return to the civility shown them by the of-ficers comprising the Garrison." Professor Ansted commented about the English in the Ionian Islands: "They are not always popular, for an Eng-lishman abroad has the art of seeming supercilious, and his reserve is taken for pride."

How many British nationals are nowadays residents of Corfu: five, ten, twelve thousand? Nobody really knows; not all of them stay for the whole year, and less than half may bother to register online at the Vice-Consulate. Many of them are British women married to Greek men. Some of them teach English, work in tavernas, travel companies or elsewhere in the tourist industry and learn good oral Greek. Some complain that they feel trapped once they have children and find they cannot escape the watchful eyes of a Corfiot mother-in-law or village relatives.

Henry Jervis-White Jervis (1852) had little time for the Corfiot counts and *signori*: "A poor Corfiot noble cannot understand that, in France or England, he would find his equals in the many hard-working students of plebeian names; and that his title of Count is not worth that of plain Mister in England... Looking down on the agriculturist and the trader with all the proud ignorance of a Barnabotti, the present generation of nobles is pre-eminently one of place-hunters...the petitioning, the can-vassing, the bribery, is unceasing."

Kendrick (1822), writing of Kefalonia, had been equally unimpressed: "there is but one rank amongst the nobility—that of count. This title was frequently purchased from the Venetian republic, which readily granted the insignificant honor, since it proved a good method to enrich the representatives of the government, who were venal and corrupt to the last degree."

John Davy explains one method which the Venetian Provedditori used for extracting money from the nobles. He held a dinner twice a year, and each guest was expected to put under his plate a paper stating the number of barrels of oil he intended to give his host. Everyone who could contribute was invited. To obtain favour with the Provedditori each guest had to make a generous offer (the minimum was two barrels). "It is not surprising that, at the expiration of his three years service, that functionary returned to Venice a rich man."

Kendrick writes of the burning of the Libro d'Oro by the Republican French; it was revived and repressed once again by the Russians and the French in turn, "since which, the English have restored the book in high perfection. The year 1817 proved auspicious for the counts; they came out, with all their former dignity, under the shelter of the intended constitution. Argostoli was in a high ferment on the occasion. 'Son nobile Io—lei non è', were the words that flew from mouth to mouth. Dirty half-starved men made their appearance on a sudden, to claim the right of hereditary honours. Friends were disunited, in consequence of taunts and hints thrown about 'superior respect and deference'."

"I am a noble—*he* is not"! Which do residents and inhabitants of the islands find more insufferable these days, stuck-up wannabe *signori* or boozy British "yobs" ("white-bodied neo-Visigoths" in Philip Sherrard's words, "brutish young persons" in an article by Jan Morris)?

Some contemporary Corfiots may play cricket and drink an occasional ginger beer (some of the few examples of any lasting British cultural hegemony, since as Archduke Ludwig Salvator points out in *Zante*, the English language had very little impact on the Greek spoken in the Ionian Islands in the nineteenth century), but the British and Greek communities have a very different approach to animal welfare and the treatment of pets and donkeys and to ideas of appropriate attire for a visit to a church or monastery. Greeks tend to argue and discuss issues in louder voices, and a visit to a chaotically old-style bureaucratic office can be enough to drive any Brit to despair (while he or she conveniently forgets the immense frustration of trying to get a human being to answer a telephone in the automated queuing systems back home). Greek approaches to public displays of sex and drunkenness are different from those in the north of Europe, but the widespread Greek male habit (by older men as well as the diminishing number—post AIDS—of younger *kamaki* or "harpoonists" who "spear" single young female tourists) of pestering and ogling independent Northern European women on the beaches, in the streets or even in offices, verges on molestation at times. It cannot be denied that there exists a Northern European female Shirley Valentine or Mamma Mia caricature equivalent to the Greek *kamaki*, happy enough to flick through tourist brochures featuring handsome Greek waiters and fishermen, and then to taste the real thing.

Louis de Bernières writes about the *kamaki* in *Captain Corelli's Mandolin*, young men "who lived on a diet of perpetual sex" with foreign women. Nicholas Gage, in his book *Hellas*, explains about the *kamakia*: "The harpoons are not strictly gigolos because they don't take money for their sexual services, expecting only the rewards of free food and entertainment, a few gifts, and the gratitude of their foreign companions."

The displays of wild or lewd behaviour by drunken British lads and lasses (not all louts!) on package holidays in places like Kavos, since around 1986, is not amusing to older Brits, who avoid the place. This is the sort of antisocial behaviour that few young Greeks would ever adopt (while not forgetting the globally-televised images of young Greek hoodies rioting in Athens in December 2008, after a fifteen-year-old was shot dead). David Selbourne wrote an article exposing the "almost non-stop orgy of vandalism, violence—even death". But this is nothing new. Lt. Col. Napier, writing in 1825 about Kefalonia, blamed drunkenness as one of the main causes of disease and death amongst British soldiers, as well as exposure to the sun, bare-headed. "I attribute much of the drinking and ill health among the troops to the *want of amusement*: the soldiers, uncomfortable and crowded in barracks, seek comfort in wine houses. The want of occupation in a great measure sends them to these infernal drinking shops."

The French newspaper *Le Figaro* carried an article by Sébastien Martin in summer 2008 headlining British Foreign and Commonwealth Office concern and an official report about the behaviour of British holidaymakers abroad. In 2007 a total of 4,600 British people were arrested outside the UK, an increase of 15% over the previous year. The writer claims they represent the worst nightmare of the tourist spots of the world.

Alcohol was one of the principal causes of the problem. Spain was the country most affected, but the Mayor of Laganas, Zakynthos, was reported as saying "we want no more young people walking naked in the streets, creating problems and breaking things. We don't want them annoying other tourists, putting their lives in danger." *The Sunday Times* covered the same story in an article by B. Montague and D. Gadher: Greece and the islands had witnessed 602 British people admitted to hospital by halfway through the 2008 holiday season; 41 British women had been raped, the figure much higher if cases of alleged rape are included. A spokesman for the state hospital in Zakynthos was reported as saying "we deal with a lot of allegations of rape, but often we cannot find any signs of resistance".

WOMEN IN GREECE
All this, of course, is what one learns in the course of a long association with Greece and the Ionian Islands. Things have not changed as much as it might seem, although young Greek women dress in as liberated a way as any foreign tourist. The Baron Theotoki, quoted by John Davy, commented critically that in the nineteenth century upper-class Corfiot women required a *cavaliere servente* in addition to a husband, painted their

A statue to the women of Zagori

cheeks, stained their hair and eyelashes, and avoided suckling their children, from a fear of spoiling their forms.

Leake (1835) made some extraordinary comments about the women of Ioannina, and about the way they walked:

> The Greek women of Ioannina are as uneducated as the Turkish, and are held in that degree of subserviency which is their common lot throughout Greece, and which seems indeed to have been their ordinary condition among the ancients… Young women seldom or never go out of the house before marriage, except to church, which is generally in the night… The walk of the women is particularly uncouth, not so much caused by their confinement or their dress as by a persuasion prevailing among all but the peasantry, who walk as nature has taught them, that a rolling, waddling gait, is a proof of refinement; so that it is a compliment to tell a lady that she walks like a goose.

The Murray *Handbook* says ungallantly of Greek women: "The women are very inferior both in face and figure to the men, and when they attain the age of 25 or 30, become fat and unwieldy." Kendrick was also uncomplimentary about the women of Lefkas: "The females cannot lay claim to beauty, either in form, features, or complexion: they are clumsy, of a displeasing corpulency, having sallow complexions, which they endeavour to remedy by paint."

In a diary entry of 6 January 1821, Byron noted down some thoughts about the state of women in Greece, both Ancient and Modern. In the modern times "They ought to mind home—and be well fed and clothed—but not mixed in society. Well educated, too, in religion—but to read neither poetry nor politics—nothing but books of piety and cookery. Music—drawing—dancing—also a little gardening and ploughing now and then. I have seen them mending the roads in Epirus with good success. Why not, as well as haymaking and milking?"

Women who lived in the larger towns of some (but not all) of the Ionian Islands, which were open to Italian, French and Western European influences, had more personal space for *voltas* (promenades) in the *plateia* and opportunities for social contact, and since the 1950s (when the Club Méditerranée came to Corfu) it was inevitable that they would absorb some of the fashions and freedoms of foreign tourists, even though there was a significant time lag in the process of adopting social change.

It is a salutary lesson to read the autobiography of Elisabeth Moutsan-Martinengou (1801-32) to gain some insight into what life was like for a young unmarried woman of good family in Zakynthos in the early years of the British Protectorate, shut up like a prisoner in her autocratic and despotic father's house. She would have much preferred to have lived a quiet, solitary life in a convent. She was eager for education and learning. On one occasion she decided to try to run away, to catch the boat to Corfu, but soon changed her mind and failed to carry it through. Gradually she came to accept the fate of a woman of her class, rather than remain forever a prisoner in her father's house, and agreed to let her parents try to find a husband for her. When someone suitable was finally found, her husband-to-be began drawn-out dowry negotiations to secure the best deal possible. His attitude caused her great distress, and she felt no joy when the marriage contract was finally signed in July 1831. She became pregnant but died on 9 November 1832, sixteen days after the birth of her son.

The early Modern Greek social drama by Andonios Matesis, *O Vassilikos* or "The Basil Plant" (written in Zakynthos 1829-30 during the period of the British Protectorate), although set at Carnival time in the year 1712, also sheds light on the changing social and ideological environment of Zante. The character of the autocratic patriarch and landowner, Darios Ronkalas, in this case wants to shut his daughter away in a convent, rather than compromise his honour by letting her marry the young man Philipakis, whom she loves but who comes from a slightly less old or wealthy "house" (let us say "upper middle class" rather than "aristocratic"). The character of Darios Ronkalos is as tyrannical a father as Elisabeth Moutsan-Martinengou's was in reality; but in the play, Ronkalos' daughter Garoufalia is already pregnant at the beginning of the first scene. With the permission of her mother, she had gone out with some of her friends to have a good time during Carnival, but lost her way when caught in a sudden downpour. She took shelter in a hut but had the misfortune to be seduced there by the inebriated but otherwise honourable Philipakis. Roderick Beaton (1994) points out that Matesis dramatizes the clash of values between the older generation of the local aristocracy and the values of the Enlightenment.

In terms of the social situation of women in Zakynthos, Elisabeth Moutsan-Martinengou was obviously no exception. The Murray *Hand-*

book confirms that "The exclusion of unmarried females from society prevails here to an incredible extent, nothwithstanding the efforts of the English authorities. It is said that many young ladies would be unable to find their way even through the streets in the immediate vicinity of their own houses." One wonders what the British could have done. A lawyer/historian in Zakynthos told me that until around 1940 women never went to funerals. William Goodisson (1822) wrote that "The Zante women are still more closely confined than those of the other islands…indeed, a Greek lady is hardly visible anywhere, excepting at Corfu, where the French had sufficient opportunity and influence to civilize them so far, as to introduce them into society."

Something of the old, restrictive attitude continued even in Corfu until the 1950s, when the arrival of the French Club Méditerranée (1952-3) brought about a gradual change in attitudes. Even then, the older generation might complain loudly that young Corfiot women were adopting French habits and behaviour and making of the island a *poutanarió alla Gallía* (a French-style or Gallic whore-house)! Hardly!

Kirkwall cites the evidence of Andreas Laskaratos, that, when he was a youth, the shoemakers were not allowed to see young ladies who required their services. "The doors of the rooms were provided with holes through which the ladies passed their feet in order to be measured." Women from the villages and poorer classes in the Ionian Islands had little opportunity for even an elementary education, and most were illiterate ("but all of them embroider well", Murray, *Handbook*, 1840).

The educational situation in Epirus was rather different, and schools, whether private, public or monastic, were run within the parameters of the Ottoman legal framework. Many were destroyed in 1822 or in 1882. In the Zagori nearly all the villages (in particular Koukouli, Tsepelovo, Vitsa, Frangades and Aristi) had elementary schools from the seventeenth century onwards, and by 1830 schools were well established; the first girls' school opened in Monodendri in 1846, and they became more general until 1880. Wace and Thompson (1914) point out that "one man beyond all others helped to spread Greek education among the villages of the Zaghori; this was a Greek priest known since his martyrdom as Ayios Kosmas". Another key figure was Anastasios Sakellarios, from Vradeto. The first, highly-regarded Zosimaia School of Ioannina was founded in 1828.

When Greek women are not being perceived as angry crones with strident, raised voices or as peasants dressed in black, the dowry system is a common theme. Henry Miller, writing in 1939, claims to have been a supporter of Greek female emancipation: "The dowry must be abolished. One must stop trading in virginity! It is a disgrace to Greece. Every Greek woman is worth her salt" (*First Impressions of Greece*, 1973).

Iakovos Polylas also comments on the dowry system in Corfu, in his story "The Error" (1891):

> One ignorant of the countryside of Corfu would be surprised to hear that women usually bring as dowry only a couple of hundred drachmas' worth of gold and sometimes a couple of olive-trees or vines, with an income of ten drachmas a year. But the country-maiden, with her sturdy body and generous soul, brings with her an invaluable treasure for the family into which she marries…we have countless examples of crushed families being resurrected by young widows.

Henry Miller tended to have an outsider's view of the peasant women "gathered at the wells among the olive trees, their dress, their manners, their talk no different now than in Biblical times" (1941).

Nicholas Gage, the Greek–American author of the influential best-seller *Eleni*, could make the same observation in *Hellas*: "For village women the well or spring is the center of life. Every crumb of local gossip is shared as they gather there, just as in Biblical times, filling large clay urns or, more likely, plastic bottles in fluorescent dime-store colors." Gage writes about Greek women, as he imagines they were in the mountain villages of Epirus, such as Lia, in the first half of the twentieth century: "Women went into labor and gave birth alone, or tried to abort themselves with herbs, wooden stakes and heavy rocks if a pregnancy occurred during a husband's long absence… Many women died in labor despite the best efforts of the village midwife… A village wife was constantly reminded that she was her husband's property."

D. R. Morier, in his novel *Photo the Suliote, A Tale of Modern Greece* (1857), writes that "Greek women, generally speaking, are considered by their husbands in the same light as that of other domestic animals, only valued by reason of the use they may be put to."

When the Reverend Hughes called on the eminent Greek teacher and scholar, Athanasios Psalidas, "I contrived to lead the conversation to what I thought a very injurious custom, viz. that of excluding women from society. I suppose nothing that I ever said shocked our host's prejudices more than this, for he vehemently defended the practice by a declaration, that women were all prone to evil, and that if liberty were granted then they would abuse it." The good Reverend was not averse to the charms of Greek women, as he seems to confess:

> We had heard that Ioannina was celebrated for the beauty and fine complexion of its females; and certainly we were not disappointed when we entered into the apartment where a party of the most charming women in this capital were collected together. They sat in a large circle round the room, superbly attired; but the liquid lustre of their eyes put to shame the jewels that sparkled in their raven tresses...masterpieces of excelling nature.

"The liquid lustre of their eyes...their raven tresses"! These were, of course, the married women. The unmarried girls were separated in another apartment. It is not long before he returns to his theme that "the female sex is regrettably degraded in Greece" through want of education, seclusion from society and an unfair system of treatment. "As soon as a girl approaches the age of puberty, she is more studiously shut up from public sight than a catholic nun." All she was taught, he claimed, was the art of embroidery, and, if the nurse or mother could read, she was "instructed in the science of relics, the history of miracle-mongers, and other absurdities which superstition has engrafted upon religion". He concluded that "ignorance and seclusion are quite as bad safeguards of innocence as freedom and cultivation".

Hughes' description of Ali Pasha's harem makes it understandable why parents might want to keep their daughters secluded in the house, out of sight and out of harm's way. Ali "possesses about 500 female victims, guarded by eunuchs and immured within the impenetrable recesses of his harem... Before age had chilled his blood his sensuality was unbounded. Wherever his satellites heard of a beautiful child, of either sex, they dragged it from the paternal roof, and massacred the family or burned the village if any resistance was offered." He also describes how the character of Ali's eldest son, Muchtar Pasha, was considered "brutal and debauched in the highest degree…his lust is so ungovernable that he has often been known to violate women in the public streets of Ioannina."

It seems that the Reverend Hughes would have preferred to have the women out walking the streets, so that the liquid lustre of their eyes could be appreciated by all (even as far away as Dorset, Thomas Hardy could conjure up Eustacia's "pagan eyes"). Hughes makes an exception for "a young Greek slave named Vasilikee, born at Paramithia, brought up in the serai from a child". Kyra Vassiliki retained Ali's affections until the end.

We might expect women travel writers to give a more sympathetic picture of women in Greece. But there have not been so many women travellers of note focusing *on this part of Greece*, to be compared with Edith Durham (Albania), Rebecca West (Serbia and Yugoslavia), Flora Sandes (Serbia), Mabel Bent (Cyclades), Dame Freya Stark (Ionia), Jan Morris (Venetian Empire, Trieste), Dilys Powell, Olivia Manning, the Australians Beverley Farmer, Joice Loch and Charmian Clift, or the American Patricia Storace. Popular novelists who have featured Corfu (or Paxos) in their fiction include Mary Stewart, Anna Weale, Ronnith Neuman, Lindsay Townsend, Deborah Lawrenson, Mary Nickson, Kim Green, Elizabeth Falconer and Erica James.

On a five-week visit to Corfu (26 March-27 April 1920), the American modernist poet HD (Hilda Doolittle, 1886-1961) wrote about her hallucinatory visions and "writing on the wall"; she also visited Prevesa and Parga. Emma Tennant has written affectionately about Corfu, and both Sophie Atkinson and Theresa Nicholas have depicted it with great sensitivity. But about Epirus, few female travel-writers (in English) come to mind apart from Eleni Gage.

In the eighteenth and nineteenth century, women writers on Greece seem more notable by their absence, although studies have been undertaken on those foreign women who did write about the country (e.g. by M. Klironomos and Dr. V. Kolocotroni). The women gave their books modest titles such as *Glimpses at Greece* and *Glimpses of Greek Life and Society*, whereas the men tended to adopt a more specific focus, like archaeology.

E. Mitsi refers to a couple of other women travellers: Lady Mary Wortley Montagu never landed in Greece, as she feared she might fall into the hands of robbers; "Montagu was afraid to disturb the ideal, the imaginary landscape of classical antiquity, by experiencing contemporary reality." She also cites Virginia Woolf's journals from her 1906 visit to Greece: "You must look upon the modern Greeks as a nation of mongrel element and a rustic beside the classic speech of pure bred races... They do not understand Greek of the age of Pericles—when I speak it."

Ionian Island Greek women writers include the aforementioned Elisabeth Moutsan-Martinengou from Zakynthos, the first Modern Greek female prose-writer, who was also a minor lyric poet and dramatist. Then there is Irini Dendrinou, a poet, short-story writer, literary critic, lecturer and translator, who was born in Corfu in 1879. Her collection of lectures on the writers of the Corfiot School is highly regarded, and I recommend her 1927 lecture on "Konstandinos Theotokis, as a writer and as a person"; they were close friends and collaborators. Of her translations into Greek I admire her version of the Serbian folksong relating to the 1389 Battle of Kosovo ("*I Mana ton ennia pallikarion*"), and of her own poems lovers of Corfu will appreciate the sonnet "*Analipsis*".

Marie Aspioti played an important role in the literary and cultural life of Corfu after the war. She was closely involved with the magazine *Prospero* (1949-54), and published *Lear's Corfu* (1965). Kay Cicellis, whom I discuss later, spent the war years in Kefalonia and settled in Athens in 1964. I have also mentioned the two works by my wife, Maria Strani-Potts; I venture to include her writing as a significant part of this tradition, although she also belongs to an even older tradition of writers like Laskaratos and Theotokis.

Chapter Four
A Tour of the Islands

Colonnade in Old Town, Corfu

THE REALITY OF CORFU

We have already considered different perceptions of Corfu, from native and incoming points of view, and from different periods of history. So how have recent newcomers to Corfu found the reality of living there?

Raul Scacchi and Gioia Maestro left Milan, Italy, and moved to Corfu nine years ago. They gave up their jobs, urban pollution and their stressed way of life; they left their country. They were entering a new century, and the time for change had arrived; they were psychologically prepared. Having made the big decision, they gave themselves time to plan and organize their new life in the village of Sinarades, and moved there in May 2001. The first period was magical, and full of the energy that came from the beauty of Corfu. When difficulties began and the novelty was over they found their own ways of dealing with it, by looking for their inner resources.

Raul is a painter and a musician, while Gioia is a poet, writer and artist. This is part of what Gioia told me.

As the Ancient Romans used to say, every place has its own *Genius Loci*...

Beauty is the *leitmotif* you can find in any diary, chronicle, book, story or article written by artists, painters, princesses, poets, musicians, etc., who spent a part of their lives in Corfu.

Unfortunately, the "dark side" of this beauty, and of the *aura* hanging over legendary personalities who visited Corfu, is that in recent times the island managed to arouse the worst appetites of those people interested only in exploitation and in a quick way to make more money, without taking any care at all of the environment, nature, balance and harmony. The last phase of modernization, the one which started in the late seventies, saw the abandonment of rural society, destroying in less than thirty years a world which had lasted with minor changes for several centuries; since then, tourism has become the first income resource for the greater part of the local population.

In spite of the huge difficulties in trying to awaken an ecological consciousness, there are still many places hidden in the town, up on the hills, by the sea or in the wider expanses of greenery and of the countryside, able to tell you tales about beauty...

My olive grove is now worried about the possibility that one day a bulldozer will destroy another big area, and the cement will prevent everybody from listening to the story.

Billi Rosen, who was born in Greece in 1942 but who also spent part of her childhood in Sweden and the UK, lived on Corfu for many years. She is the author of prize-winning novels for young adults, such as the semi-autobiographical trilogy which begins with *Andi's War*, set during the Greek Civil War; it has been translated into seventeen languages. Looking optimistically at the hills in Corfu in September 1987, she wrote in the foreword to her novel: "Thanks to tourism, Greece has become prosperous to a degree unimaginable even twenty years ago. These days all children sit down to three square meals a day, and wear shoes every day of the week."

We have heard the opinions of many British people, but it is harder to find out what the once desperate Albanians think, the Greek Roma

(Gypsies), some of whom collect scrap metal and sometimes beg for money, or the West Africans touting pirated DVDs and CDs around the coffee-shops. It is even harder to explore the views of the imported and much-exploited Filipino maids or the young Chinese girls who speak hardly a word of Greek or English, who find themselves stranded on the larger islands, serving as tongue-tied shop assistants in Chinese discount-clothing stores. Who looks after them when they fall sick or need specialist medical attention? Who helps them with the bureaucracy?

One also wonders what attracts distinguished visitors like Mr Gorbachev, who until recently liked to stay in the same hotel each summer. The Russians and even the oligarchs are coming (and investing: Russians have bought the site of the former Club Med at Dassia; a Fairmont Hotel will be in operation there from 2012, and will certainly attract a Russian clientele). How long before they displace the Brits? In terms of percentages of tourists, the British percentage is dropping, and the number of visitors from former East European countries is on the increase (the Czech Republic, Slovakia, Romania). This is not a trend that pleases the shopkeepers, who prefer the bigger-spending northern Europeans (the drop in the value of sterling may be changing that, as far as the British are concerned). The national daily *Kathimerini* reported in April 2008 that there was a 50% rise in bookings for Corfu from Russians and a 12% rise from Romanians (but a significant increase also came from the Swiss).

These reports indicate what some foreigners think, but what are the thoughts of those Greeks who remember what the Ionian Islands were like in the 1960s, before the selling and pimping of their beautiful natural environment by every opportunistic friend of the Junta, or by every other *mesiti* or go-between?

This question is addressed in an allegorical Greek language novella called *The Pimping of Panorea* by Maria Strani-Potts. It is a fairy-tale for adults, in which a Greek island is personified by a beautiful young girl, Panorea. Her family (the inhabitants of the island) invent ways to exploit and sell her beauty as a commodity, acting as pimps for their own financial gain—to such an extent that they bring about her utter devastation and, eventually, their own destruction. Spiros Plaskovitis' novel *The Façade Lady of Corfu* imagines—with some grounding in reality—that the two small islands of Vido and Lazaretto might once have been subjected to a shady sale (with the connivance of politicians) by a Greek consortium, to rich Saudi-Arabian business interests, for improper tourist development. The conspiratorial sell-out is prevented at the last minute by a bomb explosion, and so the joint ministerial order giving the go-ahead to the development plan is lost in the pandemonium. Whether this was a left-wing act of terrorism, the work of financial competitors or a settling of scores is not made clear. It seems, according to local lore, to be truth, not fiction, that it was the Left that saved Lazaretto Island from being sold to foreign interests.

KEFALONIA

As the largest and perhaps most beautiful of the Ionian Islands, from the point of view of relatively unspoilt nature (am I being disloyal?), Kefalonia (Cephalonia) and its turbulent recent history deserves more space than we can give it here.

On my first visit to Kefalonia in 1994 I experienced a paralysing vertigo when driving on a high mountain ridge over Mt. Aenos, the Black Mountain. How much worse it must have been when Lt. Col. Charles J. Napier was the British Resident (1825): "Men will not risk their safety by travelling on a bad mountain road, where, should their feet make a false step, they would be thrown down a precipice of many hundred feet, into the sea."

Ruin of Sassia monastery on Kefalonia

During my second visit in May-June 2008 I found the experience more enjoyable. I realized how much we still owe to the pioneer road-builders like de Bosset and Napier, and that became even clearer when reading Napier's memoir and Helen Cosmetatos' book on *The Roads of Cefalonia*.

Arriving at the port of Sami (where the film of *Captain Corelli's Mandolin* was shot, in part), you naturally make your way to the capital, Argostoli and the museums. What strikes visitors most forcibly at the Focas-Cosmetatos Museum-Gallery is likely to be the exhibition of photographs of the 1953 earthquakes. There were three major earthquakes: the first, on Sunday 9 August, devastated Ithaca at 9.41 a.m.; the second, on Tuesday 11 August, with its epicentre in the sea between the islands of Kefalonia and Zakynthos, struck at 5.15 a.m., wreaking havoc in Zakynthos and Eastern Kefalonia; the third came on Wednesday 12 August at 11. 25 a.m., the most powerful of all measuring 7.2 on the Richter scale, and within 28 seconds Western Kefalonia, including Argostoli and Lixouri, lay in ruins.

Of the books which deal with the earthquakes, one of the most notable fictional accounts is Kay Cicellis' *Death of a Town*. It begins:

> At 5.30 in the morning, not a single Lixouriot had woken up. Not even Napoleon Vourdouvanos, who was always among the earliest risers. This is why the earthquake of 11 August was so unreal. It got mixed up with dreams…

Kay's father was from Kefalonia, although she was born in Marseilles. She then lived on the island for nearly four years, between the age of fourteen and eighteen. She also writes (e.g. for *Descant*) about nature, the seasons, and about the character of the people. She does not agree with the view that the Kefalonians are temperamentally like the other Ionian Islanders or the Italians.

> They are a more somber and violent race. The Cephalonian temper is proverbial… When I lived on the island, I remember there were always vague echoes of frightful crimes committed somewhere in the vicinity, crimes that rapidly turned into myth. Not only *crimes passionels*, but murders caused by strange contorted notions of honour, an enraged,

tenacious sense of property, an exacerbated social sensitivity. The Cephalonians are (or perhaps were?) the most class-conscious community in Greece, where class-consciousness is relatively rare. An old heavy feudal past weighs on the place.

She writes about the land-owning nobility and the peasants: "The landowner and the peasant spoke the same rough language, shared the same crude way of thinking; and yet they were miles apart. There was unbearable arrogance on one side, and unbearable servility on the other, masking a real, and justified enmity." But it is the force of nature that impressed her most deeply: "I suppose there are tourists now, hotels, new roads; why not? But somehow I think that the pulse, the *thrust* of nature, which once reached me so clearly and powerfully, must still make itself felt there."

Other factual texts on the earthquakes include *Old Skala, Memories of the Earthquakes of 1953* by Jean Baker. There is much relevant information in Robert Bittlestone's *Odysseus Unbound*, and in the monograph by Dr. Joseph Partsch, who spent six years (1885-90) researching past earthquakes, especially that of 1867 which destroyed 2,642 houses, damaged another 2,946 and caused 224 deaths. One of the theories at the time was that the earthquakes were caused by the collapse of large underground caves. There also exists a book of photographs by Giannoudi-Avgerinou (2004) which draws on a different photographic archive from the selection displayed at the Focas-Cosmetatos Museum-Gallery. One can feel guilty looking at some of these images: they seem so artfully composed or even posed, pictures of heartbroken, stunned men and women weeping beside the piles of stones that were their houses, and a painted crucifix that stands out so symbolically from the rubble that was once a church; it is as if the pictures were designed to arouse compassion in newspapers and the media, and help with the national and international earthquake appeals, such as the BBC appeal on 16 August 1953 by Captain Percy Gick.

Robert Bittlestone's *Odysseus Unbound* is particularly graphic on questions concerning Kefalonia's earthquakes, especially the catastrophe of August 1953, as a result of which "around 450" lives were lost. He says that records began in 1444, and cites the major quakes up to 1983 (most of them offshore). "Statistically speaking the next major earthquake in Cephalonia is not due until 2048, but there is a very wide degree of variation in these predictions." He lists all the years with earthquakes of magnitudes 4.0 or above, using Papazachos *et al.* as his data source.

Soon after my last visit to this exhibition I felt a tremor which awoke me with a start, and then (on 8 June) I experienced a small earthquake (6.5 Richter) when I was in Lefkada. I then began to realize the horror and terror of a major, destructive earthquake. There was no need for the photographers to *stage* anything in 1953, or to pose people among the ruins. They simply photographed what they found: utter devastation; nothing had been left standing.

After the earthquakes of 1953, the civil engineer Takis Paulatos designed and oversaw the construction of many public buildings. He did the job far more successfully and gracefully, to my eyes, than the less coordinated and more haphazard works carried out by civil engineers in Zakynthos. The one exception might be the St. Theodore Lighthouse situated near the chapel of Aghios Theodoros; modern concrete simply cannot replicate the delightful original circular stone-built neo-classical Doric rotunda, which was designed for Napier by Lt. J. P. Kennedy, who placed the foundation stones of the original lighthouse on 12-13 March 1829. An old sketch by Kennedy shows a colonnade fringing the central cylindrical building with 22 columns 12 feet high; but although the new construction follows the general design of the original, and is presumably earthquake-(if not grafitti-) resistant, it is still better viewed at a distance.

Nicholas Enessee is less positive about the way the capital was rebuilt after the earthquake, and about the way that many houses were demolished with total insensitivity, while irreplaceable antique furniture and effects were still inside (in Zakynthos, fires were started by such demolition explosions). Rebuilt Argostoli has little to commend it, in Enessee's judgement. That is also the view of the poet Nikos Fokas, who worked for the BBC Greek Service 1962-72. In an article on Argostoli he says that after the earthquake "a residual caricature was raised by Athenian contractors and their masters". He can hardly contain himself when he sees "the obscene two, three and eve four-storied structures we call homes, hotels or supermarkets as I walk by their occupants or customers. The baseness and poor quality of these structures are by now the rule all over Greece."

Argostoli became the capital of Kefalonia in 1757; before that the Castle of St. George had served as the capital. One of the best things to do in Argostoli is to walk across the Drapano (Trapano) or Devoseto Bridge, as it is often called, after Major Charles-Philippe de Bosset, a Swiss officer serving the British, who was appointed Commandant of the Island of Kefalonia in April 1810 (until 1814). The first version of the bridge was built in 1812, against the wishes of the Argostoli counsellors, who feared that it might enable the peasants to rise up and march more easily against the wealthy landlords and town-dwellers. They had good reason to be afraid of the peasants, as was demonstrated in 1848 and 1849, although before 1825 Napier had formed the view that the lack of roads and bridges and the dangers of travel along the existing tracks were the main reasons why there was "very little intercourse between landed proprietors huddled together in Argostoli and the poor, uncivilised peasants". Christian Miller wrote of the Ponte Novo: "In its centre stands a Pyramid with the inscription 'To the Glory of the British Nation 1813'." The pyramid was damaged in the 1953 earthquake, but the bridge itself survived. Amanda Castlemain wrote in *Athens News* in 2003 that timid drivers might prefer the long way round since locals "zoom across the bridge with reckless abandon". In 2008 the bridge was out of use; it will be restored for use of light vehicles, but was no longer in a state of repair for cars or traffic.

Kirkwall wrote that Kefalonia was destined to give great trouble both to Lord Seaton and to his successor, Sir Henry Ward, as the island had been unsettled for some years. "As early as 1843, the date of Lord Seaton's arrival, there had been disturbances amongst the peasantry, to suppress which the military had been at various times employed... The class hatred, especially of the peasantry towards the landlords, and the restless intrigues of political agitators, kept up a smouldering discontent, ever threatening to break out with fresh troubles..." The anonymous author of *The Ionian Islands under British Protection* also records that the Ionian peasants, recollecting the bad old days "even now regard their Seigneurs with a Helot mixture of fear and aversion, which from time to time,—as lately in Cephalonia,—breaks out with cruel and bloody excesses".

Kirkwall recorded the sequence of events on Kefalonia from Greek Good Friday in the spring of 1848 until the crushing of the revolt by the middle of October 1849. During the revolt twenty-one people were executed by orders of court-martial, including the prinicipal assassins, Nodaro and Vlaco. Vlaco (Thodoris Vlachos) was hanged in broad daylight in the second town of the island, before several thousand spectators. A great number of peasants were also flogged.

The Ionian Islands under British Protection also addresses the insurrection in Kefalonia. Vlaco and Nodaro "declared for the expulsion of the heretical English and the annexation of the islands to Greece. But while awaiting the consummation of this patriotic purpose, they determined to wreak their vengeance on some unpopular landlords, whose houses lay in their line of march. One highly respected gentleman, the Chevalier Metaxa, was burnt alive in broad day with all his family; some of his neighbours were cruelly tortured, women were violated, and other barbarities committed too horrible to mention." Official papers were presented to Parliament. Martial law was proclaimed in the district where the atrocities had been committed; soldiers were sent to Skala. Several people were captured, and hanged on the scene of the crime (the murder of Metaxas). Thomas Gallant (2002) discusses the murder of Metaxas and says that the Count "was widely hated by the local peasants, who considered him to be a particularly offensive and oppressive landlord".

When I visited the ruined village of Old Skala, the ruins of the Metaxas house were pointed out to me by Dennis Koumoudos, Chairman of the Unique Villas company, which is redeveloping Old Skala, ironically enough for rich British people seeking custom-built villas "in prime locations". Dennis's company had bought up a large area of the abandoned land around the ruined village, which had been destroyed in the 1953 earthquake. They had had to check all the old records and title-deeds, which is how they came to know about the nineteenth-century transactions, changes of ownership and about the seizing of houses by landlords or people to whom tiny sums of money or barrels of oil were owed. We talked about the events of 1849 and the hangings and about the activities of EAM/ELAS during the German occupation.

Kirkwall continues the story: "Of forty-four prisoners condemned to death by the Courts-Martial, the Lord High Commissioner commuted the punishment of all but twenty-one." He admits that what was really "injudicious" was "the summary infliction of flogging on some of the inhabitants of the disaffected districts for such offences as creating disturbances in the guard-rooms, obstructing the soldiers, or refusing to give evidence. Flogging is associated in the minds of the Ionians with the cruelties formerly exercised by the Turks on their brethren of the neighbouring continent. It should not have been inflicted." Naturally enough, it excited the bitter and lasting animosity of the sufferers, even if it smothered discontent.

I am not sure I would want to buy an expensive villa in Old Skala, however tastefully constructed, having read these accounts. Maybe there should be a memorial for both the murdered and the hanged of the 1849 events, as part of the redevelopment, just as there is a memorial for the dead of the Acqui Division above the St. Theodore Lighthouse? However sympathetically Old Skala is redeveloped, it is unlikely that the descendants of the original villagers will return. Jean Baker writes that "From time to time, villagers are seen wandering round old Skala, tending their olive trees and remembering lost friends and times. Perhaps one day they will return to their beloved hillside which is, for many, the true Skala."

What better topic, after war, earthquakes and violence, than love and romance? At the Focas-Cosmetatos Museum and Gallery you can learn fascinating information about life in Kefalonia and Argostoli before the Second World War.

Kantades, or love ballads, were apparently still being sung non-commercially until thirty years ago, but even then quite rarely, not in the traditional way for "flirting" or wooing beneath the beloved's window. In the old days, the louvered shutters, primarily intended to control the flow of air, would be discreetly opened by the unobserved young woman being serenaded, for her to see who was serenading her; they would be opened wider if the girl liked the boy or quickly closed if she wanted him to go away. These *kafasoparathira* were known as "jalousies", perhaps derived from "jealousy", or *gelosia* in Italian.

When fans were in fashion, there was a special fan-language or flirtation dialect, which existed as the only means of flirtation or secret communication between young people being closely supervised or chaperoned by their parents. The language of the fan is described in the book *I Palia Kefalonia* (Vol. 1, Argostoli). The fan was a key element in the "mating ritual" in the main square of Argostoli: "The signals were obvious to anyone who cared to interpret them. If the girl held the fan with her right hand in front of her face she was telling her young admirer 'follow me'. On her left hand it meant: 'I want to meet you'. Heaven forbid that she touched the fan on her left ear (leave me alone) twirl it on the right hand (you are annoying me) or on her left hand (there is someone else, so go away). But if she tapped lightly her left cheek she was saying 'I love you' and if she pointed the fan closed towards the young man she was asking 'Do you love me?' Wide open it meant 'wait for me' and if it tapped the lady's lips—jump for joy—'kiss me'."

Prior to the Second World War, flirtatious behaviour on New Year's Eve involved young people spraying their "opponents" or objects of desire, with perfume (usually eau de cologne diluted with water), ostensibly so they should "smell good for the New Year". This took place while they promenaded on the long "Lithostrato" cobbled business street. The men tried to spray cologne in the eyes of young women to influence them to say "yes". The custom of the "War of the Fragrances" and of "Fragrant Eros" as master of the New Year's Eve celebrations is mentioned in D. Poulaki-Katevati's historical book, and she cites the chapter on "The War of the Fragrances" by Y. Voutepsis.

Nobody tried to spray eau de cologne in my eyes when I was strolling along the Lithostrato in Argostoli, I have to say. But I was able to look around and see how clean the streets were. It really is a tidy island compared to Corfu and Zakynthos. The road cleaners and rubbish collectors are active, even at the weekends. Could it be that there is a better system and more civic pride here (as well as philanthropic foundations and benefactors leaving bequests) because many émigrés have returned from overseas? Albert Mousson, who visited Argostoli in 1858, noted what a clean town it was. Kefalonians could not find work as easily as the Corfiots could, as Corfu was the centre of the administration, and there was more money there. Kefalonians, if they were not restless seafarers, had to go abroad to Australia, America and South Africa. After the 1953 earthquakes they left in large numbers, but they were generally more inclined towards emigration than the Corfiots.

We should also explore some aspects of the Kefalonian literary tradition, especially the association of the island with writers like Laskaratos and Kavadias, as well as Lord Byron.

The parents of the seaman poet Nikos Kavadias were from Kefalonia (his father was a Greek merchant). His poetry has become very popular since it was set to music by Thanos Mikroutsikos. There is a fine, sensitively sculpted bust of Kavadias gazing out to sea (or in the direction of Lixouri) at Argostoli, and there is a plaque on his *patriko spiti* in Fiskardo, in the street now named Marabou, after his famous poem. The house is the main point of interest for me in Fiskardo. Kavadias' father (who was in Manchuria and Russia) was not unlike many restless and enterprising Kefalonians, including our friend in Australia, the late Denis Kominatos, who travelled even more widely than Kavadias' father. Nikos Kavadias'

horizons, as a sailor on freighters, were naturally much wider than the
Ionian Islands, but he occasionally mentions women from Ithaca and
Corfu in his poetry, often in jest:

> And here's Nausicaa from Corfu,
> All covered with soapy lather.
> She had three murderous brothers
> Down in Mandouki, and in the Spianadha.
> (from "*Paideia*" in his *Collected Poems*)

Lord Byron was a different sort of traveller, certainly at the time of his
Grand Tour. Later, when he returned to help the cause of the Greeks in
1823, he was happy enough in Argostoli and Metaxata (the ship *Hercules*
docked at Argostoli on 3 August 1823, and he moved in September to
Metaxata, 7 km from the capital, where he stayed until the end of December). He also visited Vathy, Ithaca, crossing from St. Euphemia to
Pisaeto in August.

Twenty-five years later, Byron might have felt less welcome in Kefalonia. I paid my respects at the bust of Byron in Metaxata and at another
in Ithaca (I had been to Missolonghi on an earlier occasion). Nowadays the
genuinely Philhellenic British (like Napier and Byron, although Byron was
ambivalent about Greece) are warmly remembered and commemorated
in Kefalonia (Napier "ranks among the demi-gods", according to Lawrence
Durrell), more warmly than their compatriots in other islands, wth the
exception perhaps of Guilford in Corfu, and more recently the Durrell
brothers themselves. The Municipality of Corfu could learn a lot from the
Municipality of Argostoli, not only about rubbish collection but also in
terms of creating an informative exhibition such as the one in Napier
Garden, in spite of the fact that Kefalonia experienced the most serious uprisings against the British. As Dr. Joseph Partsch (1890) recorded, Napier's
memory lived on long after the names of Lord High Commissioners had
been forgotten and had disappeared "like dry leaves" (in spite of bronze
statues and inscriptions on plaques).

I did not have the opportunity to locate the inscribed marble slab at
Kalithea, Lakythra, with Byron's words "If I am a poet I owe it to the air
of Greece" in Greek ("If I am a poet… the air of Greece made me one",
as cited by Trelawny), but I was taken by a Kefalonian–Australian friend

to the vicinity of "Byron's Rock", where the poet used to ride, and to sit and write. The area is now built up and lacks the special sense of magic it must have had even at the time of Elizabeth Longford's visit. But as George D. Ravanis writes, Byron would have enjoyed the sunset there "and the fantastic view with Zante to the left and the great rock of Dia rising from the sea, with its tiny monastery". I was sorry not to have been able to check to see if the marble slab was still there, but one cannot see *every* rock of interest; I am sure Byron would have forgiven me. Tony Harrison, the British poet, once took me to see Byron's and Hobhouse's fading, inscribed signatures on a fallen column at Delphi. Lord Byron reportedly claimed to be uninterested in "antiquarian twaddle" and "poetical humbug" associated with the places he visited in Greece, but he, more than anyone else, set the fashion for touring Greece as "an anachronistic interactive exhibit" (K. E. Fleming's phrase).

Throughout history, Greeks from Kefalonia, Zakynthos, Kythira and Lefkas have gone abroad and made an impact. One thinks of Lafcadio or Lefkadio Hearn in Japan and Konstantinos Gerakis in Siam (also known as Falcon, he became first counsellor to King Narai of Ayutthaya in the seventeenth century).

It is gratifying that Kefalonians also pay tribute to those people who contributed positively to the development of their island, people like de Bosset and Napier. They have streets named after de Bosset, Napier and Byron, and the respectful, affectionately informative exhibition in Napier Garden does full credit to their achievements. The long despised and excommunicated Andreas Laskaratos would have been delighted to know that there is also a street named after him.

Roads are a good thing, I suppose, but within limits. Napier was keen on them, and the current British residents of the island should be as thankful to him as the local Kefalonians. As Napier said about one of the (minor) advantages of building a road up into the Black Mountain,

> On the Black Mountain a gentleman might build a villa, and pass the heats of summer in the midst of woods, and the most beautiful scenery, and from his windows would have one of the most extensive and interesting views in the world; would see the whole of Cefalonia, Ithaca, and St. Maura, with the small islands, spread like a map beneath him; and beyond them, all Acarnania, Mount Pindos, the gulph of Corinth,

Patras, Clarence, and the Arcadian mountains. His ice-house might be filled as late as the end of May, his table furnished with the finest fruits and vegetables.

Henry Holland wrote that, before Major de Bosset became governor of the island, the roads in Kefalonia were very bad, "most of them little better than rugged mountain paths". At the time of his visit in 1812, the road from Argostoli to Sami had been constructed and was "every-where perfectly passable for a carriage". But Lord Byron wrote in his journal that the route he used to reach St. Eufemia (Aghia Efthimia) in 1823, on mule-back, was "by worse roads than I ever met in the course of some years of travel in rough places of many countries". On his return to Argostoli he proceeded "by a better road than the path to Saint Eufemia".

Yes, good, well-maintained public roads are of course welcome and necessary, and you can be pleasantly surprised by those on Kefalonia; but in Corfu the asphalted roads, even nowadays, are forever being dug up and patchily resurfaced so remain treacherous for riders of scooters and bicycles. Bring back Lt. Col. Napier, Major de Bosset, Captain Kennedy and their kind; at least there was some logic in the roads they planned.

Byron enjoyed a modest rented dwelling at Metaxata. Better that, in my opinion, than to rattle around in a huge villa, or to patrol the continuous stretch of harbourside restaurants in the once delightful fishing village of Fiskardo, where one can admire the few old Kefalonian buildings (somewhat kitschily painted) which were not destroyed in the earthquake which affected the rest of the island.

ZAKYNTHOS AND ZANTIOTS

Of the people of Zante, the Reverend Richard Chandler wrote (1817): "The inhabitants are chiefly Greeks... They are divided by internal feuds, and are exceedingly addicted to revenge, perpetrating assassinations even in their churches. The Morea serves them as it were for a sanctuary, and abounds in fugitives for murder and misdemeanours."

Scottish traveller and writer "Lugless Willie" Lithgow (1632) said: "The islanders are Greeks, a kind of subtile people, and great dissemblers", comparable to what Kendrick later said of the Corfiots: "The Corfuoite gentry are subtle and adroit, cloaking their evil qualities under the mask of courteousness and apparent sincerity."

Zakynthos town

Sandys (1670) said of the Greeks of Zante that "in habit they imitate the Italians, but transcend them in their revenges, and infinitely less civil. They will threaten to kill a merchant that will not buy their commodities: and make more conscience to break a fast, than commit a murder."

Ansted observed that "the character of the Zantiots is, and always has been, somewhat different from that of the other Ionians. The people are singularly lively, active, and quick tempered, and are very excitable, even compared with other inhabitants of the Mediterranean shores and islands."

Holland held the view that the population was "intermediate between the Greek and Italian character... Even though enjoying more civil liberty, the Greeks of the Seven Isles are in some respects inferior to those of Turkey; their exterior is less dignified, their manners more corrupt, and they show less capability of again becoming a people."

It is hardly surprising that the Zantiots became so disaffected with the British Protectorate. But the British were not alone in their comments.

The American novelist Edith Wharton noted in her journal, during her 1888 Mediterranean cruise aboard the chartered yacht *Vanadis*, that "The Zantiotes are much absorbed in local politics, and political feeling runs so high, that any person who is dying is afraid to receive the Sacrament from a priest of the opposite party, lest poison be administered."

It is hard to understand these comments in the light of the character of modern Zantiots, who are well-known for their hospitality. When June Marinos (co-author with Diana Farr Louis of an Ionian cookery book) first visited the island in 1951, before the earthquake, she found it "absolutely wonderful and so civilised after Athens". Her father had advised her to go and "spy out the land" before accepting the proposal of marriage from her future husband, Themis Marinos. They had met in 1946-7 in Sofia, Bulgaria, where June was a cipher clerk at the British Legation, and Themis Marinos was one of two Greek officers serving the Greek Government as a member of the International (Allied) Military Commission for the Control of Bulgaria. June had imagined Zakynthos to be "tiny" because Themis kept saying they should go to "his island" for Easter. She thought it belonged to him. They went for Easter in 1951, visiting aristocratic old houses in town which contained beautiful paintings and furniture. Some had big ballrooms and were very Western European in taste. They also visited large country houses like Sarakina, some of which seemed "like palaces", with peacocks strutting around the gardens. They went on an excursion to the beach of Lagana; there was nothing there except for a few straw huts on stilts (*kalyva*); it was the most beautiful beach June had ever seen. There were no private cars on the island. There were just two or three taxi-families, former boatmen who used to transfer visistors from the liners to the quay; once ships could approach and moor at the harbour, the government compensated the boatmen and enabled them to become taxi drivers.

Zakynthos possesses a tradition of semi-improvised open-air folk or street theatre (*omilies*) and early Modern Greek drama, if we take into account the satirical character comedy in verse, *O Hasis* ("Hasis, or The Tiff and the Patch-Up", 1790-95), by Demetrios Gouzelis, which provides us with some delightful and entertaining insights into the customs, worldviews and everyday life of the Zantiot townsfolk, at least of the nouveau riche and the common people, as Zisimos Sinodhinos says in his introduction to his new edition of the play. "Every Zantiot has a little of Hasis inside him," claimed Grigorios Xenopoulos (1867-1951), the novelist, short-story writer and playwright, in 1927. Dionysios Romas (1906-81), the historical novelist and expert on Zakynthos, said that the play presents "a concise psychography (or psychological portrait) of the Zantiot".

I have looked for collections of the texts of old *omilies*, which seem to have been performed from around the mid seventeenth century during the period of Lent by amateur actors, with the female parts always played by males. I have only been able to find books containing new works by contemporary writers working in the old tradition, but it is gratifying to know that this has not died out.

If one visits the Roma Mansion and Museum in Zakynthos town, one can get some idea of what the interior of an aristocratic town house might have been like before the terrible earthquakes of 1953, which completely flattened the town. The mansion was built in the seventeenth century by the English merchant and consul Robert John Geoffrey, and was later given as a dowry to Robert Sargint. During the British Protectorate it was the *residenza* of the British Resident. Gladstone addressed the people of Zakynthos from its balcony during his fact-finding mission; then it was bought by the Roma family in 1880, and was the home of Dionysios Romas, the writer, but was badly damaged in 1953.

Themis Marinos arrived on the island two days after the earthquake occurred. By that time June was working at the British Embassy in Athens and she managed to get Themis a permit (through the offices of the British Ambassador) on the first boat, so that he could find out what had happened to his family. Luckily people had come out into the squares after the first quake (he found his brother Anthony camping in a tent in Solomos Square), and nobody was killed in Zakynthos, apart from a few looters who were buried inside falling houses. The death toll in Kefalonia was significant (nearly 500 people). The first to respond to the SOS calls and to bring help and emergency aid were the captains and crews of some nearby Israeli ships (they took the opportunity to express thanks for the fact that the Zantiots had protected the island's Jews during the German Occupation), followed soon after by British naval destroyers and other ships, which brought food, tents, blankets, essential equipment like generators, as well as medical supplies.

Richard Chandler reported that the Zantiots were familiar with the calamity of earthquakes. John Davy, writing about the frequency of earthquakes on Zante at one time, says the inhabitants attributed them to such causes as "the presence of a party of French jugglers" or to "the absence of the Bishop". He quotes the researches of Count Paolo Mercati, who listed the strongest earthquakes of modern times, from 1514 until 1810. A more recent and presumably more accurate publication by Zoe Mylona gives dates for serious or catastrophic earthquakes from 16 April 1513 until 23 October 1791. As Mylona says, "Apart from anxiety over the frequent catastrophic earthquakes, the Zakinthians also lived under the constant threat of attacks by the Turks." That is not an imaginative landscape that most of us would like to inhabit, I suspect. But she does admit that "In the early 1950s there was large-scale destruction of the buildings in the castle when services of the prefecture pilfered material from them in order to construct buttress walls, quays and other public works in the town and harbour of Zakynthos."

Dodwell (1819), writing about Lefkas, said that "most of its towns and villages were overthrown by an earthquake, in the year 1469, which also did considerable damage to the neighbouring islands, particularly Cephallenia and Zakynthos. The capital of the latter island was nearly destroyed by the same scourge forty-five years afterwards, according to Michael Ducas."

Professor Ansted wrote of the great earthquake in Zakynthos in the year 1514 (1513?) that "rent the castle hill from top to bottom... The last great earthquake took place so lately as 1840." He also noted that "there have been none of importance very lately, and perhaps for this reason the next may be serious." Ansted also quoted Sir Howard Douglas, the Lord High Commissioner, who left a detailed account of the earthquake of 6 November 1840; in summary, Douglas wrote of the dreadful calamity and "extraordinary concussion" which irreparably injured the whole town and island. When he arrived in port, he perceived that "a terrible and general calamity had fallen upon Zante".

Ansted himself described the Bay of Zante, "far exceeding in style and variety of its public buildings, any of the island capitals... The streets are numerous, wide, decently paved, and full of shops... Zante contrasts favourably with all the other cities of the Ionian Islands... There are in it many fine old Venetian houses still inhabited by the families in whose possession they have been for centuries, and these give it an air of solidity and respectability that is not felt elsewhere... The churches of Zante...are on the whole the best and richest of those of the Ionian islands."

Unfortunately, what damage the 1953 earthquake and fires (and earlier earthquakes) failed to do, unplanned tourist developments have managed to complete. One yearns in vain for the Zante described and illustrated in the two-volume study by Archduke Salvator. For me, nowadays, Kefalonia and its capital Argostoli offer a more agreeable landscape and townscape. Neither the offspring of the *nobili*, nor the *civili*, nor the *popolari*—the three basic classes of Venetian Zante—have managed to halt the touristic developments and generally ugly modern architecture of the island, even though houses are earthquake-proof and at least have tiled roofs.

Even within the Marinos family, there are at least two points of view about tourism. Tourism developed on Zakynthos "from scratch", with the letting of simple rooms, argues Themis, and then by a process of gradual and unplanned development. Tourism brought jobs which enabled people to stay on the island. Agriculture is still strong and varied, and far better developed and maintained than on Corfu. The olive trees are more productive, the fruit being picked when green, rather than allowed to fall when black. The oil is of a far higher quality than the acidic oil of Corfu. The Zantiot vineyards are also a delight to see, but it seems contradictory to argue that, on the one hand, Zante was always a highly civilized and prosperous Western European island, and at the same time to make excuses for the devastation of unplanned tourist development as a result of having "started from a completely blank sheet" after the War and/or the 1953 earthquake.

The human and cultural capital and the sense of taste, e.g. for neo-classical architecture, should not have been destroyed, if it is true, as claimed by the "Fioro di Levante" Choir on its website, that it is in the nature of the Zakynthian people to be devoted to "all that is beautiful, in all forms of expression", and that this "knows no bounds". As in Corfu, the civil engineers, architects, builders and municipal authorities must bear much of the responsibility for the environmental degradation.

Those who have the opportunity to study photographs of the town after the 1953 earthquakes will not perhaps be quite so harsh in their judgement. While one can understand that reconstruction in the 1950s and 1960s should have been fairly basic, earthquake-resistant and functional, by necessity, the greed-driven tourist developments of the last twenty to thirty years are another story.

IN PRAISE OF PAXOS

Smaller islands than Corfu, Kefalonia and Zakynthos may have suffered less from the political events (and earthquakes) of the twentieth century, but they also endured foreign occupations, lack of medical facilities, difficult communications, shortages of water, and so on. In the nineteenth century life might have been harder for the inhabitants, if relatively peaceful, although some of them also accepted refugees from more violent places on the mainland ('Turkey-in-Europe', Ottoman Greece).

John Davy was kind to the Paxiots: "Of the inhabitants of the olive-growing islands, those of Paxo are considered as distinguished for mild and amiable manners, and for absence of vice. Their olive-plantations are better attended to than those of Corfu and Santa Maura." As a result, no doubt, "the oil of Paxos is esteemed the best in this part of the world" (Murray, *Handbook*, 1840).

Olive trees could also give rise to many legal disputes, which is why every Paxiot is still determined to paint his or her initials or symbols of ownership on every tree (and rock), especially since the value of land has risen so dramatically over the past thirty years.

Gaios village centre on Paxos

Kendrick (1822) pointed out that "a few years of undisputed possession of the fruits of a tree substantiate a claim to permanent ownership, or, at least, to ownership as long as the trees last, and thus anyone having been lucky enough to appropriate a neighbour's property for a time without notice, becomes the legal owner of the tree he has robbed. This, however, gives no claim to the land on which the trees grow." I can vouch for the fact that such practices still occur.

De Vaudoncourt wrote that "many of the inhabitants of Prevesa and some Souliots, have taken refuge in Paxo, and increased the population", while Dodwell wrote that "the inhabitants live chiefly by fishing, and trading with the neighbouring islands" and he comments on the absence of running water in the summer.

Davy describes aerial angling, or sky fishing: "Should the season of the year be spring, the traveller may have an opportunity of witnessing a singular species of angling, in which, I was informed, the natives indulge from the lofty cliffs, not in the sea beneath for fish, but in the air for birds-swallows- which then crowd about the cliffs, and which they catch with a fly, attached to a fine hook and line, thrown and managed very much in the same manner as in common fly-fishing."

I have visions of some of my wife's ancestors from Bogdanatika "standing or sitting on the dizzy margin" of the lofty cliffs of Eremitis, taking swallows on the wing. At other times I imagine them trying to escape from pirates or desperate for water in the dry season.

Apparently this curious type of fishing was also practised in Zakynthos (Murray *Handbook*), where swallow-fishing was done from the tops of houses and steeples; the fishing-rods having long lines with the flies and hooks floating in the wind.

Ansted writes that "Paxo is without springs of water sufficient to supply the inhabitants, and what there are seem to be inconveniently placed, while some of them are brackish. Large cisterns, or tanks, have been constructed out of the rock to store the water in dry seasons, and these seem to have proved useful." To Paxiots of an older generation, the building of swimming-pools, demanded by those who now rent villas on the island, is anathema.

Davy recommends an excursion to the cliffs and caves of Paxos. He notes the neat white-washed houses, fruit-trees and olive-tress of Gaja (Gaios), and makes the point that poverty is uncommon, as "almost every one has some property of his own in the country, either in land or olive-trees; indeed they commonly estimate their property by the number of their trees". The women of Paxos are apparently as idle as the men, "ignorant and superstitious, as must be the case where education is neglected. Few of them can use the needle and make their own clothes."

The Reverend Hughes accompanied Sir Charles Gordon to Paxos:

> It is an arid rock, eighteen miles in circumference, without a plain or meadow within its territory: it possesses not a single fountain or spring of fresh water...yet with all these apparent disadvantages it has within itself the means of producing greater wealth to its inhabitants than all the rest of the Ionian islands: these means depend solely upon its olive trees, which give such excellent oil, that it bears a high premium throughout the Levant, and affords a most profitable exchange to its cultivators.

Hughes found the houses neat and commodious, but the inhabitants (around 4,000) were not in affluent circumstances at the time of his visit; they had suffered during the French occupation and even more because of the British cruisers "which captured their vessels and put a stop to their commerce and navigation". They tried to go for a walk in the evening but had to scramble over rocks, as there was not a single road in the whole island, so that "a horse in Paxos is as scarce an article as in Venice". As the Paxiots were unable to take any exercise by walking or riding, Hughes suggests that they were perhaps "the most constant worshippers of the Dii Penates in the world" ("couch potatoes", worshippers of the household gods—perhaps he overlooked all the physical labour in collecting the olives, or in rowing their fishing-boats).

Like almost every other writer, Hughes alludes to the legend related by Plutarch concerning the wild, loud laments announcing the death of Pan, but he recommends us to read about it in the poem "Horae Ionicae" by Waller Rodwell Wright, the section beginning

> By Paxu's shores (thus ancient legends say)
> As once a Grecian vessel held her way...

Much less familiar is the story of Massiga Mitsiali (1895-1981), the first female doctor of the island, who deserves to be better known. There is a short tribute to her by Nikos Boikos: "Massiga was born in Magazia towards the end of the 19th century. She went to school in Paxos and Athens and being a good student, she was sent to the medical school of Vienna by her uncle Dotsolos, who was a doctor. She became a pathologist and returned to Paxos to work and live here." During the Second World War Italian occupation, "Massiga travelled the whole island every day on her donkey and checked on sick people, advised mothers with sick children, tried to show an optimistic face to the discouraged and never took a reward for her efforts." My wife remembers that in the 1950s Massiga used to be paid in kind, with sausages.

Apart from Nikos Boikos' tribute, a fuller biography was written by E. Apostolopoulou-Michaelidou (2008). Massiga is buried in the Mitsialis family tomb near Eremitis, alongside Anastasios Mitsialis, translator of Salvator's *Paxos und Antipaxos*.

It was Count (Archduke) Salvator who was the first to devote himself to a serious, in-depth study of Paxos. He even tells us that the bouzouki (he spells it Busukki) had become a popular instrument on Paxos at the time, alongside the violin and mandolin. Musicologists tend to think the bouzouki came to Greece with the refugees from Asia Minor, after 1922.

Kendrick commented that "The manners and customs of the Paxinotes are rather different from those of Zante: a greater degree of freedom is permitted to the females here, nor is there to be distinguished any of that barbarous jealousy. In the town itself there is absolutely a conversazione! It certainly created much surprise in me to find that such an advancement in civilization had taken place." The town of Gaios then consisted of an irregular cluster of houses scattered on the beach.

Ansted was unusually positive about the Paxiots: "Its inhabitants are among the best-looking and most comfortable of the whole group." Archduke Ludwig Salvator (1897) commented that "the inhabitants of Paxos are famous on account of their beauty and the women are considered the most beautiful in the Ionian Islands and amongst the most beautiful in Greece".

We must not forget that the first settlers on the Diapontian island of Fano (Othoni) "were a party of twelve pirates obliged to fly from Paxo, having been outlawed, and who, on settling on Fano, following the example of the early Romans in procuring wives, went to the nearest port of the Albanian coast, and, on the pretext of buying linen, seized and carried off the women who brought it to their boats; and the tale proceeds further to say that they took the same measure to procure a priest, whom, after the performance of the marriage-rites for which he was brought, they impatiently threw him into the sea in returning, and drowned" (Dr. John Davy).

The Murray *Handbook* states that detachments of one or two British regiments were usually quartered there, but considered it a perfect banishment.

The Paxiots became enthusiastic for Union with Greece. Kirkwall records that Gladstone, the High Commissioner Extraordinary, learned that "the strong desire for the Union existing in Paxo dated from the time that two Corfu editors were confined on the island by Lord Seaton, soon after his Lordship had established the so-called freedom of the press".

For those who aspire to buy a plot of land and to build a house on Paxos, Peter Bull's *It Isn't All Greek To Me* is an entertaining read, one of the first in the genre. Another classic account of Paxos is *The Stars Over Paxos*, by John Gill (1995). It makes uncomfortable reading for Little Englanders and some locals alike, but it contains superb descriptions of the unforgettable Paxos night sky, the often rough crossing on the much-missed *MS Kamelia*, and many other aspects of life on the island, its history and legends, an island which can seem alternately like paradise or claustrophobically threatening to the "interloper" or non-native.

Chapter Five

FOREIGN RULE AND OCCUPATION

THE END OF THE BRITISH PROTECTORATE
Liberal British administrators in the time of the Protectorate understood that the rule of foreigners would create enemies and opposition in the Ionian Islands, but they believed that such feelings of enmity could be diminished by the fair exercise of justice, by making much-needed improvements and by efforts aimed at conciliation. Ansted discovered what Gladstone would also find out: "In every island I was told that...there had been little justice and no real protection." The benefits derived from association with the British were only grudgingly admitted.

Solomos, the "National Poet of Greece", became reconciled to the British in Corfu, at least to the otherwise unpopular Sir Henry Ward and to the more Philhellenic British—and to the daughters of Sir Henry (Alice) and Sir John Frazer (Frances). Diamantina Roma married Sir George Bowen, and Nina Soufi (née Palatianou) became Lady Adam, the wife of Sir Frederick Adam. Charles James Napier is sometimes said to have married a Kefalonian woman called Anastasia. In fact they were not legally married; Anastasia was his kept mistress, and so their child, christened Emily Cephalonia Napier (d. 29 February 1908), was born illegitimately. Elizabeth Longford (1975) says he fathered two girls, Susan and Emily, by Anastasia. Napier married the widow, Elizabeth Kelly, in April 1827; she died 31 July 1830. Napier had been taught Modern Greek by a Greek priest and scholar. Anastasia must have given him the opportunity for plenty of practice. In 1825 he wrote in his diary the oft-quoted observation, "Now I am once more amongst the merry Greeks, who are worth all other nations put together. I like to see, to hear them; I like their fun, their good humor...their wit, their eloquence, their good nature are their own."

Andreas Laskaratos was similarly generally well-disposed to the British, and spent time in England. Other examples include Lady Hankey (Catherine or Catterina Varlamo) who had married Sir Frederick Hankey when he was serving on Corfu, and the daughter of Nikolaos Mantzaros, Caterina, who married Henry Charles Charlton, a merchant, on 10 August 1843. Charlton was born in Majorca. His father, Joseph, was a wine-merchant who arrived on Corfu in 1815 (thanks to Kostas Kardamis for this information). Andreas Kalvos married an English woman, Charlotte Augusta Wadans, and spent many years of his adult life in England, in Louth, Lincolnshire (from 1852 to 1869). He had been briefly married to another English woman, Theresa Thomas, earlier in his life, while having an affair with his student Susan Ridout. George Seferis seems to have felt sorry for Kalvos, married to an Anglo-Saxon woman, living in a damp and foggy atmosphere in Louth, in draughty rooms, with the smell of bacon and eggs ("Kalvos", 1960): "18 years without a Greek word; even his dreams in a foreign language." Seferis arranged to have Kalvos' remains exhumed and taken back to Zakynthos—with those of his English wife, who also was not consulted on the matter. The point to emphasize here is that Anglo-Ionian weddings were not uncommon.

We should not forget that in one of Kalvos' Odes, "The Patriot", addressed to his beloved birthplace, the island of Zakynthos, the poet also expresses his love and admiration for other countries including Albion/Britain, and the freedom, power, glory and wealth of the city built beside the banks of the River Thames:

> The Aeolian breeze carried me there.
> Rays of most sweet freedom
> Nourished me and gave me comfort.

But, as Holland and Markides (2006) point out, after Gladstone's mission, and by 1861, "Social contact between British officialdom and expatriates and the Ionian classes, once reasonably free and easy at such venues as the Corfu racetrack, now tailed off almost completely."

That was not always the case, as Kirkwall (1864) points out; it was all a question of attitude:

> I became popular with the Cephalonians to a degree that perfectly astonished me. They are an amiable and easily pleased people, when kindly and considerately treated. "The English," said Lascarato often to me, "have been generally disliked, because they have treated the Greeks with contempt, and contempt never did any good."

Laskaratos, on the other hand, seems to have felt considerable contempt for the gentlemen of Zakynthos. In a letter to his Danish friend

Hansen, on 14 January 1867, he wrote to say that they had no right to criticize his attitudes towards religion because they themselves followed no religion at all. "They are only hypocritical Pharisees, murderers by nature, evil, shameless Sodomites, without any familial feelings, without humanity, always ready to do the most brazen and contemptible things in order to fulfil their bestial desires." What is slightly confusing is that Laskaratos, in his correspondence, seems to believe that General Ferdinand Whittingham wrote *Four Years in the Ionian Islands*, and that Viscount Kirkwall was the editor of the work; Kirkwall is in fact given as the editor on the title page.

If early nineteenth-century Greek attitudes to the Ionian Islands were mixed, attitudes towards the *Anglokratia* (British rule) are still mixed. The *signori* and local aristocracy might have found much to their advantage by sucking up to the British in the hope of a Government position or favours. The peasantry and those actively seeking independence or union with Greece (like the Rizospastes or Greek Radicals party) felt differently. As usual, the British believed that the natives were profoundly ungrateful. Had not the British, their benevolent protectors, built networks of roads, water supplies and aquaducts, modern prisons, hospitals, foundling homes, savings banks, mental hospitals, convalescent homes, schools, lighthouses, barracks, garrison churches and palaces? Had they not improved ports and docks, built quays, drained and cultivated marshes, introduced a sense of fairplay and justice, and the game of cricket?

There seems little doubt that the people of Kefalonia are still genuinely grateful for the achievements of de Bosset and Napier, and this is evident from books, street names, statues and busts, museum exhibits and other exhibitions.

Kirkwall pointed out that the greatest benefit that Sir Frederick Adam conferred on the Corfiots was the supplying of abundant water to the town. He also reminds us that in 1352, Boccaccio's novel *Landolfo Buffalo* refers to the scarcity of water in Corfu, and describes a Corfiot woman having to clean her kitchen utensils with sand and salt water.

Tertius Kendrick (1822) admitted that the islanders "are dissatisfied with British integrity, which they desire not, and would feel happy if permitted the means of prolonging their litigations in court". Discussing the people of Lefkas, he says, "It is clearly evident that a just and upright government does not meet their wishes. Gladly would they avail themselves of one that was Venetian in its kind."

Thomas Gallant (2002) points out that "Greeks held a fundamentally different view of 'the state'. To them the state consisted of a bundle of resources to be exploited for personal and partisan purposes." Holland and Markides (2006) then say: "The British Protection had never succeeded in rooting itself into the social foundations of the Islands, as even the old Venetian primacy, with all its failings, had."

Grigorios Xenopoulos has a short story called "*O Typos kai i Ousia*" ("The Form and The Substance"), in which a member of the old noble-class of his island, a stickler for formalities and decorum, was posted to Corfu as a judge during the time of the British Protectorate. When the Union of the Seven Islands with Greece took effect, he was delighted, because he was a patriot and had secretly supported the Radical, Unionist party. But he felt obliged to resign as a judge. The Kingdom of Greece is happy to employ him in a new capacity as Eparchos, or Sub-Prefect, in a province of the Peloponnese. He feels sure the people of the province will reap the benefit of the Ionian Island civilization which he will represent in his own person, with an even greater degree of dignity, strictness, formality, and ethical behaviour than ever before. Deputy Nomarch! Sub-Prefect! Fondly imagining the importance of his post, as it might have been in Venetian or British times, he presents himself for a briefing with the Nomarch (a down-to-earth character, a "Romios" from mainland Greece), gushing with gratitude for the great honour which has been bestowed upon him. He expects a boat to be sent to transport him to his new post. But the impoverished Greek State is not Britain or Venice. He is obliged to catch instead the first available ship, but is greatly disgruntled to find that, although the captain and the crew are made aware of the importance of the personage they are carrying on board, they make no effort to send a signal or to display a flag to announce his distinguished presence to those on shore or on the sea. The old Greek seadog of a captain has never seen anyone like this Sub-Prefect, either on his own island or on Corfu, because he looks a little like Sior Nionios, a popular caricature of an old-fashioned nobleman wearing a top-hat, who keeps insisting he is travelling "in his official capacity". The dialogue between them is extremely funny and the captain soon bursts out laughing, before turning very serious, exclaiming in exasperation that they should not have to display a flag or signal every time they transport such an old goat or imbecile as the Sub-Prefect. He cannot find the words to continue. The story ends with the Sub-Prefect catching the next boat back to the island he has just left, and presenting his resignation to the Nomarch, saying that as a Seven Islander he is not accustomed to such behaviour, and that at his age it is difficult to learn new ways of doing things. "Let our children learn from you, Romioi!"

"You're handing in your resignation because of such a small formality?" shouts the Nomarch, when he learns the reason.

"Yes," replies the former judge, fearlessly, "because I have always stood on formality and I am of the firm opinion that the Form bears witness to the Substance. Without the one there is not the other. When captains can get away with verbally abusing Eparchs or Sub-Prefects and can call them old goats because an elementary omission has been pointed out, it means that your deputies are not doing their duty, or risk embarrassment and trouble when they do so… I can't tolerate either course, so I resign."

The story neatly encapsulates the differences between the "New Greeks" and the Seven Islanders after the Union in 1864.

But were the old formalities and the strict British administration so ethical and just, in substance and practice?

The anonymous author of *The Ionian Islands under British Protection* asserts that by firm actions and policies, "We have gained more in respect than we have lost in love, so utterly incapable are all Orientals of appreciating and relishing any other but despotic Governments and energetic measures… All Orientals have much in common with children; they are always either in ecstasy or in misery."

John Dunn Gardner (1859) writes of the Ionians, "They want to be well ridden, and will then like their master, but with a loose rider on their back, they become tricky and restive."

Reading between the lines of Lord Nugent's introduction to *The Ionian Anthology*, especially Vol. 5, it is easy to put a gloss on certain expressions. "Free Government" means "The British Protectorate"; "Good customs" equal "British customs"; "The Vices of Ancient Governments" refer to any non-British government; "Vicious and debasing systems", any non-British administration; "General prostration of enterprise", the results of a non-British economic system.

Kendrick says, "Our own prompt and vigorous administration carried great weight with it in the eyes of the Zantiotes, who approved not our system in hanging so many wretches that richly deserved it."

John Capodistrias, the Russian-trained (and thus branded as pro-Russian) Corfiot who became the first President of Greece (assassinated 9 October 1831), was initially in favour of British protection, and wrote to Lord Castlereagh on 23 September 1815 along those lines, expressing the opinion that a liberal administration would ensure domestic tranquillity (see W. P. Kaldis). By 1819 he had become aware of local Greek disapproval of the British administration under Sir Thomas Maitland, says Kaldis, and when he went to London he spoke to Lord Bathurst, Secretary of State for the Colonies, about his dissatisfaction with Maitland's policies. "In Capodistrias's view Maitland was not acting in a manner consistent with Britain's promise to encourage constitutional liberty in the islands. Maitland's government, symbolized by a gallows in every public gathering place, was arousing increasing hostility."

In Capodistrias' *Letter to the Tsar Nicholas*, he writes of returning to Corfu to find his country "oppressed by the tyrannical rule exercised by General Maitland" and mourning "the hardships suffered by her neighbours, the inhabitants of Parga, as well as the Souliots and Roumeliots formerly in the service of Russia, who underwent the most pitiless and unreasonable persecution. The sacrifice of Parga was completed before my eyes. I had the unhappiness of seeing the people of Parga arriving on the shores of Corfu, expatriated because of the bad faith and faulty calculations of the British agents, compelled to abandon to Ali Pasha, in return for a paltry sum of money, their ancient homes, taking with them only the bones of their fathers."

It is troubling to read this eyewitness account, written by a Corfiot at the time. He writes of "the regime of violence under which the inhabitants of the Ionian Islands suffered". The Epirot refugees in Corfu blamed him for bringing the English to the islands. "They coerce us on all sides. They want to get rid of us completely. You know that, after Souli, Parga and the Islands were our only refuge… Parga is in the hands of Ali Pasha. What will become of us? How can we settle in the Islands when the English deny us even the means of making a living by our flocks?" When Capodistrias went to London, he expressed the complaints of his people and told ministers that "General Maitland treats my compatriots as though they were Indians." He warned them of the dangers of reactions, future difficulties, and the fruits of despair.

Thomas Gallant makes the point that "When Greece took possession of the (Ionian) islands in 1864, it inherited the feudal regime. But not for long: after a series of tumultuous rural revolts, feudalism was abolished, but the remnants of the sharecropping system remained in place."

It could be productive to apply modern landscape archaeology methods and theories to some of the islands, to see how the landscape, agricultural cultivation and contemporary building developments have been determined by past feudal, sharecropping, legal inheritance and dowry arrangements (with individual olive trees forming part of some dowry arrangements). There have always been arguments about inheritances and borders. From disputes over ownership of individual olive trees to the ownership of access tracks and even individual boulders, there has been plenty of litigation and business for the lawyers, in the absence of a comprehensive national land registry (it is instructive to observe what is happening as people start to register their properties—the process began in 2008—especially when there are so many overlapping and contested topographic maps and political scandals).

As in the Ionian Islands nowadays, and most certainly in Corfu, it seems that Kefalonia always had an excessively large number of lawyers: "The number of advocates or lawyers in this island are very great. A stranger would be somewhat puzzled to know how they managed to pick up a livelihood" (Kendrick).

It is illuminating to compare observers' perceptions of social trends over several centuries. R. Montgomery Martin (1837) writes about the islands that

> Lawyers are exceedingly abundant, and it has been calculated that every tenth individual is connected with the legal profession, who, no doubt, have sometimes reaped rich harvests when suits have been protracted through successive generations.

Greek attitudes to taxation are also enduring, it would seem, if we are disposed to accept the fairness of Ansted's remarks:

> It is a characteristic of the islanders that they will not, if they can possibly avoid it, pay any direct tax. The tax gatherer is unknown; and it has always been found almost impossible even to collect the rents of property belonging to the State... The people have never been accustomed

to direct taxation—even for lighting the streets, maintenance of roads, or other purposes of public utility.

The situation has changed, greatly so, since Greece joined the European Union, but the underlying attitude can still be detected in the tendency of the people, the local politicians and municipal authorities to tolerate illegal building, to sidestep the planning process, or in the apparent lack of real commitment to invest in, improve or maintain public spaces, infrastructure and utilities.

It might be explained by differences in national priorities and temperament, or by the fact that the Greek people were exploited for hundreds of years by ruthless tax-collectors under the Turks and the Venetians. It had became a sign of honour to outwit the Pashas' or the Sultans' agents or those of the Provedditore Generale. In spite of that, Ali Pasha undertook an impressive amount of public works, including the construction of roads and khans (roadside lodges with a courtyard, sheds for horses and some rooms to provide shelter for travellers, and where some very basic food and drink could be obtained), bridges, causeways and buildings. Henry Holland, when he was granted an audience with Ali Pasha, complimented him "on the excellent police of his dominions, and the attention he has given to the state of the roads". But, as J. R. McNeil writes (1992): "In the early nineteenth century the local tyrant Ali Pasha (d. 1822) built good roads, but they did not long survive him. Cobblestone tracks (*kalderimi*), suitable for mules but not for wheels, served as the only routes for most of the modern history of Pindus. Wheeled traffic could not routinely cross the Zygos until the late 1930s." He continues: "In the Pindus, carriageworthy roads existed in the time of Ali Pasha, who used forced labor to build and maintain them. But these fell apart after 1821, and only stone paths suitable for mules remained. The first road linking Zagori to Ioannina opened in 1919."

Tim Salmon (1995) suggests that in the Northern Greek mountains, "since the 1950s and the aftermath of the Civil War...the principal inducement for road-building was a desire to undermine the mountains' impregnability as a base for any future guerrilla activity". He laments the bulldozing of traditional tracks. The Colonels' Junta also saw much road-building in Epirus, facilitating access by bus and car to the Zagori villages, for instance. J. R. McNeil says about the Eastern Zagori, "Roads built within the last twenty years afford easy communication with Ioannina so on a Saturday night in the summer those working afar can come back to the village for a variation on venerable social traditions."

During the British Protectorate of the Ionian Islands, Lt. Col. Napier (Commandant of Kefalonia, 1822-30) was scathing in his criticisms of what he considered the wasteful excesses of expenditure ("this puerile waste of the public treasure, for private amusement") by Sir Frederick Adam in Corfu, on buildings such as the second palace (*Mon Repos*, but called by Napier "Sir Frederick's Folly" or "Nasicaa's New Palace") [Napier's spelling]. He considered that it was "of no public utility whatever, but…built purely for the private amusement of Sir Frederick Adam". In a footnote he goes on: "While correcting the press, I hear that Lord Nugent has declined to live in this splendid Palace, which is to be converted into an hospital for idiots! This is very appropriate. I dare say it will hold them, though it was not built for *so many!*" One assumes that is not a quotation that would endear itself to Prince Philip, who was born there on 10 June 1921.

Napier also turned his attention to the road to Palaiokastritsa: "It will hardly be doubted that the convalescent hospital, established at Pallio Castrizza, was a mere pretext to make a pretty road through Corfu."

Professor Ansted praised the place for its healthiness as a retreat during the intense heat of summer, "far removed from all danger of malaria". The fear of malaria was a significant factor in the landscape of people's imagination.

Napier was proud of his own record of economical roadbuilding on Kefalonia, in comparison to Adam's efforts on Corfu: "His Excellency was silent, as is his custom when he discovers that he has imprudently ventured to make any assertion that requires ratiocination, not rank, to support it."

The mutual put-downs, and the endless competition between the islands, give us some flavour of the hostilities that arose between the British officials at the time. There was a distinct lack of praise or gratitude expressed, even among them. Detailed exercises in self-justification seem to have been the norm. Napier was also proud of the quay he had constructed at Argostoli in Kefalonia, where the town's shoreline had had a "ragged, filthy edge" and the street beside the sea was impassable when the winds were strong. He is capable of more sentimental and poetic prose when not haranguing Sir Frederick Adam. Napier's new quay and the street beside the sea became "The favourite promenade of the inhabitants; for the harbour is like a lake, and, in the still moonlight of that calm climate, becomes a perfect mirror. The sounds of music, and of oars, with the songs of boatmen, float along its smooth surface with the most pleasing effect." He goes on to quote a passage from Wright's poem "Horæ Ionicæ".

The lovely British-built road and pavement walk, the Strade Marina, which ran along and around the bay of Garitsa (Castrades, or Gastrades, the oldest suburb) and down to the lighthouse, was a similar success with the inhabitants of Corfu. The pavement has been closed at times because of storm-damage, lack of maintenance in the past and lack of money to carry out repairs. The 1840 edition of the Murray *Handbook* says that "the favourite promenade at Corfu is the one-gun battery, and here all the beauty and fashion of the city assemble every fine evening. This battery is erected on an abrupt precipice, overhanging the sea." Unfortunately the road and walk to Kanoni have in recent years lost most of their charm.

THE THREAT OF ALI PASHA

General G. de Vaudoncourt considered that it was fortunate for the islands that the naval forces of Great Britain were so near at hand when the risk was great, or the Seven Islands might perhaps have fallen under the power of the ambitious Ali Pasha. It is unlikely that Ali Pasha would have treated the islands or the islanders with great care or tenderness in his "successive aggrandizedment" if he had succeeded in adding them to his territory, to judge from how he dealt with the Suliots, the Chimariots, or the people of Parga, Gardiki, Hormovo and Prevesa. Massacres and torture might well have occurred. He would happily raze whole villages to the ground. His barbaric methods are said to have included the use of racks and gibbets, stuffing gunpowder into the ears and nostrils (e.g. of the Suliots) and igniting it. He would impale victims alive, strip their heads of skin, roast them alive on a spit (as with a man called Prifti, who, in the poem by Hadji Seret, "became a kebab in the frying pan"), drown women in the lake (sometimes in sacks), have all the hair shaved off women (e.g. the women from Gardiki or Kardhiq), the hair trampled underfoot and used to stuff sofas, cushions and mattresses, as demanded as an act of revenge by his mother Khamko and sister Chainitza (also spelt Khamco and Shainitza).

Statue of Ali Pasha in Tepelini, Albania

Mothers who had lived in opulence, young maidens whom Hymen was about to bless with the objects of their tenderest affections, were delivered over to the brutal violence of the soldiery... (T. Richards, *Life of Ali Pacha*)

The Reverend Hughes delights in telling us that, after the hair had been shorn off the heads of the Gardikiote women to stuff Shainitza's couches, "Shainitza's head reclines upon the raven tresses of its daughters". Hughes also relates the story of the massacre at Hormovo and the roasting alive of Prifti, with a spit run through his body, but he does not believe the story that Ali did this with his own hands. Ali wreaked his revenge on Gardiki on 15 March 1812: 730 Gardikiotes were massacred in cold blood, most of them killed by Ali's Greek troops; they were left unburied.

Ali Pasha's intentions were explicit. Woodhouse (1968) says, "His particular ambitions were first to crush the independent Greek community of Souli, against which he waged a series of wars in the closing years of the

18th century, and then to acquire control of the Ionian Islands and their mainland dependencies, including Parga, Butrinto and Preveza."

De Vaudoncourt wrote: "Ali Pacha scarcely took the trouble to disguise the projects he had formed on the Venetian towns of the continent, and even on Corfu and St. Maura, to the conquest of which the possession of the above towns was to lead the way." The five towns were Butrint, Igoumenitsa, Parga, Prevesa and Vonitsa. "He stands in need of the Ionian Islands, and they have always constituted the object, more or less secret, of his wishes."

The Reverend Hughes shared this opinion about Ali's intentions: "As long as he lives he will exert all his energies to gain a footing in the Ionian Islands, and upon his death-bed he will bequeath these sentiments to a successor." Hughes then visited Prevesa (once the potential "Portsmouth of Albania" for Ali Pasha) in December 1813, fifteen years after Ali Pasha's attack and overthrow of the town, and wrote:

> Its inhabitants are now reduced to about 3000, and these for the most part worn down by famine and disease, stalk like spectres about the deserted streets over which the gloom of departed prosperity is spread. Most of the houses, and all the churches, except one, have been levelled to the ground; the greatest part of the present inhabitants dwell in the suburbs, under sheds literally constructed of hurdles, open to the sight of every passer-by, and exposed to all the winds of heaven.

Hughes also gives an account of the horrors of the attack on the French and the Prevesans, the scenes of murder, rape and pillage. The heads of four sick Frenchmen were even cut off in hospital. Ali Pasha had an Episcopal ally, it seems, a Christian bishop, Gerasimo of Ithaca (then living in Lefkas), who, with Captain Botzaris, discovered a multitude of people in hiding. The poor wretches were taken to Prevesa, thrown into prison and then transported with two hundred other victims across the Gulf of Arta "to suffer death in cold blood by the hands of an executioner". After the massacre, which the Bishop had not expected, the Bishop was sent by Ali to Corfu, where he deserted, never to return to his native country. Not surprising, given that "the ghastly heads of those who had been so dear to him lay weltering with 300 others in a pool of blood". It has to be said that S. Katsaros (1984) and C. Perraivos (1857) accuse another ecclesiastic, Ignatius, Archbishop of Arta (born in Mytilini) of being a secret informant of Ali Pasha, and of acting with George Botzaris in a treacherous way which led to the Prevesa massacre. Katsaros reports that Ignatius eventually made his way to Corfu, where he took Perraivos to court on account of the latter's accusations against him. Ignatius later disappeared from Greece altogether, which leaves us with a few loose ends, including the question as to whether Ignatius and Gerasimo were perhaps one and the same person!

If Ali Pasha had conquered or obtained Corfu and the Ionian Islands by other means, he would certainly have added many more women to the 5-600 already scattered around his harems in Ioannina, Tepelena and Kerkalopoulo; but he might have shown more tenderness to the youths he would have added to his seraglios, for "he is almost exclusively given up to the Socratic pleasures" (de Vaudoncourt). He selected Greek youths "as his confidants and even his principal officers". Corfiot sailors manned his gunboats on the Lake of Ioannina, but Ali's grandfather, Mukhtar, had taken part, and lost his life, in the 1716 Siege of Corfu and the assault on the fortress, another reason to suggest that he might have harboured a grudge against the island. Leake writes that "it is believed in Albania that his sword is still kept at Corfu, among the trophies of that expedition". That in itself might have given Ali Pasha a strong motive for retrieving his grandfather's sword, and for using it again. (It disappeared during the French occupation of Corfu.) The Reverend Hughes heard that Ali offered a large sum of money to gain possession of it, but without success. Hughes was convinced that Ali "would cede half his continental dominions for the possession of Corfu, which would render him more independent of the Porte than every other acquisition".

Apart from his Corfiot sailors, Ali Pasha also had a band of musicians attached to one of his regiments of troops; he told Monsieur Pouqueville that he had "stolen them", i.e. he had bribed them to desert from various regiments in the Ionian Islands (Hughes).

When Ali attacked the Suliots on one occasion, according to Leake (Additional Notes):

> Moskho…the wife of Tzavella and mother of Foto, particularly distinguished herself on the day of battle. She broke open some cartridge boxes with a hatchet; and then loading herself and the women with car-

tridges, distributed them to the Suliotes in the trenches... When Ali threatened to roast alive her son Foto, who was in his hands, she replied, that she was young, and could have other children, and that she would eat a bit of the roasted flesh rather than betray her country.

This episode is also cited in an article entitled "Brave Women" in *The New York Times* of 8 February 1880. Leake then summarizes some lines by the Albanian Muslim poet Hadji Seret, from Delvino, who wrote about the exploits of Ali in demotic Greek (November 1805): "The author...remarks that Mukhtar, his grandfather, distinguished himself at the siege of Corfu (in the year 1716), where he entered the castle by assault, and hung up his sword upon the gate." Those parts of the poem that Leake quotes, translates or summarizes make fascinating reading, in relation to the Zagori, Hormovo (in modern Albania), Suli and Prevesa.

There is a curious play called *Ali Pacha; or, The Signet-Ring: A Melo-Drama, in two acts*, which was performed at the Theatre Royal, London in 1823, written by the American John Howard Payne (who wrote the song, "Home Sweet Home"). Some scholars argue that it was co-authored or even written by James Robinson Planché. In the introductory remarks to one edition, by "D-G", the actor who played Ali Pasha (W. Farren) is praised, as well as the author: "To have conceived a monster of greater ferocity than Ali Pacha, would have been to paint a devil that the infernal regions could hardly have been hot enough to hold." Payne took some licence with the manner of Ali's death, staging a grand explosion (in the style of the monk Samuel, originally from the Aegean Islands, and the Suliot heroine Despo Botzi), rather than murder by an emissary of the Sultan. In Act I, Ali reduces Ioannina to flames and ashes, before Ismail and the Sultan's army can reach it. In Scene III, Zenocles (son of the murdered Patriarch of Epirus) exclaims in passionate sub-Byronic tones:

Oh! Men of Greece, can ye alone crouch tamely to the barbarians, and invite the yoke, while distant nations madden at the story of your wrongs, and burn to vindicate your cause? Sons of heroes, start from your lethargy! Crush the insulters of the land of glory, show the expecting world that Greece is not extinct, and give some future Homer themes for a mightier Iliad... Here, in the sight of Epirus, shall the spoiler's blood bathe the soil he has made desolate!

More controversial is the dialogue between Ali and Zenocles in Scene III:

> *Ali:* I once oppressed the Greeks—'twas then my policy. Now, a common danger unites us against a common foe.
> *Zenocles:* Thou the ally of the Greeks! Think'st thou my countrymen will disgrace their holy cause by owning such a leader? Thou art their first foe. "Let Ali perish!"—Such is the cry of all Greece.
> *Ali:* What? I forgive the Greeks! I deceived thee. I was born to be their scourge. I live to see the traveller seek, on the wreck of ancient Greece, the ruins of the new.
> *Zenocles:* Oh! Ill-starr'd nation!

Payne was a master, says D-G, of scenic illusion and display. The play is short, but Payne makes Ali's death a grand spectacle. Ali fires a second pistol into a powder barrel, at the same moment that Ismail and the two other officers fire on him. The citadel is blown up. Zenocles appears amid the flaming ruins with a banner. In the play, therefore, Ali ends his life much like the Suliot heroes, Samuel and Despo.

There are other portrayals of Ali Pasha in folk literature. Victor Hugo captured something of the way in which Ali was imagined in Western Europe at the time in one of the poems in his sequence "The Orientals" (1829):

> Un jour Ali passait : les têtes les plus hautes
> Se courbaient au niveau des pieds de ses arnautes.
> Tout le peuple disait : Allah !

Here is an English translation as "The Pasha and the Dervish" (1839):

> Ali came riding by—the highest head
> Bent to the dust, o'ercharged with dread,
> Whilst "God be praised!" all cried;
> But through the throng one dervish pressed,
> Aged and bent, who dared arrest
> The pasha in his pride.

Ali Tepelini, light of all light,
Who hold'st the Divan's upper seat by right,
Whose fame Fame's trump hath burst—
Thou art the master of unnumbered hosts,
Shade of the Sultan—yet he only boasts
In thee a dog accurst!

K. E. Fleming (1999) is highly critical of the lurid and often apocryphal "Orientalizing" and much repeated anecdotes about the "despot's" life, character and cruelty, as contained in most biographies—and their treatment of the stories about Kyria Frosini, the Gardikiotes, the Suliots, and about his demonized mother, Khamko. "Ali, then, has not been so much described as imagined and in these imaginings as much is revealed about the assumptions of those imaginers as about the figure of Ali himself." She is probably right, and the point is taken, but in this book I am indeed dealing with the way in which Ali (and the Greeks) have been portrayed and imagined; I am not attempting an academic or critical account of the arguably "voyeuristic" or "titillating" nature of exaggerated, novelistically-embellished or didactic traveller's tales, as she variously describes them. Here we are concerned with that very "western European cultural imagination" and those attitudes of cultural superiority found in stories, which she is eager to dismantle and dismiss as merely entertaining, or unworthy of being placed on bookshelves alongside works of serious scholarship (such as her own). A corrective was certainly needed, and it is invaluable to have such a strong focus on Ali's diplomacy, military strategy, economic, agricultural and trade policies and public works, instead of on his cruelty and sexual preferences, and on the stereotyped projections of Westerners.

In the end, Fleming reluctantly seems to admit that many of the stories about Ali (even if accounts differ) are true, or not without veracity, e.g. Frosini's drowning is "almost certainly a true story" and "the fact that descriptions of Ali are Orientalist does not mean that they are wholly inaccurate, and it is evident that his cruelties and avarice, his wild rages and dictatorial government, although stock characteristics of the Oriental despot, were also quite real."

I wonder what Fleming would make of G. K. Chesterton's poem "Lepanto" (1911), considering its pejoratively Orientalist and anti-Muslim

Tomb of Ali Pasha in the Kastro of Ioannina

description of Mahound/Mohammed and its glorification of Don John of Austria (and the Crusaders of old: "It is Richard, it is Raymond, it is Godfrey at the gate!"), and the defeat of the Ottoman navy of rowed galleys at the Battle of Lepanto or Navpaktos on 7 October 1571:

> Mahound is in his paradise above the evening star,
> (Don John of Austria is going to the war.)
> He moves a mighty turban on the timeless houri's knees,
> His turban that is woven of the sunsets and the seas...

Fleming herself is also capable of a little tabloid titillation and of gratuitously repeating a lurid tale (footnote p. 98, based on a note of Leake), as I do now myself, in typical Orientalist fashion, concerning the fate of Ali's three hundred French prisoners from the garrison at Prevesa, which he attacked in October 1798:

> For those who wonder at the impractibility of transporting three hundred severed heads over several hundred miles to Istanbul, the tech-

nique was this: The skin was peeled off the skull and packed down for transportation. Before presentation to the grand vizier, the skins were stuffed with straw, then moistened with water to revivify them.

On checking Leake's note in *Travels in Northern Greece*, we find the following:

> Of 175 inhabitants of Prevyza, who were taken in the place and accused of having abetted the French, three only were saved. The heads of the Prevyzans, and those of the Greeks and the French killed at Nicopolis, amounting to 300, were sent to Constaninople. By heads is to be understood the skins only, which are stuffed with straw and moistened before they are presented to the Grand Vezir.

The same technique was apparently *not* used when Ali's own severed head was sent to Istanbul. It was sent on a silver dish and put on public display for three days.

Kastro of Ioannina

Arthur Foss (1978), also criticized by Fleming, quotes the Reverend Hughes' description of scenes of cruelty carried out in the space between the bazaar and the Kastro of Ioannina: "criminals have been roasted alive over a slow fire, impaled, and skinned alive; others have had their extremities chopped off, and some have been left to perish with the skin of their face stripped over their necks".

Foss could have gone further. Hughes also writes that "our own resident, as he was once going into the serai of Litharitza, saw a Greek priest, the leader of a gang of robbers, nailed alive to the outer wall of the palace, in sight of the whole city". On the road to Arta there was an area where a large number of gypsies lived. The Pasha always selected his executioners from among them; nearby there was a large plane-tree which served for a public gallows and "ten or twenty robbers at a time have been seen dangling in clusters among the branches".

The story of Dionysios, the so-called "Dog-Sophist", is intriguing in this respect. A defrocked bishop, he practised astrology and necromancy and believed that he was "fated by the stars to deliver his country from the Ottoman yoke". He led an uprising in 1611, heading a crowd of drunken followers which entered Ioannina singing the *Kyrie Eleison* and which proceeded to plunder and kill about a hundred Muslims, burning several houses. Hughes relates how the Turks rallied, slew many and took prisoners "for exquisite tortures". Dionysios, the Skilosophist, had hidden in a deep cavern in the Kastro. Some Jews discovered him; he was flayed alive, his skin was stuffed with straw and sent to Constantinople. As Foss points out, one result of the uprising was that Greeks lost the right to live in the Kastro, their place being taken by the Turks and Jews. The Reverend Hughes describes how Ioannina was "treated by the Turks like all other conquered cities after this rebellion". The principal conspirators, together with many innocent persons, were "impaled, sawn asunder, burnt alive". Every Greek church within the Kastro was razed to the ground, the Christians being banished for ever, by special firman. The Jews were permitted to retain their habitations and were given immunities on account of the assistance they had rendered the Muslims.

In the long run it did not pay to become a friend, doctor, lover or wife of Ali Pasha. As Byron commented, "he has the appearance of any thing but his real character, for he is a remorseless tyrant, guilty of the most horrible cruelties… He has been a mighty warrior, but is as barbarous as he is successful, roasting rebels &c. &c." (*Letters and Journals*, Vol. 1).

In spite of his barbaric cruelty (however embellished by Orientalist travellers), Ali is often credited as being a supporter of the Greek Revolution. It suited his strategy in his own independence struggle against the Sultan. G. de Vaudoncourt revealed how much Ali Pasha relied on the talents of Greeks for his administration as he could not trust some branches to "ignorant Albanians", and did not wish to place other branches in the hands of Turks whom he mistrusted and hated. "His constant project…is the independence and entire separation of his dominions from the Ottoman empire." The Greeks needed him in turn "to paralyse the efforts of the Porte", and flattered him with the title "King of Greeks", but only until the time that they could reconquer their own liberty.

The Murray *Handbook* of 1884 states that "The career of Ali Pasha exercised a great influence on the Greek revolution, which he indirectly promoted… His rebellion against the Porte, by weakening the central power, afforded an opportunity to the Greeks for successful revolt."

George Bowen (1852) repeated this view and added that "if his power had remained unimpaired, he would easily have crushed the insurrection; and it was his rebellion against the Sultan which was seized by the Greeks as the most favourable opportunity for them also to rise in arms."

This point is also developed by K. E. Fleming:

> Ali's declaration of independence from the Porte…provided an opportune occasion for the Greeks, too, to try their hand at freedom… The protracted battle between Ali and the sultan's troops…tied up Ottoman troops at a critical moment in Greek revolutionary history… When in the last years of his life he appealed to the Greeks in nationalist terms, claiming to be a member of the Filiki Etairia…he did so…because he saw that his own success might be entirely contingent on the success of the planned Greek insurrection against the Ottoman Empire.

Fleming adds a footnote: "In the event, the opposite was true: the success of the first outbreak of the Greek War of Independence in 1821 can in large part be attributed to Ali's 'insurrection' against the Porte."

One of the most unjustly neglected works of literature concerning Ali Pasha and his war against the Suliots is D. R. Morier's aforementioned three-volume novel *Photo the Suliote, A Tale of Modern Greece* (1857). An abridged version appeared in 1951, in which the editor explains that David Richard Morier was appointed in 1804, at the age of twenty, as secretary to the political mission sent by the British Government to Ali Pasha. Morier explains in his introduction that he first heard the story of Photo when he was obliged to spend time in quarantine in the lazaret of Corfu, at the time when the republic of the Ionian Islands was under the protection of a Russian garrison; the date of his story was "now more than half a century old" at the time of writing. While in quarantine he had a "pestiferous companion, Dr. Dimitraki Iatropulo of Kallarites" (Kalarytes in Morier's spelling), a Greek "not deficient in one of the characteristics of his nation—loquacity". Rather ungrateful, considering that during his confinement David Morier noted down lots of information from the apparently competent if unqualified doctor. He is also critical of Professor Psilidhi, "who liked nothing better at all times than to display his own little wit, being a Greek to the very marrow for vanity and conceit..." But Morier was more complimentary of the Greek spirit in the following:

> The Greeks are, by nature, a laughter-loving race. Endowed with a volatility of spirits, which centuries of oppression have not been able to condense into a becoming gravity, they slip away from the grasp of their oppressors and with the levity of corks reappear on the surface of the billows which, it might be supposed, had sunk them for ever... Immeasurable self-conceit was a principal ingredient of their national character, and a source of support in the tribulations they were daily exposed to, while they remained under the dominion of the Turks.

Morier drew on his own journals and experience of the region, including the gorge of Suli. Locations described in the novel include Zitsa, Suli, Kallarites, the Kastro of Ioannina and the Acheron River; his descriptions of Kallarites are particularly evocative.

COLLABORATION AND RETRIBUTION

I recently had a discussion with a Corfiot academic about the concept of "collaboration". To what extent can it be said that some Greeks "collaborated" with the Ottomans, or with the British for that matter, or came to an "accommodation" with them? Professor Thomas Gallant (2002) argues that it was not a simple matter of either *resistance* or *accommodation* in the Ionian Islands; he prefers to write of the experience of "*dominion*".

"Collaboration" does not seem to be such a useful concept in relation to those who took part in either Ottoman or British administrations, or even in connection with Greek women who may have married officials from the occupying or "protecting" powers. On the other hand, when we read about the actions of Athanasios Vaghias, of Suliot traitors like Pilio Gousses (Pelios Gousis/Pylio Gusi) and Koutsonikas, of George and Kitsos Botzaris, of the actions of Ignatius, Archbishop of Arta, or of the great wealth acquired by someone like Signor Alessio, and his status—almost like a sovereign or pasha over the villages of the Zagori—we have to ask ourselves where the borderline lay. It is a grey area. Kyra Vassiliki, the Greek slave brought up in the serai, became one of Ali Pasha's wives in 1816, and was considered charitable and kind. According to the Reverend Hughes her kind disposition was "frequently shown in mitigating the severities of her lordly lover over his subjects".

Kirkwall (1864) writes that Sir Thomas Maitland appointed his friend, Baron Theotoki, President of the Primary Council. "This Ionian, an amiable man, and a pleasing author, had been the object of much obloquy for the manner in which he supported the English Protectorate in the Islands." As Brian Dicks writes (1977), "The Senate was headed by a president, appointed by the British sovereign on the recommendation of the High Commissioner. He was drawn from the ranks of the Ionian nobles, bore the title 'Highness', and was received with full military honours. The president was the most important person in the Ionian State after the High Commissioner... the first president was Baron Emanuel Theotokis, a member of a famous Corfiote family and a firm friend of Britain."

The Zantiot composer Paolo Carrer wrote a four-act opera *I kyra Frosini*, based on the libretto of 1868 by Elisabetios Martinengos, itself inspired by Valaoritis' poem "Kyra Frosini"; in the current CD booklet of the opera, Nikias Lountzis contributes an essay called "An Enchantress from Jannina", in which he asks whether Frosini was "An Adultress and Collaborationist or a Symbol of Virtue?" He says, "I do not know what induced the people of Jannina first, and then the enslaved Greek nation in its whole to proclaim an adulteress a martyr. Was it female charm, their hatred for the tyrant or the people's yearning to create a fable that the rest of the world would believe?" Lountzis thinks her death was probably her own fault: "Coarsely insulting her social-historic environment, Phrosyne became an adulteress and she was considered to be a collaborationist because of her passion... It is my belief that the artists who dealt with her were ravished by her dignity rather than her charm."

William Haygarth (1814) and Kostas Palamas (1925) saw things differently, as did the creator of the folksong "The Drowning of Kyra Frosini" (c. 1801):

> Have you heard what happened at the Lake of Ioannina,
> How they drowned the leading ladies, and Kyra Frosini?

Haygarth thought only of her doomed innocence, artless nature and tragic fate, addressing her spirit as "O hapless Fair!" C. Santas (1976) suggests that to Palamas she symbolized *the Greek soul*. He quotes Palamas: "Like the national soul, fallen, sinful, she does not begin to have a clear understanding of her lofty destiny until she is enslaved."

The concept of "collaboration" seems to have acquired greater significance in the context of the Italian and German occupations of the Second

Memorial to the Battle of Kalpaki, 1940

World War. C. M. Woodhouse (1948) wrote of minor collaborators like the Chams, and the Vlach "Legionaries" established by the Italians in 1941 to strengthen their sense of kinship and identity with the Romanians. The idea was to create a semi-autonomous Vlach state, according to Woodhouse, but the experiment was a failure and was abandoned in 1943.

Women, especially prostitutes, who were known to have consorted with German or Italian soldiers during the Second World War risked the fate and public humiliation of having their hair shorn off after Liberation, and of being paraded in the streets. In Corfu, three women who had become known as "The Three Graces" had to be winched secretly on board a departing boat bound for Italy.

Even in Corfu, at the end of the war, there were some summary executions of alleged collaborators, some by "hit squads" from the mainland, without any hearings or trials. Collaborators with the Italians who were tried and sentenced to prison included a fanatically pro-Italian journalist who was later buried in the Catholic cemetery, and a compromised interpreter. Songs were sometimes made up by the people to pour scorn on "arse-lickers", scoundrels and collaborators, or on women who entertained Italian and German officers, such as:

A blackbird which never could fly very high,
Knew how to crawl, to eat, lick and lie.

Another one, in Greek, about a non-Greek woman who was a generous hostess, won admiration for her ample backside:

Zito o Zervas, zito o stolos,
Zito kai tis V——as o kolos.
(Long live Zervas! Three cheers for the fleet!
Hurrah for V——as' arse, they say is so sweet!)

In February 1942 Ioannis Capodistrias, who was a descendant of George Capodistrias, the brother of Count John Capodistrias (1776-1831, the Corfiot-born first Governor of liberated Greece, assassinated at Nafplion, whose tomb can be seen at Platytera Monastery), was appointed as Prefect (Nomarch) by the Italian occupiers in the Second World War, and later was tried and sentenced to five and a half years in prison for collaboration (he was lucky to escape a sentence of execution; he died a very poor man in 1959). He had not helped his cause by making a speech in praise of Mussolini, pandering to the Fascists and welcoming the possibility that Corfu should become part of the Kingdom of Italy. The Italians occupied Corfu from April 1941 to September 1943, although their intention was probably to place the Ionian Islands firmly under their influence rather than to incorporate them into the 'new Italian Empire' (Enessee argues that the plan was, indeed, to incorporate them).

A black armband appeared on the statue of Count John Capodistrias the day after his namesake's appointment as Nomarch. Count John himself had initially supported and approved the British Protectorate (his letter to Lord Castlereagh of 2 September 1815, and the treaty of 5 November 1815), but this was a different matter altogether. There has been further controversy over the roles of the Mayor, Nomarch and Chief of Police during the German occupation, at the time that Corfu's Jews were deported, and about the proclamation signed by them on 9 June 1944.

The novel *Blood Libel* ("I Sikofantia tou aimatos") by Vasilis Boutos caused great controversy in Corfu, because it dealt, in fictional form, with the deportation of the Jewish community of Corfu in 1944, and with the role of the Mayor of Corfu at the time. In Ioannina, the role of the Greek gendarmerie in assisting the Nazis with the removal by lorry of the Jewish population in March 1944 (1,725 people sent to Auschwitz) has been discussed by German historian Christoph Schminck-Gustavus (2008).

The British can be grateful they were spared the shame, the bitter and divisive experience of occupation during the Second World War (apart from the Channel Islands, which had a comparable history to that of Corfu).

PROVINCIAL DESPAIR, PROVINCIAL PRIDE

The poet Kostas Karyotakis committed suicide in Prevesa in July 1928, shooting himself at a beach called Aghios Spyridon (he had already tried to drown himself in the sea at Monolithi), as a result, apparently, of his dislike of the government of the day, and because certain confidential papers had been leaked to an opposition paper, causing him to be transferred to Prevesa. He hated the prospect of the posting in that then dull provincial town and was waiting in vain for the transfer to be repealed (he was there for less than a month when he took his own life). He had served as general secretary of the union of the Ministry of Public Welfare; there was much friction and disagreement with his superior at the Ministry, who was prone to castigate him, and Karyotakis must have felt oppressed and depressed. For most of his life he had moved around from one provincial city to another, initially accompanying his frequently transferred father, a civil engineer with the Ministry of Public Works. A poem of 1927, "*Thelo na figo pia apo dho*", expresses the desire to move away to a new, unrecognized place, to become like gold dust in the atmosphere, a simple, free element. He achieved his wish.

Karyotakis also wrote a poem called "Ideal Suicides", which is about the contemplation and postponement of suicide. In his poem "Sleep", he had also seemed to express a death-wish:

> Will we be granted that gift, that fate,
> To disappear and die one night
> On the green shore of our native country?

David Ricks (2003) writes that the whole of Karyotakis' last collection is in effect a suicide note, but notes that the poet's suicide has given Prevesa an undeserved notoriety.

In a piece of prose anthologized in a Greek high school reader ("Katharsis"—"Purification" or "Atonement"), and assumed by the editors to have been written in Prevesa, Karyotakis writes of his life in the provinces, and of the people who oppressed him: "Scoundrels! I feed on the bread of exile. Crows tap on the window of my room. And in the tortured breasts of peasants I see the spirit gaining in strength, a breath of wind which will increase in force to sweep you away."

Robert Liddell (1965) comments that the poem "Prevesa" is popular as a hideous picture of provincial life, but admits he likes the place.

Leake considered Prevyza (*sic*) "one of the best towns in Greece", in spite of its drawbacks and poor housing; he liked the abundant gardens containing fig, walnut and apricot trees, as well as the olive plantations. Karyotakis wrote a charming, happy nature poem about an orange tree, which might well have been written in the vicinity of the orange groves around Prevesa. Pouqueville (1820-22) wrote enthusiastically about the town as it was under the Venetians, with its orchards and extremely clean houses, its fertile soil, a safe haven for tens of thousands of Greeks who remained free in that corner of Epirus. After Ali Pasha attacked it, it was soon inhabited by Albanians, to whom Ali distributed the houses, the furniture and the fields of the former Greek owners.

Everybody I spoke to in Prevesa during a two-day visit in March 2008 agreed that the town has become an attractive place to live and has developed out of all recognition in the last fifteen years. Old editions of the *Blue Guide* describe the town as "unprepossessing", but in my opinion anyone would be delighted to work or holiday there nowadays; in many ways it is an ideal location. It even boasts a statue of Karyotakis, and you can look at the house where he lived so briefly, in the centre of the old part of town. The present Nomarch (Prefect) is proud of the town's association with Karyotakis, in spite of the poet's less than positive attitude towards the "Kirios Nomarchis" (I wish the translators had kept to that sarcastically-respectful designation) and other civil servants and local officials of his day. He clearly found it a stifling place to live at the time, with its army garrison and with little to do on a Sunday but go and listen to the band or stroll along the quay and look at the ships.

The poem "Prevesa" has become even better-known since it was so expressively set to music by Dimos Moutsis ("I Preveza", sung by Christos Lettonos, on the album *Tetralogia*). It has been translated by Kimon Friar, Rachel Hades and others. Here is a verse from a new translation by Keith Taylor and William Reader:

> Walking slowly on the wharf you say,
> "Do I exist?" and then, "You do not exist!"
> The ship arrives, raised flag.
> Perhaps His Honour the Governor is coming…

In that poem Karyotakis did for Prevesa what one of his masters, Baudelaire, did for the island of Kythira.

UNIFICATION AND COMMUNICATION

How did mainland Greeks see the incorporation of the Ionian Islands into the Greek State in 1864? It "enriched the country's upper strata with…a petty and impoverished aristocracy" (J. Koliopoulos and T. Veremis, 2003). One thinks of the Karaghiozis shadow-theatre character, Sior Nionios. William Miller (1905) suggests that "The Corfiotes, and the Ionians generally, resemble the Italians more than the Greeks in many ways. They cling to their Venetian titles, they have more aristocratic ideas and more Western polish, and they are not regarded with universal favour by the men of 'old' Greece, who apply uncomplimentary names to them."

Theodoros Kolokotronis' memoirs (1846) suggested that "it was not until our rising that all the Greeks were brought into communication. There were men who knew of no place beyond a mile of their own locality." Men living in villages on the mainland "thought of Zante as we now speak of the most distant parts of the world. America appears to us as Zante appeared to them. They said it was in France..."

This simply is not true, according to Thomas W. Gallant (2001). While I agree with Professor Gallant that it is true that many villagers were not as isolated as Kolokotronis suggests—they would indeed travel to panigyris, weddings, market towns, and often had occupations that involved travelling around; they may have been transhumant Sarakatsani shepherds or members of Vlach caravans (not to mention the painters, doctors and men of the Zagori who would travel far afield to earn their living)—yet the average villager would not often venture much further than an hour or two from his or her home.

Christos Christovasilis wrote a short story called "Koutsoyannis in Ioannina" (1898), which describes in a vivid, amusing way the visit of a shepherd down from the mountains for the first time in his life, exploring the big town during the period of the Turkokratia. He wants to buy a flute, but is awestruck by the size of the bazaar and by all the goods on display. Having lost his cousin Kostas along the way, he is delighted to find friendly faces happy to serve him many endless courses of food in a *khan* (hostelry), not realizing that he is expected *to pay* for what he has eaten. (An almost ruined *khan*, which could and should be restored as a modern hostelry in the old style, is still standing—just—in the centre of Ioannina.)

If Ioannina seemed such a remote place to a shepherd who lived a mere six-hour jouney away, the "Frank Islands" might have seemed very remote indeed to many a mainland Greek at the time of Kolokotronis, although he himself had spent time in Corfu, Lefkas and Zakynthos. Kolokotronis says that at the end of 1820 he spent eighty days with Capodistrias in Corfu. In 1821, according to Kirkwall, Kolokotronis, "who in 1806 had taken refuge in the Ionian Islands, left Zante to join the outbreak on the continent".

Chapter Six

FROM ISLAND TO MAINLAND, CORFU
TO EPIRUS

Zagori, Epirus

MAINLAND VS. ISLANDS

Nowadays, because of the impact of tourism, we tend to imagine the
Ionian Islands and the mainland coasts of Epirus (and Aetolia-Acarnania)
as separate entities, but for Aristotle Valaoritis, whose father was an Epirot,
the mainland was only a stone's throw away, and he often went to Acarnania. We have to remember that, for him, much inspired by national
events, the events of Suli especially had happened in a geographically close
region. We sometimes forget that Lefkas is virtually a part of the mainland
(to which it was once joined before an artificial channel was dug between
the two by the Corinthians), and that the other islands are bound to their
mainland ports more than they are to each other. Paxos may look to Corfu,
but it is close to Parga too. Corfu is inextricably linked to Igoumenitsa, as
Zakynthos is to Killini (and to Patras, like Kefalonia). Solomos was very
aware of the proximity of Missolonghi.

Trying to travel from one island capital to another can, at times, be either expensive, inconvenient or complicated, e.g. from Corfu to Zakynthos, let alone from Corfu to Kythira (no longer in the Region of the Ionian Islands, but administered from Piraeus). If the Athens central government, or indeed the regional government, cared more about inter-island communications, especially during the winter months, they might have ensured better communications (e.g. from Paxos to Corfu). In the old days regular government steamboats connected all the islands and helped to maintain a sense of regional and cultural identity. Air travel via Athens is not the same thing, although a vital service. One doubts whether the situation will improve when all the Ionian Islands are administered by a single Nomarch, or Prefecture, as it is planned for the future.

The regional budget for the Ionian Islands gives much higher priority to the development of the road network than to sea links, but one may question if this is the right priority for a European Region which consists of thirteen inhabited islands and 32 islands in all. (The extent of the region is 2,307 square kilometres and the total population is around 228,572 inhabitants.)

In 2007 the Region of the Ionian Islands published a handsome book in Greek and English called *History and Culture of the Ionian Islands*, which contains some invaluable essays and illustrations. Some might say that the European Union and Greek regional budgets could have been better spent on improving sea links and communications between the islands, but I believe this substantial book contributes to a sense of regional and cultural identity. The Region of Epirus produced an equally impressive companion volume, *History and Culture of Epirus* (2007). One hopes that they will be made more accessible, in paperback editions.

MAINTAINING THE ENVIRONMENT

Many visitors and those who have chosen to make their home in Greece have expressed their disappointment at the general indifference to the local environment. Gerald Durrell's biographer, David Hughes, quotes him as saying: "Corfu is its coastline, that's all. The visitors don't spend tuppence. They eat in the hotels, they flake and redden on the beach all day, they patronise the town once by buying a couple of postcards. That's their contribution to the economics of the island, otherwise it all goes to tour operators and hotel managers. So Corfu is still poor. And it's ruined. Do you wonder that I'm a conservationist?" Gerald Durrell's comments ring even more true today, when so many tourists stay in all-inclusive hotels, with everything paid for in advance: meals, drinks, excursions and even their ice-creams.

Lawrence and Gerald Durrell (with Rose Moore and Felicity Baxter) wrote a letter to *The Times* on 14 July 1984 headed "Land abuse on a Greek island", expressing great concern for the wild flora of Corfu and opposition to the use of herbicides to suppress growth beneath the olive trees. They thought that this practice was a folly, which threatened to eradicate much of the native flora. "Spraying results in extensive areas of scorched and dying vegetation."

Gerald wrote about the problem again in his 1987 article for the *Sunday Times* magazine series "Impressions in the Sand". His rueful reappraisal of Corfu does not make for comfortable reading. In the 1960s he had been to see the Mayor and a committee was duly formed, but nothing happened and Gerald gave up in 1965. He was particularly opposed to the "indiscriminate spreading of noxious chemicals against the olive fly...killing all the fauna and flora which had been one of Corfu's greatest beauties and interests", as well as the widespread use of DDT which was being "put down on any areas that looked like a swamp or a wetland". More recently, ecologists have opposed the devastating consequences of spraying olive trees from above.

The history of concern about olive cultivation is a long one. Back in 1816, General G. de Vaudoncourt's *Memoirs of the Ionian Islands* said about Corfu that "agriculture is there much neglected, and the olive trees are even abandoned to themselves without being pruned or manured. If the necessary care and attention were paid to these trees, as well as to the preparation of the oil, the quality would not only be infinitely better, but the harvest would also be more abundant."

Dr. John Hennen (1830) commented that "the olive tree, to an English eye, appears grossly neglected; the fruit is not plucked when ripe, but is allowed to fall on the ground, a process which commences generally in October, and often lasts until April. The trees are never regularly pruned nor trenched, and they are so thickly planted, that there must be a considerable deficiency of healthful ventilation."

Kendrick (1822) said much the same. He wrote about the laziness of the peasantry but said that was not the only reason for the neglect. "How many olive trees are there on the island that are never pruned or even manured! Were it otherwise, the harvest would be five-fold to what it is at present."

Professor D. T. Ansted (1863) harped on the same theme: "It is not the custom of the Corfiot to work when he can remain idle, and he has, therefore, left his tree to the accidents of time and weather... The total absence of pruning and training after once grafting, and the habit of only collecting the fruit when quite ripe, and never gathering it as in Italy, have combined to leave the tree to adapt itself to circumstance; and so far as picturesque beauty is concerned, no lover of fine trees can regret that such a course has been pursued."

As Thomas Gallant writes (2002), "With near unanimity the British bemoaned the incorrigible laziness of the Greeks." He quotes Jervis on the typical Corfiot: "Indolent beyond belief, he is satisfied with the food which Providence affords him off the neighbouring olive tree; which he patiently waits to see drop to the ground."

What nobody mentions is that in times of poverty or food shortages, the typical Corfiot is perfectly content with a hunk of bread, some *feta* cheese or an onion and a handful of olives, the small black Corfiot variety, even if it does not make very high grade oil after it has fallen from the tree and been gathered from the now ubiquitous netting on the ground. Neglect and the spraying of pesticides combine to make the cultivation of the olive a problem when tourism has taken over as the main industry of the island.

Maybe it is time now to accept that the olive tree of Corfu is no longer a viable or much-cultivated agricultural asset worthy of European Union financial support. This is not the case in Zakynthos or the other islands. Should it not be admitted that the Corfiot olive plantation has become more of a picturesque natural forest, worth preserving for its intrinsic beauty rather than for its crop? If that is so, it is too late for the seaside olive groves of Barbati.

THE MOUNTAIN LANDSCAPE

Those who find it hard to tolerate environmental damage and tourist developments on the islands can escape to the mountains on the mainland.

One such is Tim Salmon, author of *The Unwritten Places* (1995). He did not warm to the sleazy new cement-built and materialistic Greece to which he had returned in the mid-1970s: "That was one reason for turning to the mountains, long the unassailable bulwark of Greekness and independence, now the very last repository of those more innocent values... I also believe that Greece's salvation and national pace of mind will only be achieved when all that the mountains stand for is repossessed and revalued." For Salmon, who has also written two editions of a walker's guide to the Pindus Mountains, Hellenic identity is connected with the mountains.

C. Santas, in his book on Valaoritis, says that the mountains in poems and folksongs are symbolic of the Greek character. They are the rugged places "where the enslaved Greeks could breathe the air of freedom, where they could rally against the enemy".

The Reverend Hughes maintained that "perhaps there is no part of Greece where its language has been preserved in greater purity than the mountainous districts of Epirus, or where more efforts have been made to restore it than in Ioannina". He was astonished by the novelty and sublimity of the mountain scenery around Suli, in Epirus, with the broken rocky masses, wild precipices and chasms.

William Haygarth was just as struck by the landscape. In Part I of "Greece, A Poem, in Three Parts", 1814 (part of it written in Athens in the winter of 1811), he writes of Nature and of "the wilds of rude magnificence". He, too, is inspired to write of the rugged rocks and fastnesses of Suli and of the Pindus Mountains more generally. He addresses "Eternal nature":

> O let me seek thy haunts upon the brow
> Of Pindus, where thou dwell'st 'midst solitudes
> Of stern sublimity...

There is a beautiful illustration opposite page 11 of the poem, entitled "Summit of Mt. Pindus". Haygarth describes the scene as one to exalt the mind to serious joys and solemn meditation. "Nature here...calls the sons of Virtue." The concepts of "virtue in the mountains", and the suitably of the environment for meditation, have not escaped many writers: "Virtue is in the mountains, in the stony villages", as Peter Levi wrote in one of his poems, "In Memory of George Seferis, 3". Haygarth was deeply affected by the landscape of the Pindus Mountains:

The passage of the Pindus presents some of the grandest scenery that is to be met with in Greece... The general style of its scenery is sublimity... The savage grandeur of mountain districts appears to have been always selected by the Greeks for the residence of those deities which preside over the powers of the imagination. On Helicon, on Parnassus, and on Pindus, they placed the abodes of the Muses... the prominent features of that district of Epirus in which the entrance to the infernal region was placed, are particularly calculated to overwhelm the imagination with the terrors which it was necessary to excite. With equal felicity the Muses are described as dwelling in silence and retirement amidst the sublime scenes of Pindus.

Kostas Krystallis (1868-94) was one of the famous Epirot poets (like George Zalokostas, from Sirako, in the Tsoumerka, which Hammond says was largely Vlach in speech, although it was "seldom heard" by the time McNeil was there) who yearned to fly like an eagle up to the mountains:

Every evening, every dawn, I want the cold wind
To come from the gorge, like a mother, like a brother,
To caress my hair and my broad, bared chest...
I want to walk beside precipices, along ridges, high peaks...
(from "To a Golden Eagle", my translation).

In his prose works Krystallis wrote extensively about the Vlachs, about the Pindus Mountains, about Samarina and Malakasi.

THE VLACHS OF METSOVO AND PINDUS

According to A. J. Wace and M. S. Thompson (1914), Sirako was once spelt *Siraku*, and Kallarites *Kalarl'i*. They also point out that when the new Greek–Turkish frontier was established in 1881, it followed the line of the river, and that Kallarites remained Greek while Sirako remained Turkish.

I visited Sirako and Kallarites in February 2008, when the cold north wind was blowing and the snow had fallen higher up (as in a well-known Zalokosta poem), and found them both extraordinarily beautiful villages of stone houses and mansions climbing one above the other, similar to those in the Zagori, set among the snow-capped peaks of the Tsoumerka mountain range; but not a soul was in sight, midweek, and every stone

Restoration on Bridge of Plaka

house was closed. Sirako feels a lot higher than its 1150 metre altitude. I would also recommend the journey and the sights in the neighbouring countryside, such as the Kipina Monastery at Christi and the elegant Bridge of Plaka over the Arachtus River (of historical interest because the river marked the boundary between Turkey and Greece 1881-1913, and the customs house is where the Plaka Agreement, a temporary truce or armistice agreement between rival Greek guerrilla groups, was negotiated and signed on 29 February 1944). Extensive restoration work is being carried out at these and other sites.

Leake (1835) describes his visit to the two impressive Vlach villages: "At Kalarytes all the men speak Greek, and many of the women; but the Wlakh is the common language both in the towns and among the shepherds."

Of the Vlachs of Metsovo, Edward Lear writes (1851):

In general their employment is that of shepherds, and as such they move with their flocks from district to district. But in certain parts of the mountains settled colonies of them exist, who possess large flocks of sheep and goats, and are distinguished for their industrious and quiet habits of life. Many of the men emigrate as labourers, artisans, etc., to Germany, Hungary, Russia, etc., and return only in the summer to their families. They retain their language.

A folksong collected in the Zagori (P. Aravantinos, 1996) is the lament of a virtually abandoned wife who has been married, by her family, to a Vlach:

> Mother, why did you give me in marriage to a Vlach?
> Twelve years he was away in Vlachia, and just three nights at home.

She wakes up during the third night, a sad and bitter night, two hours before dawn, but finds her husband gone. She laments on her empty bed that her master has left them and gone on his travels "into the lonely wilds of Vlachia, to black Bucharest".

One of the most stirring folksongs to be heard in Northern Greece is a song about the Vlach village of Samarina, perhaps the highest village in Greece, situated in the Pindus Mountains. Although located geographically in Macedonia, the song which has made it famous, "*Ta Paidia tis Samarinas*", is also part of the repertoire of most Epirot music groups which feature the *klarino*, the folk-clarinet. According to Tim Salmon, the song is about the warriors the village sent to help the besieged at Missolonghi in 1826. The village is the subject both of Wace and Thompson's book (1914), and of a publication by the Cultural Association of Samarina (2007), containing many previously unpublished photographs from the Wace and Thompson archives.

The Missolonghi connection is implied by the words about *doufekia* (long rifles or muskets). Various versions of the song exist, but this is my translation of one version from Epirus; my favourite recorded version is sung by Siatras.

> Listen all you brave young klefts, you poor lads of Samarina,
> When you go up to the mountains below Samarina,
> Don't fire your guns, don't start singing songs!
> (Even though you're stained with blood, lads);
> And if my mother asks you, or my poor wretched sister,

Don't say that I got killed, don't tell them that I'm dead!
Tell them that I got married, that I'm hitched for life-
A stone slab for a mother-in-law, the black earth as my wife...

William Haygarth (1814) describes the setting of Metsovo as "very striking, spreading down the side of a hill, and completely surrounded by mountains, amongst which the summit of Pindus forms the principal feature. It contains about a hundred houses, and is inhabited almost entirely by Greek merchants, who make long journeys to Russia, and other parts, to procure and dispose of merchandise."

G. F. Bowen (1852) depicts Metsovo in November 1849. On the opposite side of the *khan* where he lodged "rise clustered on little terraces, and interspersed with rocks and beds of torrents, the houses, somewhere about a thousand in number, of the large Wallachian village of Metzovo. To a fanciful imagination, they might seem as if they had been suddenly arrested in hurrying down the steep face of the mountain, and fixed, as if by magic, in the whimsical arrangement which they now present."

J. R. McNeil (1992) writes about the historic heart of Vlach culture in the Pindus and about notable villages like Sirako, Kallarites, and Pramanda. "Sirako is...a classic shell village... The government is building a road that approaches Kallarites from the south, progressing slowly through difficult terrain. By the time it is finished there may well be no one left... These Pindus villages are typical of scores more in their depopulation... They are shell villages, soon to be ghost towns, as the elder generation dies off. Their children are less likely to return to the Pindus for their golden years, and so further rapid population decrease is almost certain." Later he concludes, emphatically, "In the Pindus the dance is over."

McNeil also mentions that the Turks burned Sirako and Kallarites after destroying Ali Pasha's authority. There is a folksong about the burning of Sirako in June 1821 (again quoted by P. Aravantinos). Then it was burned again, by the Germans, in 1944. The folksong about 1821 says that that the Vlachs may have abandoned Sirako, but ends on a note of confidence and certainty that they will return: "When the weather changes, they'll build new homes, they will build new churches, new monasteries."

Wace and Thompson (1914) suggest that the Greek–Turkish frontier established in 1881 "caused a further decline in prosperity as it interfered with such trade as still remained. Many families from both villages have now settled in various towns of Greece, and have severed all connection with their former homes." When Pouqueville visited Kallarites in the early nineteenth century, there was considerable trade with other parts of Europe and many wealthy merchants lived there (there were 580 Vlach families in 1815). The well-travelled Vlachs spoke a number of foreign languages, and had good libraries with many books in French and Italian, as well as the Greek classics. Pouqueville admired how tidy and house-proud the Vlach families were in these remote mountain villages, like eagles' nests. Their way of life was very different from that of the Suliots.

The Mountains of Suli

Claude Fauriel (1824) suggests that one day the Suliots could return to their unapproachable mountains to live there again, but why should they choose to go back there, he asks, since the whole of Greece will be free? Spiros Katsaros argues (1984) that the Suliots were much better off in Corfu, anyway. To the Corfiots, he suggests, in the period 1804-14, the Suliots were simply armed Albanian refugees, who were displacing them from their properties. There were 3-4,000 of them, foreigners requiring to be housed at short notice, prepared to squat illegally whenever necessary, needing to be taught Greek, and how to behave in a "civilized" way, the Corfiot journalist and historian argues. They were gradually transformed into "proper Corfiots", they slowly adjusted and were assimilated, and no longer wanted to return to their mountain villages in Epirus, which had so few creature comforts or facilities; their descendants may not even know that their relatively recent roots were in the Suliot villages. That is not the myth of the Suliots that the school textbooks started to teach after the War of Independence, says Katsaros. In the official history books, the Suliots are forever gazing nostalgically across the sea to their Epirot mountain homes. On these questions Katsaros is at odds with another Corfiot writer about the Suliots (himself of Suliot origins), D. Karamoutsos.

It remains my ambition to explore in more depth the mountains and traces of the famed villages of Suli. Bowen achieved that aim (1852). "We rested for some time among the dismantled homesteads of the Suliotes... The walls of their houses are still partly standing; the boughs of their fig-trees, now run wild, are still hanging over the doors; their hearths are still black with the smoke of former fires; crumbling stairs still point the way to fallen chambers. But no one now dwells in the houses, or prunes the fig-trees, or sits by the hearths, or climbs the stairs."

Unfortunately there are many mountain villages in Epirus where such descriptions still hold true, as well as in Kefalonia after the earthquakes.

MOUNTAIN CULTURE

I feel confident that the dance is *not* over in the Pindus Mountains generally. Houses are being restored in many areas, new homes are being built. New life will return one day, thanks in part to the financial assistance of the European Union and to the availability of Albanian stonemasons.

McNeil's table of the changing population numbers for Sirako shows considerable variations between 1805 (2,790) and 1951 (just 47). The highest numbers were in 1812 (3,500) and the 1890s (3,500). Kallarites had 2,650 in 1820, but 640 by 1853. Pouqueville records that Kallarites had 580 Vlach families in 1815.

McNeil provides a serious, realistic and depressing assessment of village abandonments and future population prospects. Yet why do these villages look so beautiful, prosperous and attractive now, even when deserted of people, on a cold day?

Have things changed since Professor McNeil visited them? There is now, as I have said, much evidence of newly-built guest houses, of other building and restoration work, at least partly funded by the European Union (60% grants are not uncommon). They may be destined to become summer resorts and weekend retreats during the winter, but the people are still proud of their culture and their built environment, even if they prefer to spend most of their time in cities like Ioannina and Athens. I would count these villages among the most beautiful locations in Greece (although even here, high in the mountains, there are signs of environmental problems).

Some people love the poems of Krystallis, influenced as they are by the demotic song. His short poem "I wish I were a shepherd" ("The summer in the mountains and the winter in the plains", playing on his flute) is popular in Greek school anthologies, as is "To a Golden Eagle". His article about "Easter in the Pindus" (1892) could not be improved upon as a lyrical description of the importance of Easter, after the melting of the snows, the reawakening of nature and the mountains, the joyful time of the return from foreign countries for the *xenetismeni* (seasonally expatriated or self-exiled) men to their wives and families. The Reverend Hughes failed to share the spirit of Greek Easter when he was in Ioannina on Easter Sunday 1815, and he calls the raising up of the wooden image of Christ in the churches "a solemn piece of mummery". He had little patience for the "long continuous exclamations" of "Christos Anesti", "Christ is Risen", and "It is True that Christ is Risen".

If many Epirots share the sentiments of Krystallis, others empathize with Dimitrios Sarros and his unbounded love for his native village, in this case Vitsa:

> I swear to you, I make a solemn oath:
> If they told me to exchange my village
> For a royal kingdom, I'd never do it.

In another poem he expresses the nostalgia of those Greeks who lived and worked "like exiles abroad":

> I'll be a shepherd back there, where I really belong
> I'll get a thousand-odd sheep and five hundred goats.

Mountain culture could slowly revive in Greece. I prefer to be optimistic. People are investing in that vision. Who does not feel a sense of wonder when coming across a lone shepherd or goatherd in his heavy black *cappa* and carrying his *glitsa* (crook), looking after his herd of sheep or goats with their well-tuned bells?

The shepherd's or goatherd's "symphony of bells" is one of the most wonderful sounds in the world, but Lt. Col. Napier (1825) blamed the keeping of goats for the greatest ills on the island of Kefalonia: "Thousands of goats prevent the growth of every thing like a plantation, and, what is worse, are the cause of more litigation, ill blood, crime, and idleness, than any other source of mischief in the island: neither vineyards, fields, nor gardens, can escape the devastations of these animals... I will say, that no measure of government would do so much good to this island, or be more welcome, than a tax upon goats, which would gradually clear it of this curse." One can imagine the cultural conflict that arose from views like that, almost as great as the more recent arguments about the preservation and protection of breeding sea-turtles on Zakynthos.

We may not aspire to become shepherds or goatherds, but we can certainly recharge our batteries and benefit from a closer communion with Nature. As Christophoros Milionis writes in his introduction to Nikos Desyllas's beautiful photographic book on *Epirus*, "What really remains intact is Epirus' nature, with its inexhaustible variety and its strong colours."

While making allowances for local pride and poetic embellishment, the fact is that as European countries become more crowded and over-populated, wild, empty spaces and mountainous areas will become more attractive to ecologically and environmentally minded people, quite apart from dedicated mountain-trekkers and river-rafters, as well as to hunters, unfortunately, who have a powerful union and political lobby.

For lovers of literary associations, there are evocative descriptions of Kallarites' mountain landscape in the David Morier novel *Photo the Souliote*: "Whoever has seen an eagle's nest perched on the crags of the high rocks, may form an idea of the situation of Kalarytes, as viewed from the opposite side of the deep ravine, on the upper brink of which its houses seem to grow out of their rocky foundations." He describes the stone walls of the houses, "consisting of the splinters of rock, the scrapings, as it were, of the natural foundation, laid upon each other without any cement, but a little mud, and covered over with a roof of the same rough material". He tells of the making of an "enormous pyta, or flat pie, not quite a yard in diameter". (Little has changed.) He also gives us a vivid impression of dancing in the village square, with its gigantic oriental plane tree spreading its shade "to the very edge of the woody precipice which formed its boundary on the other side". The dancers, holding each other by the hand, circled round "led by the chief cutter of capers, flourishing the embroidered handkerchief, and displaying all the grace and agility usually exerted on these occasions".

That is the sort of scene which would draw tears to the eyes of the Epirot men obliged to make their living in foreign countries. The nineteenth century was as much a period of *xeniteia* as the twentieth, although the countries where Epirot men went to work tended to be different. The landscape of their imagination remained the native village or mountain range. Even for those contemporary Greeks who have settled in big Greek cities, the pull of the village is strong, especially in August.

Some people still manage to "find themselves", to discover their own true identities, on Greek mountains or islands, or sailing the high seas, such as the aforementioned poet and seaman Nikos Kavadias, whose parents came from Kefalonia.

One Corfiot poet of distinction, Lorentzos Mavilis, who was born in 1860 in Ithaca, lost his life in action at Driskos, above the Lake of Ioannina, dying from bullet wounds at St. Paraskevi, in the struggle to liberate Epirus from the Turks in 1912. There are statues in his honour both in Corfu and in Ioannina. As he wrote in his most famours sonnet, "Lethe", if we must weep, we should weep and lament for the living, who want to forget, but who can never do so. He seems to have suffered the same fate as his English friend and Philhellene Clement Harris (1871-97), who was in Corfu when he decided it was his duty to volunteer to fight in the 1897 war against the Turks. He enlisted in the Hellenic army at Arta, Epirus. His unit fell under heavy fire and he was killed at Pentepigadia, in April 1897. Mavilis addressed a sonnet to Harris, "a poet and martyr", sent to the Elysian Fields and a hero's death, felled by a Turkish bullet. Harris wrote in his journal on 15 April 1897 that his enlistment was "not an act of madness, but the least a man of honour could perform towards a country crying for liberty in the name of the Cross". If there is no statue dedicated to Clement Harris in Corfu or Epirus, there ought to be one, although Woodhouse (1968) writes that the war declared on Turkey in April 1897 and later developments were a "disastrous failure" which ended in "humiliating defeat…the intervention of the powers was needed to rescue the Greeks from the consequences of their own folly".

At least one Englishman could see a funny side to Greek expansionist aims. A. D. Godley, the classicist and humorous poet, included the poem "Graeculus Esuriens" in his *Lyra Frivola* (1899). The Greek Navy, following good British practice and precedence in the Ionian Islands and elsewhere, annexes the Isle of Wight, after the Greek Admiral has despatched an ultimatum to the Prime Minister:

With Hellas (Freedom's chosen land) we purpose to unite
Some part of those dependencies—let's say the Isle of Wight.

His poems provided humorous moments and relief for readers and fellow classicists at the end of the nineteenth century.

In the case of another, far less frivolous British writer, we return to

Tim Salmon (1995) for descriptions of the Vlach shepherds of the northern Pindus Mountains and Samarina (in Macedonia) who fascinated him and provided some almost Zen-like moments: "Alone on my mountaintop I hunkered down out of the wind and ate my bread and cheese... I listened to...the thousand tiny noises that make up silence. I thought no thoughts. In fact I think I was hardly conscious of myself as a separate, differentiated, centre of consciousness... I felt complete and at one with my surroundings, content just to be: a kind of peace that is vouchsafed me, at least, only in the mountains and only when I'm alone." As night falls he hears the sounds of a flock returning, "The tremolo of sheep bells mellifluous and fluid as running water over the drumming of the big bass bells worn by the billy goats and the tinkling soprano of the brass bells worn by the nannies."

The aggressive shepherds' flocks guard dogs could frighten him as much as any less experienced mountain-walkers or trekkers faced with the ferocious Molossian breed of mastiff once used for military purposes. (The ancient breed is said to be extinct, but I'm not so sure.) It was far from all peace and lonely meditation in the mountains, as Salmon participated in the Vlach *dhiáva* journey from the mountains to the plains.

A couple who abandoned Corfu for the Pindus Mountains are Roy and Effie Hounsell, who settled in 1991 in one of the Zagori villages called Koukouli. In their book *The Papas and the Englishman, From Corfu to Zagoria* (2007), they do an excellent job of describing local customs and characters, hikes in the Vikos Gorge and up to the Dragon Lake, rebuilding a house and their small adjoining guest-house in Koukouli, the village where they live year-round, and they make a persuasive case for settling in the Epirot mountains rather than on one of the more over-developed Ionian Islands. Few have been brave enough to follow their example, because of the cold winters and snowfalls. They spent eight happy years at Paleomagazia in Corfu, but "The distant BOOM of a disco shattered the illusion... Corfu had sold its soul to cheap tourism. The time had come to leave."

Roy describes the Albanians living rough in the village of Koukouli (Zagori), men who had come on foot over the mountains and entered the country illegally, hoping to find work and a better life by doing all sorts of odd jobs and using their skills as stonemasons to repair buildings. Now that many of them can enter Greece legally, they are not so different from the many Brits who work in the black economy in Corfu, helping with building projects of one kind or another.

Do the Epirot mountain villagers make a great distinction between foreign newcomers, be they British, German or Albanian? One wonders what they make of Corfiots. The musical traditions could not be more different than those of Corfu and the Pindus Mountains. The languages they speak, and the vocabularies, are different too, the Corfiot and Epirot accents being far removed from one another. Corfu has many words of Italian origin; the Epirot dialect has many specialized words for the natural features of mountains, for varieties of edible wild *horta* (greens) and of course for the professions of shepherd or goatherd.

In the past the Zagori villagers might have looked at the semi-nomadic or transhumant Sarakatsani shepherds with a degree of suspicion. They used to live in wicker and rush huts or tents. John Campbell and Paddy Leigh Fermor have described their old way of life, before they settled in villages and became part of the mainstream of Greek life. Some of them waxed lyrical about the "sierras of the Zagora, beyond Vitza and

Vikos Gorge

Monodendri where they grazed their flocks in summer" above the Vikos Gorge in Zagori (Zagora is what Leigh Fermor calls the area), "all their eyes lit up like those of the children of Israel at the thought of Canaan… You didn't need wine there—the air made you drunk; and as for the shade, the grass, the trees and the *water*—why the water came gushing out of the living rock as cold as ice, you couldn't drink it it was so cold, and you could drink it by the oka, and feel like a giant. Words failed them."

Words fail me sometimes, too, when I want to describe the Vikos Gorge and the village of Vitsa, which we have known since 1983. The quality of the air and water, the peace and quiet, the trees and vegetation are an environmentalist's dream of the good, natural life. Robert Liddell (1965) describes it as a handsome village on the edge of a precipice.

ZAGORI

Where exactly is Zagori, geographically? Hammond (1967) gives a good definition: "Zagori is the high basin of flysch between the Mitsikeli range on the west and the main Pindus range on the east… Zagori is an exceptionally healthy highland area, which is rich in fruit and in pasture but suffers from a dearth of arable land." Hammond demonstrates that in the Hellenistic period the canton of Zagori, as well as the highland area of Pogoni, belonged to the Molossians, within the frontiers of Molossis. He identifies ancient Bounimae (which worshipped Odysseus as its founder) with Voutsa, or Vounimes, in East Zagori.

In the words of Homer (Teiresius to Odysseus in the underworld, *The Odyssey*, Book 11, tr. S. Butler), "you must take a well-made oar and carry it on and on, till you come to a country where the people have never heard of the sea and do not even mix salt with their food, nor do they know anything about ships, and oars that are as the wings of a ship". It must have seemed strange to Homer to conceive of a people whose imaginative landscape did not encompass the sea and ships.

If Voutsa (Vounimes) was so far from the coast that people had never seen the sea or ships, it is hardly likely to have been the case with the summer inhabitants of the village of Ancient Vitsa, in Central Zagori. The cattle-breeders who lived there in the summer most likely went down to the coastal plains with their herds during the winter, just as the transhumant Sarakatsani shepherds did in more recent times. But they would also have depended on a diet of meat and milk. For more about the excavations and important discoveries at the cemeteries of Ancient Vitsa (between Vitsa and Monodendri), the distinguished archaeologist Dr. Ioulia Vokotopoulou's three-volume *Vitsa, the Cemeteries of a Molossian Settlement* (1986), with a summary in English, is essential in order to make sense of the site. It was a settlement of nomadic stockbreeders, probably from May to September each year, from the ninth century to the fourth century BC, during which period the site was continuously inhabited. It was apparently burned down and then abandoned in the third quarter of the fourth century BC. (In terms of the location and the stone used, the remains, to a casual observer, look very little different to the ruins of houses built in the eighteenth century AD).

The Greek Ministry of Culture's website lists the rich offerings that were found in the graves of the eighth century BC and the Classical period, with many imported bronze vessels. Apart from the settlement itself, around 177 graves were revealed and excavated. "In both cemeteries, men were buried with their armour (iron swords, knives, spear heads and daggers) and women with their jewellery (fibulae and pins, necklaces, rings, hair ornaments). Almost every grave contained two of five vessels."

Elizabeth Longford (1975) describes Byron's and Hobhouse's week-long ride from Zitsa to Tepeleni. Although Byron visited Zitsa (not Vitsa, in the Zagori), Longford describes the typical Epirot mountain scenery she saw for herself at nearby Monodendri and at the edge of the Vikos Gorge:

> Scenery every bit as formidable and glorious as the renowned Ravine of Vicos (only a little way off the travellers' route) opened before them and closed behind their swaying backs, to disclose yet another vista of unscalable crags on which some monastery had nevertheless been miraculously balanced. The now abandoned monastery of Vicos makes an admirable setting in which to remember Byron. The long-silent bell is wakened into eerie life; voices shout "Byron!" across the gorge and Echo makes answer; after rain the river dashing below is a strange pale green, just as Byron and Hobhouse saw the rivers of Epirus, instead of sparkling with the crystal clarity of summer. The scrub oaks in the gorges are lavishly festooned with lichen.

I always remember Byron in this environment. It is truly "Landscape such as Byron loved". Byron and Hobhouse did at least catch sight of the mountains of the Zagori from Zitsa: "Those to the north-east, the hills of Sagori, seem a long ledge of rocks, running nearly from west to east." J. C. Hobhouse (1813), in his "Letter VIII", describes Zitsa in glowing terms: "Perhaps there is not in the world a more romantic prospect than that which is viewed from the summit of the hill."

Byron writes that he "went over the mountains through Zitsa a village with a Greek monastery (where I slept on my return) in the most beautiful Situation (always excepting Cintra in Portugal) I ever beheld" (12 November 1809, to Mrs C. G. Byron). Reading "Canto II" of *Childe Harold's Pilgrimage* and the famous stanza about Zitsa (XLVIII) always gives me pleasure, and I make no apology for quoting some lines here:

> Monastic Zitza! From thy shady brow,
> Thou small but favour'd spot of holy ground!
> Where'er we gaze, around, above, below,
> What rainbow tints, what magic charms are found!

The Reverend Hughes thought Byron's encomium much too lavish and the view inferior to many others in Epirus.

George Bowen describes the white walls of the monastery of Zitsa which "glimmer through the foliage of a grove of aged and gnarled ilices, the sacred tree of Dodona, and crown the summit of an isolated hill… the view from the monastery of Zitsa is very magnificent". The Abbot of the monastery was somewhat suspicious of the travelling "Franks", supposing them to be spies with political objectives, visiting the country before coming to conquer it.

Edward Lear (1851) had greatly looked forward to seeing Byron's "Monastic Zitza", but was caught in a torrential rainstorm and high wind. He felt disappointed by Zitsa on 5 November 1848: "the surrounding scenery, though doubtless full of varied beauty, does not seem to me sufficient to call forth such raptures of admiration, even if selected as a spot where an imaginative poet, reposing quietly after foregone toils and evils, might exaggerate its charms".

I have driven to Zitsa to revisit the Monastery of Prophitis Ilias, where Byron had stayed two hundred years ago in October 1809. An attractive approach is from Vitsa, crossing the main Ioannina–Kalpaki–Konitsa highway at the iron bridge near the turning up to the Central Zagori villages, at the 19 km mark from Ioannina. While I do not think that Byron exaggerated the beauties of the spot as it was in 1809, I would agree that, nowadays at least, there are more remarkable beauty spots in the region, such as Vitsa itself (or other Zagori villages) and Sirako in the Tsoumerka. But he was right to praise the Zitsa wine.

Almost exactly the same sensations and impressions as Byron felt then can be conjured up even today by walking down the path towards the Vikos Gorge from the main square of the village of Vitsa, or the steeper steps down to the gorge from Monodendri.

Robert Liddell (1965), like many other tourists and visitors, thankfully (for the Vitsini) bypassed the more beautiful village of Vitsa, with its many hidden secrets, to go to Monodendri: "The moment of greatest wonder was when I took a short walk alone…and went a few hundred yards behind the village to a spot whence I could see into the stupendous gorge of the Vikos, one side lit by the last rays of the sun. Rocks of such grandeur that they would need no legendary or historical associations, nor call forth other words than *Magnificat anima mea…*"

Theo Angelopoulos, the Greek film director, made viewers feel the rain rushing down the stone paths and *kalderimia* of Epirot villages in his first black and white feature film, *Anaparastasis* (*Reconstruction*, 1970), which was filmed in the villages of Vitsa and Monodendri, and in Ioannina, from November 1969 to February 1970. The film deals with a reconstructed murder case, based on a true-life crime which had in fact occurred in Thesprotia. It opens with a voice-over narration telling us that the village of "Timphaia" had 1,250 inhabitants in the census of 1939, but only 85 in the census of 1965. It comes as a shock to see what a state the village houses and the roads were in at the time of filming. People may complain about the new buildings going up, but most are done with respect to tradition, and the construction of asphalt roads in the 1970s transformed the lives of the villagers, certainly during the heavy rains and snowfalls of winter. At the end of the film, the director strikes a false note by presenting the village women in violent mood, attacking the murderess as she is taken away; this might have seemed plausible in another location (cf. stoning the widow in Cacoyannis' *Zorba the Greek*) but it is not a credible representation of the behaviour of Zagori women. As Angelopoulos writes on his website, *Reconstruction* uses the actual event—a local murder—as a point of departure for a devastating view of something far more important: the death of a village, of a whole world (www.theoangelopoulos.com).

The locations of the film would surely speak to a Southern Albanian audience as much as Ismail Kadaré's novel *Chronicle in Stone* (1971) must speak to readers in the Zagori villages. I visited the town of Gjirokastër (Argyrokastro) in Albania to see the burnt-out shell of Kadaré's childhood home, which I hope will be reconstructed one day. When a fire destroyed four beautiful old houses near the main square of Vitsa on Christmas Day 2007, I thought of the common fate and hardships that people have had to face over the centuries, on both sides of the border, when tragedy struck and sparks leapt out of fireplaces and flames consumed the wooden beams of old stone houses such as these. Nowadays it is likely to be skilled Albanian builders and masons, from towns like Argyrokastro and Berat, who will come to rebuild and restore the Greek houses. The photographic exhibitions (and related publications) held in the beautifully restored building of the Rizarios Foundation Exhibition Centre in Monodendri, Zagori, are of the highest international standard, and it is worth a visit to Monodendri for some of these exhibitions alone.

So much is written about the dramatic landscape of Pindus and Epirus that it is gratifying to find the occasional comment about the *people* (in addition to the Suliots). Davenport (1837) quotes de Vaudoncourt, on the subject of the people of Zagori: "Mild and hospitable, they have preserved the rigorous manners and character of the ancient Greeks... They are not the less brave."

J. C. Hobhouse (1813, "Letter XIV") would seem to agree: "Immediately to the north of Ioannina, the mountains of Sagori are peopled by Greeks, whose villages were long considered independent, and even now rather enjoy the protection than feel the power of the Pasha. The Sagorites, who live on the flat summits of the hills, anciently called Lingon, are most of them petty traders, and their commerce with foreigners has given them a gentleness of manner and disposition to be found in no other inhabitants of Albania."

These are sentiments with which I am happy to concur. J. Koliopoulos and T. Veremis (2002) make the points that it is a misconception to assume that Greek peasants led identical or similar lives in Greece in the past; that their lives varied significantly, depending on whether they were islanders or inlanders, coastal peasants or mountain-dwellers; that there were many other variables, including political or administrative conditions. "Venetian rule in the Ionian Islands had left its mark on the life of the local people; so too had a measure of autonomy and certain immunities granted by the Ottoman overlords to mainland communities like…the Mt. Zagori villages in Epirus."

We do not usually talk about "Mt. Zagori" (or "Zagoria" for that matter; Zagori is an old Slavic, Serbo-Croatian or Bulgarian word that means "Beyond or behind the mountains", and is first recorded in a document referring to this region in 1321, according to Max Vasmer, 1941), but the point is valid. What I am not clear about is when Slavic placenames were introduced in Epirus, specifically in the Zagori. Dr. Pouqueville suggests that it was the *Sclavonians* who introduced the term "Zagori". It seems unlikely that the Slavic-sounding village names (e.g. Tsepelovo, Kapesovo, Vitsa, Dovra, Baya, Tservari—the last three have Greek names now, but the 1823 edition of *The Life of Ali Pacha* contains a map showing Veitza, Dovra, Dzidza) date back to the times of the earliest Slavic descent or incursions into Illyricum (late sixth century AD) or Epirus (seventh century); more likely they were introduced many centuries later, either during the period of Bulgarian incursions, or in the times of Serbian rulers like the Tsar Stephan Dushan (1308-55) or Thomas Preljubović (ruler of Epirus 1366-84), *or* as a result of early sixteenth-century raids. But, as noted, the name Zagori, denoting this region, is first recorded in the fourteenth century (1321), as is the village of Vitsa (*Veïtsa, Vezitsa*), first mentioned in 1319 and 1361. Wace and Thompson (1914) observe that the names of Slavonic origin are common both to the Greek and the Vlach villages, indicating "that there was once a Slavonic domination and probably also settlement in the region concerned".

Ali Pasha lost the support of the people of Zagori when he united the forty villages as "Tchiftliks" under his Vizirship, "for the purpose of forming an inheritance for his third son, Sely Bey… In vain did their chiefs implore, in vain did they represent that they had been proprietors from time immemorial" (Davenport, 1823). In spite of this injustice, the Zagori villages managed to retain a great deal of independence. The district was also much respected because it had "from time immemorial, supplied a considerable part of Turkey with medical practitioners, who are known by

the denomination of Caloiatri, or good physicians". Although their knowledge was largely traditional and empirical, and although ignorant of the
principles of medicine and anatomy, they were widely valued and ac-
knowledged to possess considerable manual dexterity in surgical operations. "It was one of these quacks," writes Davenport, "that Ali selected as
the instrument of his crime." Ali promised him forty purses as a reward for
the destruction of his enemy, Sepher Bey. The cunning doctor carried out
the crime, but on his return to Ioannina he was seized and hanged by
command of Ali, who was anxious to rid himself of such a witness.

I have written about aspects of the history of Vitsa (Zagori) in my
book *Corfu Blues* (2006). After it was published, I became aware of the
fascinating poem, written in Greek, by the Albanian Muslim Hadji Seret,
quoted and translated in part by Leake in his notes on Chapter One of
Travels in Northern Greece. In the poem, Ali Pasha's dying father Vely warns
his dependants, his young son and his protectors against losing the revenue
of forty purses accruing from the district of Zagori, which was to be his
principal inheritance, as the paternal property. After the chiefs, village
headmen or primates of the Zagori submitted to him,

> They went and submitted, and kissed his hand,
> And said, Behold, we have come upon receiving your message.
> We pray, my lord, that you may live,
> And be confirmed in your post, and command us....

Ali later proceeds to Zagori, where men, women and children come out
to meet and adore him, and to "kiss his sock".

Wace and Thompson (1914) also remind us that in Turkish times the
Zagori "was directly dependent on the Vali of Yannina and it was one of
the ancestral dominions of Ali Pasha". It was known as the *kinon* or *vilayet*
of Zagori, and enjoyed many privileges, until they were taken away in
1868.

The Reverend Hughes believes that in Ali's early days he was a leader
of a band of bandits, and that in his capacity of *kleft (klepht)* he so infested
the mountainous district of Zagori that Kourt Pasha took up arms to
defend the country. Ali Pasha once told the Reverend Hughes that when
he was young he had lived upon the mountains in the midst of snows and
exposed to storms, with his *touphéki* on his shoulder and his Albanian

capote, but that he never cared about the cold. In any case, before long the Zagori chiefs switched their allegiances to this rival Pasha (Kurd or Kourt Pasha of Berat), and Ali inflicted a terrible punishment upon the people, according to the poet. Leake warns his readers that "it is important to remember, that as a poet the author uses exaggeration, and that as a Musulman, he regards the Christians as an inferior class, upon whom the treachery and cruelty exercised by his hero are little else than laudable proofs of wisdom and power."

Ali's punishment of the Zagori is as he had forewarned the chiefs:

> From the four quarters he gave them the musket;
> The Rayas were destroyed and dispersed.

This part of history/legend does not feature much in Greek Christian historical narratives, as far as I know. But if the people of Zagori did not feel greatly threatened by Ali Pasha and his Albanian soldiers once they had come to an understanding (Ali succeeded in gaining many adherents among the Greeks of Ioannina and the Zagori), they continued to be troubled by *klefts*, especially after they lost their privileges in 1868, and this situation continued until 1913. On the subject of *klefts*, more generally, it should be explained (cf. George Bowen, 1852) that to be a *kleft*, or robber, was until those times no more considered a disgrace than to be an outlaw in the time of Robin Hood. On the contrary, the *klefts* were "looked upon with favour by the mass of their Christian fellow-countrymen, as their only avengers on their Mahomedan oppressors...in the worst times they kept alive some spirit of the old Greek spirit, and their exploits are the burden of countless popular songs and ballads".

It was not Robert Liddell, or Elizabeth Longford, or Paddy Leigh-Fermor who first inspired me to visit the Zagori or Vitsa, en route from Thessaloniki to Corfu. Although the Murray *Handbook* had already drawn my attention to "the romantic highland district of Zagori", it was another book about mainland Greece, the *Companion Guide* by Brian de Jongh (1979), that persuaded me to visit the region. Had it not been for his excellent guidebook, I would probably never have taken the trouble to make the detour which gave my life something of a new focus, and certainly a new perspective on nature and architecture. About Vitsa (which he spells Vitsi) he writes of "Its well-preserved grey stone houses, roofed with tiles shaped like lozenges, ellipses and polygons, clinging to the mountainside". At Monodendri, near the Monastery of Agia Paraskevi, "an abandoned threshing-floor forms a kind of belvedere". (I have always been enthusiastic about threshing-floors in isolated places.) Further above the village, de Jongh describes the "uninhabited lunar landscape of strange rock formations, like dolmens, weathered into horizontal, parallel and angular folds of such regularity and finish, that one has the impression of gazing at a forest of man-made structures of varying sizes. The feeling of hallucination provoked by this geological phenomenon is haunting."

The rock formation of Oxia is as amazing as the view from the lookout point down into the Vikos Gorge. From the village of Vitsa there is a track, known as the Vitsa Steps, which joins an ancient *kalderimi*, which winds down the wooded mountainside to the Misios stone bridge arching across the (seasonally dry) Vikos branch of the Voidomatis River at the bottom of the Vikos Gorge. When I stand on top of the Misios stone bridge (built in 1748 by the wealthy benefactor Alexios Misios) in the Vikos Gorge, which links the villages of Vitsa and Koukouli, I often wonder if some masterbuilder's wife was also buried in its foundations by the *kioprulides* (bridge-builders) to make it strong.

LOCAL LEGENDS

There is a remarkable Greek short story, "*Ta Magia*", in a collection about Dovra (the old Slavic name of Asprangeloi, Zagori) and about the Vizir's expedition in 1814 to the Dragon Lake (Drakolimni). The story is by the respected poet and prose-writer Frixos Tziovas (b. 1920), and opens his collection *Exodos Yia Panta*. Tziovas served as a teacher both in Dovra, where he was born and went to elementary school, and in Vitsa. Dimitris Hatzis (1913-81) also records another version of the expedition that Ali Pasha made to the Dragon Lake in his short story "*Drakolimni*", in the collection *Thiteia*. According to the legend Hatzis relates, Ali Pasha wanted to know what creature was hidden in the lake, so climbed up alone (but with his trusty guards) taking boats and long ropes which could reach the bottom of the lake. Legend had it that the dragon of the lake, who had lived there since the world was created, protecting the mountain against foreign invaders, got angry, causing a sudden hailstorm, earth tremors and darkening of the skies. The terrified Ali Pasha turned on his heels and took off back down the mountainside. You would be unaware of these stories

Strange geological phenomena in the Vikos Gorge

and legends if you simply climbed up to the Dragon Lake from Mikro Papingo and took a swim amongst the harmless Alpine mountain newts (the real mini-monsters or dragons of the lake).

Studying the collected works of Kostas Krystallis, I found other versions of the legend of the dragons which were said to inhabit not one, but three of the high "dragon-lakes" in the Pindus Mountains. Krystallis relates that Ali Pasha was greedy for money and, after crossing the lake by boat, tried to drain and empty it by creating a hole in the side of the mountain for the water to escape down to the River Aoos, to see if there was any treasure hidden at the bottom of the lake, as the peasants used to say. An enormous hailstorm forced him to abandon the work. Krystallis also tells other folk-legends with mythological dimensions, based on the stories of the local people, concerning dragons and other supernatural creatures. He admires the way the Greek people have developed such a high degree of fantasy and imagination related to the landscape and strange geological phenomena. They did not understand how lakes could be formed near the summits of mountains, and had no idea how deep they were. The dragons

Bridge of Arta

sometimes had animal or human faces, and some were monsters. They fought battles between themselves, spat fire, hurled rocks and trees and shook the mountains.

There has also been a tradition (at least in song and legend) of human sacrifice in many parts of the Balkans, but especially relating to the building of the Bridge of Arta over the Arachtus River. Spiros Mandas (in *The Bridges of Epirus*, 1984) refers to a strange custom that persisted until well into the twentieth century: women who had the misfortune to give birth to a dead child would go to the nearest river and throw one or more *arkoudes* (upright stones set at the edge of the cobbled path across the bridge to protect and mark the sides) into the water from the top of the bridge. This became such a problem in the case of the Misios Bridge, with so many stones removed, that in 1938 they had to be replaced by low walls (*pezouli*).

In relation to the Bridge of Arta, Spiros Mandas suggests that it was Nature's revenge that the victim should be the wife of the masterbuilder, the chief offender against the laws and invincible forces of Nature; he had to be made to suffer, to make a sacrifice for trying to dominate the powers of Nature.

Roderick Beaton (1980) says that versions of the ballad have been collected from all parts of the Greek-speaking world, as well as from Bulgaria, Albania, Serbia, Romania and Hungary. Ismail Kadaré (1987) makes a case that the "mother-version" of the ballad was Albànian. The legend of human sacrifice, he argues, was first associated with the castle of Shkodra. He goes on to suggest the theory that the Legend of Immurement may have travelled south to Greece with the caravans of "barbarian" masons from the north (the Albanian territories) who were apparently employed to build the walls of Greek cities in antiquity, and the ballad is likely to have been the creation of these "mason rhapsodists", he suggests. It is perhaps more likely that they brought the legend and a version of the ballad with them in the fourteenth or fifteenth century AD, when they came down through Epirus on the way to Central and Southern Greece, where many settled and were ultimately assimilated. Philip Ward (*Albania*, 1983) suggests that the ballad was widely established by 527-65 "when the Greek ballad of the bridge of Arta must have been composed", and may be associated with a Homeric or post-Homeric age. The Shkrodra legend of the immurement of Rozafat, or Rosapha, was first related by Barleti in 1504 (Ismail Kadaré, 1987; Pettifer, *Blue Guide Albania*, 1994).

Of all the legends dispersed around the Balkans, this is the one that captured people's imagination, more than any other. Greeks, understandably enough, believe that the ballad spread from their territory to that of other Balkan peoples, Albanians, Bulgarians and Serbs, who then adjusted or adapted it to suit their own circumstances and building structures.

Five and forty masons and sixty sturdy helpers...
All day they build the bridge, all night the bridge crumbles down.
(in Basil Photos' *Epirus and the Epirotic Muse*)

Rennell Rodd's version has the same number of masons and workmen, but Robert Liddell's translation has it as "A thousand masterbuilders toiled to build the bridge of Arta", as in the Greek version ("*To stoichion tis gefyras*") printed in Nugent's *The Ionian Anthology* and in one of the versions in Manousos' collection of songs, *Tragoudia Ethnika*. There are said to be at least 330 versions or variations of the theme of the song in Greece alone.

Passow's version (1860) appears to have been collected in Corfu. *The Ionian Anthology* mentions Fauriel's collection as a source for some other songs published. Manousos includes three versions (Corfu, Kefalonia and Cyprus) and many variant lines. He says the song was well-known up in the Mt. Pantokrator region of Corfu. Introducing it, Manousos says every Corfiot believes that the spirit or shadow of the first person who passes by when the first stone of a new building is being laid remains in the foundation, and that he or she will die within a year. To protect passers-by from death, the people slaughter a lamb at that moment, a black one, or better still a white cockerel. They slaughter it on top of the foundation stone, amid the great rejoicing of the workers, also inserting some coins with the first stone, for good fortune and prosperity. Then the head of the household and the rest of the family get out of the way, because if anyone touches any of that blood, it is said that they will die. Manousos also records that people say the Bridge of Arta shakes when people use it, and that they never cross it carrying musical instruments out of respect for the memory of the unfortunate woman.

Manolis Kalomiris (1883-1962), who was married to the Corfiot Hariklea Papamoschou, and who composed a poignant setting of Mavilis' sonnet "Lethe", also composed the opera-like musical tragedy *The Masterbuilder*, in which he cites *forty* apprentices and *sixty-two* builders in his chorus of gipsy women and builders. Roderick Beaton comments that the folksong concerns a masterbuilder with a varying number of craftsmen and apprentices. In the folksong a bird sings and speaks in a human voice:

> Unless you sacrifice a human, the bridge will never stand.
> But don't sacrifice an orphan, a stranger, or a passer-by,
> Only the chief mason's beautiful wife will do;
> She comes late in the afternoon and brings his supper.

For an authentic feel of the way one version of the traditional folksong was sung, I like the 1930/1931 recording made in Athens by Vasileios Papantoniou.

Apart from the play by Nikos Kazantzakis, there are five other Greek theatrical works based on the theme of the Bridge of Arta, according to

Spiros Mandas. There is also a one-act opera, *The Walled-Up Wife* (2005), by American composer Gilda Lyons, which deals with the theme of immurement or 'foundation sacrifice'.

I feel that it is unlikely that the good people of the Zagori villages would have contemplated such a thing as immurement, or of walling-up a woman (although they were effectively walled-in when their husbands were away working in far-off lands). During the Civil War, worse things may have happened, of course.

Chapter Seven
NEW PERSPECTIVES

Beach on Corfu

THE LEGACY OF THE COLONELS
When Peter Levi (1980) visited Corfu during the period of the Military
Junta around 1970, he found the island "thrilling and disappointing...
The caves and the villages that Lawrence Durrell had made famous were
ruined and vulgarized, Palaiokastritsa was already becoming an insult to
the eye... There are certainly unspoiled corners even in Corfu, but they are
mostly owned by the rich or the eccentric or the very lucky."

By that time "the police governed Corfu very roughly". It had not been
quite so rough when I lived there in 1967-8. Even Peter Levi, when he visited
Greece in 1967, had determined "to keep an open mind about the
Colonels". He soon changed his mind, when evidence of beatings, impris-
onments, repression and torture reached the outside world, through
Amnesty International and other organizations. When he himself was arrested and interrogated about his identity for an hour, he felt frightened and
had visions of spending a night in Corfu prison, "a notoriously evil place".

Corfu prison certainly does not look like a bed of roses. It was particularly bad during the Metaxas Dictatorship and during the late 1940s, as a result of the Civil War. I visited it in October 2007 with the Lazaretto Society. Built by the British, the interior of the octagonal building has been partially modernized and is supposed to be high security. The sight of the isolation holding cell ("Golgotha"), where condemned communists (political prisoners) spent their last night before being transported to the island of Lazaretto for execution, is still a grim reminder of a relatively recent period. At the end of 2008, the Corfiot magazine *Free News* (December) reported that the prison was so overcrowded it was at "Zero Hour", with cells four metres square containing three prisoners each, and the prison (capacity 120) holding 215 inmates. The Corfu MP Nikos Dendias became the Greek Minister of Justice in January 2009; it seemed possible that he would solve the serious problem of overcrowding and bad conditions in Greek prisons, until PASOK won the October 2009 election.

Osbert Lancaster published a poem in 1968, "On Not Going to Greece, Easter 1968". Its last lines could have been applied to Corfu's Pano Spianada (Upper Plateia), or to any other square in Greece:

Christos Anesti! But I would not care
To greet My Lord in Constitution Square.

The Corfiot poet Theotokis Zervos (b. 1943) understands what life was like as a student leader in Thessaloniki in opposition to the Colonels. Arrested as a leading student activist, he belongs to the generation of Greek writers who experienced imprisonment and exile.

The legacy of the Colonels and their investments in tourism is all around us. The landscape of Corfu really began changing for the worse at the time of the Colonels, when supporters of the regime obtained large loans for the development of hotels and tourist resorts. Spiros Plaskovitis describes the mindset well in *The Façade Lady of Corfu*.

Patricia Storace, in *Dinner with Persephone* (1996), visits Corfu at Easter sometime in the 1990s:

We take an ugly road out of Corfu town, past rows of cheap beach hotels and supermarkets flanked by white plastic versions of classical sculpture and billboard cut-outs of slim-waisted men from Minoan frescoes. Next to a half-finished building, amid a pile of iron and concrete rubble, a man turns a lamb on a spit. A wall near him is covered with sprawling graffiti... After fifteen or twenty minutes, the coast becomes the recognizable jewel-like coast whose beauty was perhaps, in the end, a fatal gift to the island. The bays curve like a beautiful woman's cleavage, and are watched by hideous concrete hotels that hover over them like voyeurs.

Was it really so much better before the British built roads in the nineteenth century? John Davy (1842) writes:

> The new roads, where completed as in Corfu, appear to vast advantage, compared with the old: they are, in brief, excellent carriage-roads, made of the best materials; whilst the old ones were bridle-paths, or, if regularly constructed, paved,-the pavement generally out of order, and in many places broken up, totally impractical for wheels; indeed, until the new roads were opened, there was not a single carriage or even cart in use in all the islands.

What bliss, one might think: Corfu without cars or even carts! According to the National Statistical Service of Greece, in the year 2007 (for a total island population of 125,400) there were 45,123 passenger cars circulating with plates registered in the *nomos* of Corfu (not including vehicles circulating with other Greek or foreign plates, and not including the influx of coaches, lorries and cars which arrive by the ferryload from the mainland and from Italy during the tourist season, which greatly increases the number of vehicles circulating on the island), against 11,689 cars registered as in circulation in Kefalonia and 15,221 in Zakynthos. In addition, Corfu can boast 13,377 registered trucks, 365 buses and nearly 24,000 motorcyles/scooters (apart from the abandoned vehicles dumped to rust in the olive groves). The fast car ferries (often moving faster than permitted) create waves which undermine the Old Fortress. In 2008, Helena Smith reported in the *Guardian* that "the island's infrastructure had deteriorated through years of neglect. Its road network—originally built by the British and seen as a feat of engineering—had become pot-holed death traps with more tourists dying on them every year."

The British Protectorate built roads "on the Macadamized plan" (this does not mean they were coated with *Tarmacadam*) and we suffer the consequences. One thing has not changed, however: the pavements are still generally out of order and in many places broken up. Ansted was already complaining in 1863 that "the natives" hardly seemed inclined to keep in repair the roads which the British had built.

Although Corfu airport technically became international in April 1965, it was not until 1972 that the new international passenger facilities were completed, enabling mass tourism, package holidays and charter flights to contribute rapidly to the simultaneous environmental destruction and economic exploitation of the island, the creation of wealth and employment at an unacceptable cost. Two dates are very significant in terms of the history of the development of post-war tourism in Corfu: the opening of the first of Club Med's straw hut villages, in 1952 (a tented version had been tried in Majorca) and the opening of international flight facilities at Corfu Airport in 1972.

An article by Nicholas Tomalin in *The Sunday Times* (1972) records the arrival of "the first really large tourist jetful to arrive at the island. The very first chartered Boeing 707... If it took only three hours to fly over 200 of us there from Gatwick, Corfu must now be readily accessible to all the

Plane landing on Corfu

tourist-producing nations of northern Europe. Within five or ten years it will be swamped." The results are powerfully described in the allegorical novella *The Pimping of Panorea* (*To Poulima tis Panoreas* in Greek) by Maria Strani-Potts.

If the whole island of Corfu seems to resemble a permanent building site nowadays (and has done so for the past 40 years), the town must have seemed like that during—and almost continuously since—the sixteenth century, as Venetian and other military architects worked on improving and strengthening the town's fortifications, defences and vulnerable urban spaces (e.g. as a result of Turkish sieges); this work was gruelling and almost endless, and frequently involved the demolition of houses, stores and existing buildings. The citizens possibly complained as much then as they do now, even if the building works were ultimately for their own protection. It was akin to slave labour. The flattening of hills, the demolition of buildings and the construction of new ports may have had a purpose, but it is seldom appreciated when the work is underway (see Corfu Cultural Society, 1994).

In his introduction to the 1977 edition of *The Traveller's Guide to Corfu*, Martin Young writes about the large number of monstrous hotels that had been built in the previous five years in unspoilt and beautiful corners of Corfu and warns that "unless the new Greek Republic is more concerned than its predecessors with preserving the 'beautiful' and the 'good', it seems certain that in less than a decade it will no longer be possible to recommend this still lovely island to the discriminating few".

But Elizabeth Longford could still write in 1975: "Those who know any of the Ionian Islands will say that it cannot but be the brightest star in the galaxy, so beautiful does it seem: be it Corfu, Levkas, Ithaca, Cephalonia, Zante or another. Those who know them all will nominate them together as the Islands of the Blessed…"

THE END OF RURAL POVERTY?

Would Greek diaspora/expatriate poets use the term "peasant" quite so often as the British and Americans do (in Greek the equivalent but less loaded word is *agrotis*, countryman, although *horiatis*, villager, carries something of the same connotation)? Would they focus on "black-garbed crones", given that the wearing of black is normal and unremarkable for a woman in mourning?

One would expect them to see differently, or to use a fairly matter-of-fact, neutral descriptor; they would not perceive the Orthodox Church as quite so quaint and superstitious as non-Greeks tend to do. In *A Place For Us*, Nicholas Gage describes his mother, Eleni, as an "obedient peasant woman". But he resented, as a young refugee, "the black-kerchiefed *yiayias* (grandmothers) straight from the villages, who attacked me with wet sloppy kisses and pulled my cheeks until they burned". Later, when he was planning to make a return visit to Greece, his sister Olga advised him to beware of "the magic of the village hags", which suggests that some Americanized Greeks did absorb a degree of prejudice.

Dr. Augustinos Sordinas' essay on "Old Olive Mills and Presses on the Island of Corfu, Greece" (1971) describes the unchanging brutalisation, poverty and misery of peasants on Corfu:

> Until the end of World War II life in the traditional Corfu village was stupefying. The average peasant lived in preposterous squalor and a truly stultifying aesthetic and intellectual void. Perennially hungry or underfed...clothed in rags, poorly sheltered, usually malaria-ridden and consumptive and totally illiterate, the normative peasant was motivated by simple deep-seated urges which I can best describe as constant "food-hunger" and "land-hunger". It was a life of constantly unfulfilled wants, chronic malnutrition, and traditional fear of the weather, the usurer, the latifundist or their urban counterpart the oil-dealer. In short, suspicion of humanity and distrust toward everything, nature included. The profound impact of all these syndromes upon the alienated and brutalized peasantry and their effect upon the ethnographic present cannot be exaggerated.

Peasants forced by the Venetians to help build Corfu's fortresses must have been even more brutalized.

One can get some sense of the credibility of this account when reading the short stories of Theotokis (e.g. "*Pistoma!*" or "Face Down!") and of Polylas, as well as the libretto of Spiridion Xyndas' opera *O Ipopsifios* ("The Parliamentary Candidate"), performed in Corfu in 1867. Polylas' story "*Ena mikro lathos*" (1891) describes the poverty of the villagers Maria and Petros, who are constantly in debt, especially if one of their modest harvests fails, if someone in the family falls sick, of if their only son fails to return from military service when expected in time to help in the fields; the hardship they suffer if they have an urgent need to call a doctor, or to visit one in town, a difficult journey of three hours in the blazing heat of the sun. Many poor families spent their life-savings or lost their houses and land paying doctors' bills or buying medicines like quinine, and if misfortune fell, they might also lose the ability to provide dowries for their unmarried daughters.

> "What a wretched life we lead here in the village!" said Maria to herself... In the off year when the olives don't bear fruit, they [our husbands] have to get into debt to feed their families. And it often happens, in payment for all our sins that the southerly wind will spoil the fruit or the cold April winds will shrivel the grapes in their budding. And the usurer will threaten them with imprisonment, so as to make them sign for ten instead of one; twenty, even fifty- oh! Black souls! May they one day have God as litigant.

Dr. Sordinas may be right about the miserable lives led by the Corfiot peasants, but the back-breaking work of collecting the olive crop was often carried out by the thousands of low-paid casual, seasonal, labourers brought over from Epirus, from Chameria, Paramithia, Filiates, Sayiada, Ioannina and other areas, according to Spiros Katsaros. The Paxiots, in turn, would bring over olive-gatherers from Lefkimi. A poor agricultural worker might sometimes be referred by a slighter better-off Corfiot villager as *o doulos mou* ("my slave").

The romanticization and idealization of the peasant, the fisherman, the shepherd, is just as common as its opposite, the denigration of the peasant or shepherd. Both Durrell and Miller could be guilty of both tendencies: "The peasants are incorrigible thieves and liars" (Lawrence Durrell, Letter, 1935, *Spirit of Place*). Henry Miller (1941), observing activities at the village well, writes of a "peasant woman at Corfu, a woman with six toes, decidedly ugly..."

"*Timeo Danaos et dona ferentes*", wrote Virgil in the *Aeneid* ("I fear the Danaoi [the Greeks] even when bearing gifts"), and journalists have been misquoting the line ever since, defaming the Greek character and exhorting others to be on guard when confronted by the generosity of contemporary Greeks, reinforcing the consensus idea that all acts of kindness or generosity are somehow tainted by treachery, guile, duplicitous behaviour, *rousfeti*, bribes or corruption: "Beware of Greeks bearing gifts."

It is important to understand how Greeks themselves perceive the impact of mass tourism and the casual appropriation of Greece by tourists from "the North" (in the following case, Sweden), indifferent to Greek culture. We can learn something about their perceptions from the poem "The Tourist", by the Swedish–Greek poet Nikolas Kokkalis:

A hotel in a foreign country
Which is not yours.
Soft, fine sand on a beach
Whose soul is alien to you.
A sea which you do not approach with awe,
Trees whose names you have never heard.
Games you have never played,
Houses which do not speak to you,
Scents of food which provokes no memories.
Words which you do not understand.
Thoughts you might not even comprehend,
Poverty which you merely pass by...

Consider Chapter 6 of Olivia Manning's novel, *Friends and Heroes*, part of *The Balkan Trilogy*:

Alan talked for some time about the Greeks and the countryside: "an idyllic, unspoilt countryside". Guy, interested in more practical aspects of Greek life, here broke in to ask if by "unspoilt" Alan did not mean undeveloped, and by "idyllic", simply conditions that had not changed since the days of the Ottoman Empire. How was it possible to enjoy the beauty of a country when the inhabitants lived in privation and misery! ... You prefer the peasants to remain in picturesque poverty, I suppose?

Manning's fictional dialogue then contrasts images of Greece as it was during the Second World War, the pros and cons of dictatorship and freedom, poverty, tradition and development.

Louis de Bernières' *Captain Corelli's Mandolin* puts some stereotypical psychoanalysis of the "divided" Greek character into the mouth of his

Dr. Iannis: "Every Greek, man, woman, and child, has two Greeks inside...side by side with the Hellene we have to live with the Romoi." Louis de Bernières goes to some lengths to list and identify the characteristics of the two sides of the Greek soul. In his acknowledgements at the end of the novel, he cites his indebtedness to a number of books, including Nicholas Gage's *Hellas*. Reading Gage's book, we come across a very similar passage: "The average Greek sees himself as two people... When he feels noble, courageous, or creative, he calls himself a *Hellene*... When he feels devious, obstinate, or selfish, he calls himself a *Romios*, which is the Greek word for Roman."

The broader term "Balkan" often conveys negative connotations, as fully documented in the fascinating books by Maria Todorova (1997) and Vesna Goldsworthy (1998), on how the West has imagined and imagines the countries perceived as belonging to the Balkans. The same is true of the word "Byzantine" to non-specialists; C. M. Woodhouse reflects in his autobiography (1982) on the perverse use made of the word today: "We use it to stand for the decadent relic of the Roman Empire which declined and fell. But once it had stood for an empire as great as our own was to become, and far more durable. Yet we never use the name for our own past skill and power, only for the vices which we attribute to others."

I tried asking a variety of people to write down the first twenty word associations that come into their heads at the mention of the word "Greece".

The Greek–Australian poet Komninos replied immediately from Australia with the following: "Olympics/ Chaos/ Salad and fried potatoes/ Petty bureaucrats/ Calamari/ Backgammon/ Suburban street theatre/ Cigarettes/ Souvenirs/ Souvlaki/ Diesel fumes/ Dreadful daytime television/ White stone/ Sensationalist news reporting/ Crystal clear water/ Goat bells/ Fishing boats/ Crumbling churches/ Political graffiti/ Soldiers."

The Greek-American writer Demetrius Toteras replied rather differently from California: "Twenty words: a strange request coming from you, like asking one to define their mother grammatically... My brain recognizes my face as the face that fought at Thermopylae... My eyes are still brown, my skin olive, but that doesn't tell me what I feel... when I become that dusty dirt... that hot sun, the smell of squid mixed with the scent of jasmine when all my senses are one with all that is... The moment you try to describe Greek you lose the Greek." He wrote much more than this, many more than twenty words, but it was the kind of spontaneous answer I was expecting.

Toteras had sent another email on a similar subject as part of our sporadic but ongoing (42 years long) conversation about the nature of Greekness (he was my *koumbaros*, "best man", at my wedding, a relationship which in Greece is often lifelong, like brothers): "I personally can't help who I am. I'm a prisoner of my own culture, physically, mentally, morally... I am Greek with a thin coating of Americanism—like mustard on a ball park frank... I look like a Greek... I think like a Greek... I live in the collective time-frame of history... I am related to all the Greeks that came before me... A Greek knows who he is... he is a knot on a fisherman's net... anything more than that and he is accused of *hubris*."

THE WRITING OF MODERN GREEK HISTORY
The landscape, seascape, flora and fauna, the peasants, and much of the territory of Greece have been thoroughly appropriated and occupied as the imaginative possessions of foreigners, who feel free to praise or denigrate, to admire or mock, at will. This mental colonization has been practised by some members of the Greek diaspora as well as by foreigners.

The writing of Modern Greek history has not always helped, even allowing for the comparative absence of well-maintained archives, because of the Greek need to cultivate a sense of national identity.

It is hard to be certain of the ground we stand on. Let us consider Epirus. When I was requested to act as an informal guide to the international group visiting the Kastro and island of Ioannina, I suddenly realized that I did not know the true answers to many questions asked about Epirus. Did the women really dance on the heights of Zalongo before throwing themselves and their infants, one by one, off the precipice? How was Ali Pasha killed? (Was a dagger plunged into his chest? Was he shot through the floorboards, or out on the verandah; in the breast, groin or abdomen?) What were the real circumstances of Kyra Frosini's death and how many women were drowned in all? (The nineteenth-century accounts differ, with 15, 17, 18, 19, 20 or more drowned; several accounts have Frosini expiring on the road to execution, and buried in the monastery of Saint Anagiros.) Was there a secret "underground" school in the crypt of one of the monasteries on the Island of Ioannina? Who was responsible for defacing the murals painted on the walls of the island's monastery chapels:

hostile Muslim Turks or superstitious Christian Greeks who believed the powdered plaster scraped from a saint's eyes contained magical properties which could bring good health and good luck? I had often heard both explanations.

A lot has been written about the so-called "Secret Schools".

Robert Liddell (1965) claims that "secret schools" did *not* exist in Ioannina, so that the story about the crypt of the monastery church of St. Nicholas of the Philanthropini being used as a secret underground school in Turkish times is a legend without any foundation. In fact "the Greek community openly maintained two flourishing academies" in Ioannina.

Henry Holland (1815) discusses the academies "at which, in sequel to each other, the greater part of the young Greeks at Ioannina are instructed".

Brian de Jongh (1979) is not so adamant: "In the north side chapel, believed to be the site of one of the so-called secret schools of Yannina (most of these were run openly, the Turks attaching little importance to the preservation of Hellenic culture among their subject peoples), the walls are painted with lively scenes of martyrdom…"

Does it matter? It does if you are writing a school textbook, a guidebook, or acting as a guide to a group of interested visitors.

When my wife was at school in Corfu, they used a series of Modern Greek Readers, a different one each year, anthologies of poetry and prose separated into sections like "Religious Life", "National Life", "Family and Social Life" and "Greek Nature". The one I am looking at now, published in 1957, intended for the second year of high school, contains a poem by Ioannis Polemis (1862-1924) about "The Secret School". The poet describes the tangible darkness of slavery which exists outside the school. Every night the school operates secretly within the domed church, with its flickering oil-lamps, where the enslaved children are gathered; outside, their country suffers in chains. The hoarse voice of the priest-teacher brings long-suppressed hopes to life; those listening feel the pain of slavery, of what they have lost, and contemplate what they have and should have… Out of the silence a psalm is heard, with its other-worldly melody, and the children hear the deep, prophetic voice and words of the teacher: "Do not be afraid of the dark. Freedom will dawn, like the radiant morning-star, after a long night."

Recent attempts to modernize history books for Greek schools led to a row between the Ministry of Education and the Church as to whether the "Secret Schools" really existed at all. It is quite possible that secret schools did exist in Ioannina *before* the time of Ali Pasha. After all, Sultan Amurath (Murad) II took the city in 1430. There would have been many changes of policy and periodic clampdowns during the time between 1430 and 1913.

The Albanian historian Hajredin Isufi, in his article "Aspects of Islamization in Camëri" (2004), states that the Ottoman occupation of Ioannina was accompanied by a cruel massacre, that they erected "a pyramid with 2,000 cut heads of Christian people", a fact (if true) of which I was unaware, but which would point indeed to the need for secret Christian schools in the early years of Ottoman rule. I had understood rather that Ioannina surrendered *peacefully* to the army of Sultan Murad II in 1430. "The city of Ioannina surrendered to the Turks a few months after the bloody fall of Thessaloniki on the 9 October 1430", according to the Region of Epirus' account of the Ottoman conquest of Epirus (2007). Salonica fell on 29 March 1430, according to Mark Mazower (2004): "A few months later, Ottoman troops went on to besiege the city of Ioannina." The Ottoman commander advised the Archbishop to surrender peacefully, rather than have the churches plundered and ruined and the people enslaved. "Janina obeyed and remained an important centre of Hellenic learning throughout the Ottoman period: indeed one of Murad's generals actually founded a Christian monastery there", writes Mazower, which suggests a very different scenario in terms of educational opportunities and learning.

K. E. Fleming mentions that many travellers' accounts of Ali Pasha comment on the relatively healthy status of church education within his territories. She mentions Hobhouse's (later Lord Broughton) observation in 1810 that there were two well-established secondary schools in Ioannina, to which Leake also refers.

It does seem to be the case that Ali, being dependent on Greek skills, "not only tolerated but encouraged Greek education" (Foss). One might, for instance, have expected Aslan Pasha (Pasha of Ioannina, 1600-18 or 1620) to have been tolerant and encouraging of Greek education too, since it is believed that he was a Greek Christian boy taken from the village (or combined parish) of Monodendri-Vitsa in the *paidomazomo* (the gathering of children; the Janissary child tax, tribute or levy) of 1550 or 1580, who became a Janissary (for more about Aslan Pasha and Vitsa, see my *Corfu Blues*).

∾

So, what about the women of Zalongo? What and whom are we to believe? Brian de Jongh considers the Zalongo incident rather over-romanticized and the stories about the Suliots probably over-dramatized. The folksong about the incident is included in *Folk Songs of Greece* by S. and T. Alevizos, where I first learned it. The editors introduce it thus: "In December, 1803… rather than try to escape and thus risk being caught by the Turks, the women preferred to dance to their death, each one throwing her children and then herself over the cliff."

The Dutch-born French artist Ary Scheffer (1795-1858) portrayed the women of Suli in his painting of 1827, *Les femmes souliotes, voyant leurs maris défaits par les troupes d'Ali, pacha de Janina, décident de se jeter du haut des rochers* (1803).

T. Richards, editor of *The Life of Ali Pacha* (1823), writes of the events of "Sallonga": "Thirty-nine women threw themselves headlong from the rock, with their children, many of whom were sucking at the breast."

R. A. Davenport (1837) has them dancing as they leapt: "About sixty women, with their children, were cut off from the rest, and fled towards a steep rock. There, seeing no hope of escape, the despairing mothers fondly kissed their babes, averted their faces from them, and threw them down the precipice. Then, joining in a frantic dance, they successively approached the edge of the cliff, and leaped after their mangled offspring."

C. Fauriel, in his *Chants Populaires* (1824), writes, "When there are no more children to throw down, they take each others' hands, beginning a circular dance as close as possible to the edge of the precipice; and at the end of the first turn, when she reaches the edge, the first woman hurls herself over, rolling from rock to rock to the bottom of the ghastly abyss. Meanwhile the circle, or the chorus, continues to turn, and at the end of each turn a dancer detaches herself in the same manner, until the sixtieth…"

Leake (1835) refers to the fact that "6 men and 22 women threw themselves from the rocks, at the place where the precipice is highest…

Several of the women who had infants, were seen to throw them over before they took the fatal leap."

Robert Liddell (1965) rather de-romanticizes the incident: "On this occasion some sixty women resolved to hurl their infant children over the rock and then to jump themselves, rather than fall into Ali's hands. About forty of them were killed, the others fell into trees or shrubs and were more or less injured, but survived... This is the sober account of a local historian; I do not think it robs 'the women's Thermopylae' of any of its heroism, though far more picturesque accounts have been given... The local historian (an archimandrite of Preveza) is obviously right when he tells us that there was no room to dance, and no time to think of such a thing; moreover, we know that they did not fling themselves from exactly the same spot (which, indeed, is the reason why their fates were so different)."

Leake (1835) has much detailed information about the Suliots, but on the subject of the women of Zalongo, he seems to underestimate the numbers (here he is translating and summarizing the work *A Brief History of Suli and Parga*): "Several of the women, despairing of escape, surrounded as they were on the summit of the hill of Zalongo, destroyed themselves and their children, by throwing the latter over the rocks, and themselves afterwards. Some of these women were not killed by the fall, either because they fell on the bodies of their children, or because they were caught by their clothes on the points of the rocks."

The Reverend Hughes (1820) wrote that "a party of about 100 women and children, being cut off from the rest, fled towards a steep precipice at a little distance from the convent: then the innocent babes were thrown over the rocks by their despairing mothers, whilst the women themselves, preferring death to the dishonour that awaited them, joined hand in hand, and raising their minds to the highest pitch of enthusiasm by songs in honour of their lost country, they whirled round and round in a species of frantic dance like the ancient Thyades, till they approached the very edge of the cliff; then with a loud shout of defiance, and as it were by a pre-concerted signal, one and all threw themselves headlong down."

Edward Lear (1851) wrote: "At its summit twenty-two women of Souli took refuge after the capture of their rock by the Mohammedans... as the enemy scaled the rock to take the women prisoners, they dashed all their children on the crags below, and joining their hands, while they sang their songs of their own dear land, they advanced nearer and nearer to the edge of the precipice, when from the brink a victim precipitated herself into the deep below at each recurring round of the dance, until they were all destroyed."

George Bowen (1852) contributes his opinion that the women joined hands, chanting the songs of their own dear mountains and forming a circling dance "at each recurring round of which an heroic victim hurled herself over the brink of the precipice into the dark gulf beneath".

Arthur Foss (1978) seems satisfied with the figure of sixty women, but suggests that the Zalongo story owes much to tradition: "It is here, according to tradition, that some sixty indomitable women of Souli, preferring death to torture and dishonour, danced themselves into a frenzy and then, one by one, leapt off the precipice to their destruction, having first thrown their children before them."

I revisited the site in March 2008, in the company of professional Greek guides and officials from the Nomarchia and local archaeological services, and we were told that the actual spot from which the women leapt to their deaths was in fact at Stephani Point 100 metres to the right (looking up from below, from the site of the monument, now in urgent need of restoration, as it has been struck by lightning and damaged in several places; we were lucky to see it without scaffolding). It may not be long before a *téléphérique* is also installed; a distressing thought from the visual point of view, but on reflection a necessary facility to enable access to less fit or mobile people, given the number of steps that have to be climbed to reach the monument and to see the view.

But whenever I go to Zalongo with visitors or friends, I continue to relate the story of the Suliot women's tragic dance. I find the old folksong "Farewell Sad World, Farewell Sweet Life" so moving in Greek, poetically true and convincing; I prefer it to all the historians' accounts, as objective, over-romanticized, nationalistic, sceptical or colourful as they may be. The dance has also been orchestrated by N. Skalkottas in *36 Greek Dances*.

> The fish cannot live on the land
> Nor the flower on the sand,
> And the women of Suli
> Cannot live without freedom.

The song captures my imagination in a way that the monumental sculpture of the women of Suli by G. Zongolopoulos does not. I was somewhat disappointed to read Spiros Katsaros' slightly cynical opinion (1984) that the verse quoted is not a genuine demotic or folksong, but more of a popular song composed by a lyricist, rather than by some anonymous folk-bard. He claims, controversially, that the Suliots who fought and died at Zalongo belonged to the clan of the Botzaris traitors and that the women who leapt to their deaths were the wives and daughters of the traitors who had escaped during the night and abandoned them in order to save their own skins. To me, that sounds like an insular Corfiot trying to debunk the heroic legends of the mainland opposite.

Liddell refers to the visitors' book, with comments (cited in French) by "the very worst type of French tourist": "I would have preferred to have let myself be violated rather than to have jumped." "Finally some clear-minded and lucid French people have arrived at this high spot of obscurantism and superstition." Liddell cites their comments that they "hoped to come back to find Greece purged of such *miasme* or *marasme*." Vasso Psimouli (2006) makes clear in her prologue that the mythologizing of the Suliots in national historiography, and in many foreign accounts, cast them as latter-day Ancient Greek heroes or re-born Spartans. *This fulfilled the needs of the times.*

THE HERITAGE OF EPIRUS

If Shakespeare was drawn to the story of Antony and Cleopatra, lesser dramatists were drawn to other more or less loosely Epirus-related topics like King Pyrrhus, Scanderbeg (George Castriot, "the scourge of Turkes, and plague of infidels" in the words of Edmund Spenser) and Queen Lao-damia. There have been at least three plays about Scanderbeg (by Whincop, Lillo and Havard) and three operas, but from Charles Hopkins' tragedy *Pyrrhus, King of Epirus* (1695) onwards, Pyrrhus and his Pyrrhic Victory have attained world renown.

"By the splendour of his deeds" King Pyrrhus, King of Epirus 307-272 BC, "entitled his country to the admiration of the world...taking Alexander as his model, he longed to rival him in glory and renown" (T. Richards, 1823).

Jacob Abbott (1853) writes that "the period of Pyrrhus' career was immediately subsequent to that of Alexander the Great, the birth of Pyrrhus having taken place about four years after the death of Alexander".

Abbott concludes that Pyrrhus "accomplished nothing. He had no plan, no aim, no object, but obeyed every momentary impulse... He succeeded...in killing an immense number of men, and in conquering, though temporarily and to no purpose, a great many kingdoms."

P. Devambez (1967) considers that the life of Pyrrhus would make a spectacular adventure film with "distant expeditions, courage and generosity, brilliant actions including a set battle-piece in which a charge of elephants threw panic into the ranks of the Roman army".

Prior to Pyrrhus' campaigns in Magna Graecia, he had conquered Corfu with the help of the Tarentines. R. Montgomery Martin (1833) wrote that "Pyrrhus, king of Epirus, after several unsuccessful attempts, conquered the island, and made use of its fleet and marines in his attempts on Italy, which greatly weakened the Corcyreans, whose commerce was almost completely annihilated by Teuca, queen of the Illyrians, to whom it was subject in the century before our era, and to check whose cruelties the Corcyreans were obliged to follow the example set them by the little Grecian republics, and place themselves under Roman protection... During the domination of Rome, the Corcyreans were converted to Christianity." Queen Teuca, or Teuta, reigned in Illyria from around 231-227 BC. Her pirate chieftains were almost as fearsome to the Corfiots and Ionian islanders as Barbarossa was to become in the sixteenth century AD.

Oliver Goldsmith (1805) was more generous in his estimation of Pyrrhus, whose mind, "incapable of rest, knew no satisfaction but in new enterprises". Goldsmith provided a brief eulogy: "Of the character of Pyrrhus, as a warrior, it will be sufficient to say, that even Hannibal accounted him the greatest general the world ever beheld; Scipio, according to the celebrated Carthaginian, being only the second." Hannibal esteemed Pyrrhus first, Scipio second and himself third, according to Plutarch.

After the Battle of Beneventum (275 BC), Pyrrhus prayed to Zeus, "I have defeated in battle those whom no one has defeated until now, yet they have also defeated me." After the victory at Asculum (279 BC), where he lost 3,505 soldiers against the Romans' 6,000 (or was it rather after the Battle of Heraclea, 280 BC?), he uttered the famous words, rendered variously as "If we defeat the Romans in one more such battle, we shall be totally ruined" or "If we win another victory like this, we are defeated."

Nowadays he is best remembered for these words, which symbolize "The Pyrrhic Victory", in which the nominal victor sustains unacceptably heavy losses, rendering the victory almost worthless (P. Garoufalias, 1979). Jacob Abbott records it slightly differently: "One of Pyrrhus's generals congratulated him on his victory. 'Yes,' said Pyrrhus; 'another such victory and I shall be undone.'"

In Dryden's translation of Plutarch's *Life of Pyrrhus*, the story is recounted thus: "Hieronymus says there fell six thousand of the Romans, and of Pyrrhus's men, the king's own commentaries reported three thousand five hundred and fifty lost in this action... The armies separated; and, it is said, Pyrrhus replied to one that gave him joy of his victory that one other such would utterly undo him." After six years in Italy, he sailed back to Epirus: "Thus fell Pyrrhus from his Italian and Sicilian hopes, after he had consumed six years in these wars, and though unsuccessful in his affairs, yet preserved his courage unconquerable among all these misfortunes, and was held, for military experience, and personal valour and enterprise, much the bravest of all the princes of his time, only what he got by great actions he lost again by vain hopes, and by new desires of what he had not, kept nothing of what he had. So that Antigonus used to compare him to a player with dice, who had excellent throws, but knew not how to use them." His life came to an end when he was wounded in battle by a Greek from Argos, whose mother, trying to help defend her son from a counter-blow, hurled a heavy tile at Pyrrhus (mounted on horseback) from a housetop on which she was standing, overlooking the scene.

So many aggressive, ambitious human enterprises and expeditions, simultaneously successful and disastrous, victories which are ultimately defeats! Pyrrhus and Ali Pasha are not alone in this respect. Christopher Wordsworth (1839) wrote of Ali's tomb in the Kastro of Ioannina: "A few steps leads us from the palace of Ali to his grave. It is a simple tomb of white stone, shrouded over with some wild plants growing above it. It affords a striking evidence of the vanity and emptiness of all the eulogies which have been lavished upon the political prudence and sagacity of this Napoleon of Greece. They would indeed have been worth something, could he... have foreseen this one event... that his headless body would in a few years lie upon a plain plastered slab in his own courtyard!"

Thanks to figures like Pyrrhus, Scanderbeg and Ali Pasha (who was fond of repeating that he was the modern Pyrrhus, or 'Bourrhous', as he pronounced it, although he told the Reverend Hughes that he previously had no distinct notion of Pyrrhus' character and exploits), Epirus was "on the map". Wace and Thompson (1914) record that Ali Pasha placed an inscription over his castle gate at Ioannina "in which he claims descent from Pyrrhus King of Epirus... A Moslem Albanian who claims in modern Greek to be a descendant of Pyrrhus and delights in a Greek epic of his own deeds recited to him by his own Homer is a most remarkable phenomenon." Pettifer and Vickers (2002) have suggested, controversially, that Greek historians have either omitted or distorted "the nature and ethnic background of rulers such as King Pyrrhus".

๙

After Pyrrhus, it was Byron and other nineteenth-century travellers who fixed the region of Epirus firmly in readers' imaginations. Examples of hubris and Pyrrhic-type victories seem common phenomena in this region of the world. "The inhabitants of Epirus strongly partake of the character of their country: like their mountains, they are rugged and uncultivated; still retaining their ancient reputation, they are distinguished by their great bodily strength, their activity, and their bravery in the field, qualities possessed even by their women" (T. Richards, 1823).

The women of Epirus, of Pindus and of Zagori, were renowned for their feats of endurance, for carrying ammunition over the mountains during the Second World War, just as the women of Suli had been renowned during the Suliot wars against Ali Pasha. There is a fine statue of "The Zagori Woman" on the road leading up to Central Zagori.

If arriving by ferry from Italy or Corfu, travellers usually approach Epirus through the port of Igoumenitsa (the Scala of Gomenitza, as it was called). I remember it in the 1960s as a small, insignificant and rather scruffy port; it was just a village in the 1940s. It still lacks infrastructure (such as a cinema or theatre) and evidence of planning, in spite of its development as a commercial port and as the access point to the Egnatia highway. My wife recalls that when the National Bank of Greece opened there c.1965 it had a glass frontage with indoor plants placed behind the glass window-panes, but donkeys used to butt their heads against the panes, trying to get to the greenery to eat it. Sometimes I think we are all like those donkeys, trying to get at and appropriate "the real Greece" or to consume and digest "the Greek experience".

Epirus means the continent, the mainland or *terra firma*. T. Richards (1823) described how the Greeks perceived Epirus in ancient times: "The mountains of ancient Thesprotia were considered by the Greeks, as the extreme confines of the world, the land of darkness, the region of night, the kingdom of inexorable Pluto. Being situated more to the east, and observing that the sun disappeared daily behind these mountains, they there placed the gloomy mountains of Tartarus, the abodes of the damned..."

Hammond (1967) writes that Epirus, "the Mainland" of the *Odyssey*, "was the large shadowy realm of the savage Echetus".

In the nineteenth century, at the time of the British Protectorate, as Thomas Gallant remarks (2002), "To visit Kerkyra was not to traverse into the heart of darkness", even though there was some sense of exoticism alongside that of familiarity (see, for instance, the photographs taken by Major J. D. Shakespear, 1856-60). To people with vivid imaginations the Albania and Epirus of Ali Pasha's day came much closer to a sense of the exotic, the Oriental, the unknown.

Even for Corfiots, Epirus/Albania (and Suli) were to some extent "The Other", and that remained true until more recent times. Arthur Foss (1978) says that "my Corfiot friends, when they heard that I intended to visit what they call *i steria* or the continent, were surprised that I should prefer this to remaining on their enchanted island. They themselves have little interest in or knowledge of the mainland opposite."

It was one thing to aspire to political union with mainland Greece in the nineteenth century; it was another thing to imagine spending much time in Epirus. Epirots tended to come to Corfu and the islands to do business or to settle, not the other way round. James Pettifer could begin the first chapter of his book *The Greeks* (1993) with the statement: "Few foreign visitors go to Epirus, few Greeks for that matter. Seen from Corfu, across the narrow straits, the mountains of north-west Greece are remote... Epirus is dense forest...a very long way from Athens. For citizens of that city, it is the Wild North rather than the Wild West; an Athenian would no more consider living there than a Cockney move to a rain-sodden blanket bog in Wester Ross."

George Bowen (1852), after his travels in Epirus and Thessaly (and as far as Constantinople), writes of the delightful feeling an Englishman like him experienced on returning to Corfu, then "under the strong arm and gentle influences of his own glorious country", and on seeing "familiar English faces welcome me back to Christendom and civilization".

In the past, the "Frank" Corfiots would often look down on the inhabitants of Epirus, as far south as Prevesa. If they were not "Turks" or "Turko-Albanians", Muslim Albanians, they were at best "Arvanites", Christian Albanians.

The indifferent attitude noticed by both Foss and Pettifer has slowly changed, because so many more people now own cars, appreciate the new Egnatia Highway, and are beginning to discover the beauties of accessible areas of natural beauty, like the Zagori.

IOANNINA AFTER ALI

The Reverend Hughes may have thought that the annals of Ioannina were enveloped in obscurity, but we have good descriptions of the city in the times of Ali Pasha, by the likes of Byron, Holland and Haygarth:

Unseen is Yanina, though not remote, /
Veil'd by the screen of hills
                            (Byron, *Childe Harold's Pilgrimage*, stanza LII)

In his letters of 1809, Byron describes reaching Yanina "after a journey of three days over the mountains through a country of the most picturesque beauty…" He later rode out on the Vizir's horses and saw Ali Pasha's palaces and those of his grandsons. He found them splendid "but too much ornamented with silk and gold".

William Haygarth ("Greece, a Poem", 1814), who was in Greece at the same time as Byron in 1811, wrote part of his poem in Athens in 1811. He tells us a little more than Byron did:

The situation of Ioannina, the capital of Ali, is very magnificent. Resting on a gentle descent, it extends along a narrow promontory, which projects far into the lake, whose waters are darkened with the shade of impending mountains, amongst which the range of Pindus is visible…the effect of the whole scene is striking and picturesque; the broad dome of the mosques, the slender column of the minarets, the lofty cypresses, and the range of the Vizir's palaces towering in gaudy splendour above the mud cabins which surround them, afford most interesting subjects for the pencil… Ioannina must be considered as the capital of Greece…about two-thirds of the population are Greeks, Albanians, Christians and Jews; the rest are Turks… The society is more civilized than in any other town of Greece… In the barbarous districts of Epirus, we must now seek for the glimmering of that light which once illumined the territory of Attica.

Henry Holland (1815) noted that "in this city there is much social intercourse of a pleasant kind, at least equal in its merits to any that I have found in Spain, Portugal, or Sicily; and superior certainly to what will be met with elsewhere in Greece. The vivacity of the Greeks always gives character to their society; and in Ioannina this is aided by the intelligence and acquirements they have derived from European intercourse." He informed us that the population afforded a curious spectacle in the streets and that it was "composed of Greeks, Turks, Albanians, and Jews….with the addition of Arabs, Moors, and Negroes".

T. Richards (1823) reminded us that Ioannina was a flourishing town even at the period when the Turks entered it. The year was 1430, according to modern historians, although the exact date and month seem uncertain. The Turks did not leave until 1913. Few people are aware that there is a small Turkish Military Cemetery at Koulines in Corfu. Why? Turks who were wounded in 1912 were brought to Corfu for treatment, and a number of them died here. Although surrounded by rubbish and piles of old bottles, the wall around the cemetery has been restored and the cemetery is well-maintained, with clean marble tombstones. But when I visited it was locked, and I was informed by an aggressive local that photography was forbidden.

When Leake (1835) was travelling in Epirus, his Greek host in Delvino complained of the hardships which his nation suffered from the Turks, and asked why the great powers of Europe, but particularly the English, would not assist in liberating their fellow Christians. Leake replied that it was not a very agreeable task to explain that nations seldom acted except out of self-interest, that Great Britain had a cruel war on its hands, and that the country's policy at the time was to support the Turkish Empire. We are fortunate to have figures like Lord Byron, Clement Harris and C. M. Woodhouse to invoke in defence of the philhellenic record.

The Reverend Hughes described the view from above Ioannina "with its glittering palaces and mosques, stretched along the shore of its magnificent lake... Nothing was wanting but classical authority to make us believe these really to have been the famed elysian fields of antiquity surrounding the Acherusian lake." Nowadays it is still possible to look down at the lake from above, or even from its shores, and to feel the same sensations, although the green colour of its waters suggests pollution rather than magnificence.

When Ali Pasha realized that the town was at risk of falling to the besieging Turkish army, and after his own army had deserted, he was still able to defend his fortified capital, the Kastro, and "still remained master of the navigation of the lake, by means of a small squadron of gun-boats, manned by Greeks from Corfu". Ali then "allowed his faithful Arnautes the pillage of a town, which he could no longer preserve, and which it was even his interest to destroy" (Richards, 1823). Even the harem and public baths were invaded by the "wild and lawless soldiery", in their "unbridled fury", and "their unfortunate inhabitants subjected to all the horrors of brutal violence... After the Arnautes had glutted themselves with plunder, upon an appointed signal, a most furious cannonading, accompanied with horrid outcries, announced the destruction of the city. Showers of bombs, grenades, and fire-balls, carried devastation, fire, and carnage, into the different quarters of Joannina, which no longer presented any other appearance but that of one vast conflagration. Seated upon one of the bastions of his Castle of the Lake, Ali himself directed the cannonade, pointing out the spots which the flames had not yet reached. At his voice, the fire from the artillery redoubled with the utmost fury. In two hours, bazaars, bezestans, public baths, mosques, and private dwellings, were overwhelmed by an all-devouring sea of fire." The inhabitants tried to escape, women with children tried to cross the Pindus range to Arta. Women in childbirth died in the forests, and "young virgins disfigured their native charms with dreadful gashes". His magnificent palace disappeared and the 450 females in his harem were slowly ravaged by fever and scurvy.

With such a dramatic cinematic description, one wonders why there is still no international Hollywood extravaganza (as opposed to a Greek or Albanian film or TV series) devoted to the story of Ali Pasha's life. In 1821 the general insurrection of the Greeks was very much in his interest and he helped to "foment the general spirit of revolt", even if he was really fighting for his own survival rather than for the freedom and independence of the Greeks. Perhaps some of the goriest episodes of his life are better suited to the medium of the Karaghiozis shadow-theatre, as described by Durrell in *Prospero's Cell*.

The Murray *Handbook* describes Ioannina rather quaintly as "St. John's Town" (after St. John the Baptist), or in its more common form as Yanina, or "Jack's Town". There was little to be seen of Ali's seat of power in the Kastro of Ioannina but "the shapeless remains of the ruined serai". "Ali Pasha used to enter with his boat, then get into a small carriage (drawn by mules), which rolling up an inclined plane, landed him 100 feet above at the door of his serai." I wish I'd had facts like these at my fingertips when trying to guide an international group around the Kastro in 2003. I would also have liked to read them an "eye-witness" account of the 1821 burning, as imagined by Kostas Krystallis, supposedly transcribed from an old notebook.

Edward Lear (1851) writes of Ioannina (11-13 May 1849) that he "would gladly pass a summer here…inside this city of manifold charms the interest was as varied and as fascinating: it united the curious dresses of the Greek peasant—the splendour of those of the Albanian: the endless attractions of the bazaars, where embroidery of all kinds, fire-arms, horse-gear, wooden-ware, and numberless manufactures peculiar to Albania, were exhibited… no marvel that Joannina will always hold its place in memory as one of the first in interest of the many scenes I have known in many lands."

George Bowen (1852), seeing Ioannina in the middle of the nineteenth century, wrote: "The lake and city of Joannina, the island, the shattered and crumbling fortresses, and the groves of minarets all reflected in the glassy waters, burst suddenly upon us. It was as though a new world sprang into existence."

Writing earlier in the century, when Ioannina was still at its peak, the Reverend Hughes describes "its mosques rising out of their cypress-groves and bearing aloft the triumphal crescent" which give Ioannina "an air of picturesque beauty, especially if seen from the eminence of the western side… I have rarely seen a more striking prospect than is here presented."

Ioannina may have seemed beautiful, but cruelty such as that practised by Ali Pasha did not cease in the nineteenth century. The German Occupation in the Second World War brought reprisal executions and the burning of whole villages, as well as the rounding up and transportation of Ioannina's Jewish population to Auschwitz. A former Italian soldier stationed in Ioannina for a period was interviewed by Schminck-Gustavus (2008). He describes Ioannina as he found it in the cold winter of 1941-2, the winter of hunger and starvation. He complains that the locals could not understand his Ancient Greek; the minarets made him feel he was in Turkey, not in the land of Homer and Odysseus. There was absolutely nothing in the town, which seemed to him, a member of the Italian Occupation Forces, no more than "a filthy, frozen hole". Then the Greek Civil War of 1947-9 brought more atrocities to the mountain villages around Ioannina.

Although Hobhouse records that the Turks had no form of scenic representation apart from the shadow theatre, Hughes records that "since our departure, theatrical exhibitions have been displayed at Ioannina under the patronage of the vizir, a temporary theatre being erected, and the whole corps de ballet imported from Corfu: such a scene, I will venture to say, was never exhibited in a Mahometan city since the era of the Hegira."

That in itself says a great deal about the differences between the towns of Corfu and Ioannina at the beginning of the nineteenth century, although the Corfiot writer Spiros Katsaros (1984) suggests that there was very close contact between Ioannina and Corfu at the time, and that Ioannina tried to keep up with, borrow from and copy the intellectual and cultural developments in Corfu. He claims, rather superciliously perhaps, that all the capable people from Ioannina would often come to Corfu to seek inspiration and ideas which they would take back, so that Ioannina itself gradually became a decent cultural centre, in spite of its role as the Epirot centre of the *Turkokratia*. He also quotes the views of Dimitris Fotiadis, that Ioannina was a town of "court-slaves", through and through, who sucked up to the tyrant, a "paralysed and immoral" town where Greek poets composed and printed popular demotic songs in praise of Ali Pasha's victories against the Greeks, while they were busy getting drunk and having a good time, ignoring the blood being shed all around them, the groans of pain and the unjust deaths (as if no Corfiots ever sucked up to their Venetian and British overlords!).

Dr. Konstantinos Kardamis has written about the history of theatre and opera in Corfu, as performed at the Nobile Teatro di San Giacomo di Corfu. The building was converted into a theatre in 1720, "the first modern theatre on Greek soil. Initially it seems that it staged strictly theatrical performances, but in 1733 opera was performed there for the first time." Performances continued until 1892, when it was converted into the Mayorial House.

In the twenty-first century, it is widely if sometimes grudgingly admitted in Corfu that Ioannina has shot ahead in terms of architectural and urban restoration work, and there is considerable respect for Ioannina's hospitals and university. It is a real working town, serving the wider region.

NATIONALISM, TRUTH AND RECONCILIATION

There was a recent attempt by the Greek Ministry of Education to update and correct history textbooks for the schools, to make them less nationalistic, but the plan fell foul of the Archbishop and the Orthodox Church (which called the new textbook "shameful"), as well as nationalist groups, neo-Nazis (who burned copies of the book in front of the Parliament building), and scientific journals which claimed the book was "unconstitutional" (the Greek constitution apparently says the State is obliged to cultivate national conscience). The Ministry had issued the new textbook for the sixth grade (twelve-year-olds) in September 2006; it caused a furious controversy for omitting some key historical events and for allegedly downplaying the role of the Orthodox Church in Greek history, including the existence of "secret schools" in Ottoman times. The book, commissioned when the PASOK government was last in power, was seen by many as being non-patriotic and too politically correct in relation to acts of Ottoman oppression and discrimination, victimization of Greeks such as forced conversions, Janissary abductions of children ("recruitment" rather than "kidnapping"?), and concerning Greek uprisings and acts of martyrdom.

Both the Greek and Turkish governments had realized the time had come to encourage a degree of reconciliation by removing exaggerated nationalist bias from their respective school textbooks, and to teach more critical thinking, rather than to focus on the shaping of national conscience and identity as the main goal.

The *Athens News* covered the controversy thoroughly in its March and April 2007 issues, and also featured an article on the topic by former American diplomat J. B. Kiesling on "mystic nationalism" and historical revisionism, but not just in the Greek context: "Whether students learn useful history of murderous myth depends more on their teachers than on the bravest drafting committee."

D. Kremida, in the *Turkish Daily News* (March and April 2007), quoted the Greek Education Council Chairman, Thanos Veremis, as saying that "Violence is an integral part of history, but there's no sense in continuously narrating it. That is not the aim of textbooks." Veremis is also quoted as saying that "I do not understand why we have always portrayed Turks as monsters. Why do we not explain our own excesses in Anatolia?... There are monsters everywhere."

Hercule Millas, Professor of Turkish Studies at the University of Athens, told the *Turkish Daily News* that "for decades the two sides have made efforts to change their textbooks in an effort to reconcile. In the last 20 years they have stopped using 'insulting' expressions, such as barbarian, in history textbooks."

Louis de Bernières in *The Observer* in 2005 found both Greek and Turkish nationalism irritating. He has little patience with Greek Turkophobia and with the fact that both countries cultivate and celebrate "the memory of martyrdoms and historical wrongs".

Maybe I should have omitted some of the stories in this book concerning the excesses of Ali Pasha, but they are vital to any book dealing with Greek cultural history and the landscape of the imagination.

⌘

It would have been an Orientalist's delight to see Ioannina in the days of Byron, Haygarth and Holland, with its sixteen mosques. Dr. Pouqueville thought there were fourteen mosques. In fact there were *seventeen*, according to the thorough research of K. Koulidas (2004).

George Bowen (1852) saw a hundred minarets in his mind: "the hundred minarets of the city were resounding with the calls of the muezzim to prayer". But the rest of Ioannina in was in a sad state: "The capital of Aly Pasha, which thirty years ago was the first town in Greece for learning, civilization, and splendour, has fallen into a melancholy state of decay. Its most interesting feature is the citadel, now little more than a shapeless mass of ruins, covering a steep rock projecting into the lake."

The minarets have featured in other fiction and non-fiction pieces. Kostas Krystallis wrote of eighteen minarets in his short story about the *panigyri*

Fetihie Mosque at Ioannina

of Kastritsa (1894). While Christos Christovasilis also wrote of eighteen mosques in his moving piece "Our Poor Mosque" (1929); after the exchange of populations, his family lived in a formerly Turkish-owned house, near one of the tallest, most beautiful and most historical mosques and minarets, that of Shemsheddin, the first ever built in Ioannina or in the whole of Epirus (in 1432). He laments the day that the National Bank of Greece sold it by auction to the highest bidder, and that the new owner, without any feelings or sentimentality about art or history, had it demolished or rather "killed", in the author's opinion. He had often climbed the 177 steps of the minaret. When he saw a mosque for the first time, as a child, he admired the minaret with its circular balcony, which looked to him like an enormous ring around a giant's finger.

Out of the seventeen minarets which certainly existed, only four mosques have been saved until the present day (three with minarets). At the beginning of the twentieth century there were twelve mosques. Four were demolished in the 1920s, five in the 1930s and two as late as the 1950s. With imagination, even now one can still conjure up the landscape of mosques, minarets and bazaars, and the Kastro, or fortress, of Ioannina with its impressive *serai* can easily be peopled in the mind's eye with Ali Pasha, his court, his harem, his Greek secretaries and his Albanian soldiery. A little Orientalist fantasizing cannot easily be denied us. Ioannina cannot escape its colourful past.

Whether it is an obligation for the Greeks in the twenty-first century to preserve the architectural heritage of foreign occupiers or minorities is a moot point. To what extent should Greece have preserved the Muslim heritage, be it Cham, other Albanian or Turkish Muslim? To what extent the Roman, the Norman, the Venetian, the French, the British or the Jewish? Turkish baths? All the mosques and minarets that were still standing in Ioannina when it was liberated in 1913? Slavic place-names? Venetian fortresses and arsenals? Cemeteries (Turkish, Jewish, British...)?

Nation-building is difficult enough without constant reminders of past suffering, of foreign occupation and centuries of slavery and oppression. But it is a two-way business. If people want an important Classical Greek, Byzantine or Orthodox monument to be preserved in Istanbul, Southern Albania, FYROM/Macedonia, Cyprus, Asia Minor (or in Sicily and Magna Graecia for that matter), then it is surely a matter of reciprocity and a priority cultural policy issue for international organizations like UNESCO. Countries should recognize each other's ethnic minorities, past or present, but that should not make us blind to the way that politicians will sometimes exploit these minorities, however fully assimilated, for nationalistic and irredentist purposes.

At the very least, the authorities ought to make every effort to prevent acts of trespass, vandalization or desecration of cemeteries. Recent incidents of anti-Semitism in Ioannina include the desecration of the Jewish Cemetery at Aghia Triada on 15-16 April 2002 (also vandalized in 1992), alleged trespass (in an attempt by the Municipality to expropriate part of the cemetery area), and desecration of a Synagogue on 3 August 2003 (Nazi slogans). The Jewish cemetery is in a state of wilderness and the tombs have been frequently vandalized by Greeks searching for buried gold jewellery, according to Christoph U. Schminck-Gustavus (2008), who visited it and made enquiries.

Older Corfiots still feel a sense of shame, at the least as "bystanders", concerning the fate of the Jews of Corfu and the large old Jewish cemetery (dating back to the sixteenth century, if not earlier) which was levelled after the war. Many ancient monuments and inscriptions were destroyed. Corfu's hospital stands on part of the ground, and so, ironically, does the Department of History of the Ionian University. In Thessaloniki, Aristotle University campus occupies the land which was the former Jewish Cemetery. The Corfu-born Jewish writer Albert Cohen (1895-1981), author of the 1968 novel *Belle du Seigneur* ("Her Lover"), could still profess a great love for the island which inspired him and which he never forgot.

As a result of immigration there is much discussion about the building of new mosques and other religious buildings and schools. Should existing old mosques which had been turned into museums be converted back to religious use, like some of Prague's old Jewish synagogues after the fall of Communism?

According to Arthur Foss (1978), the Aslan Aga mosque in Ioannina was "the last mosque to be used by the faithful; it was closed in 1928". The first mosque to be demolished in Ioannina was razed around 1920. Concerning Ioannina's Muslims, he writes further: "In 1973 only eight Muslims remained, living together in an ancient house in the centre of Ioannina. The local authorities, we were told, had refused to allow them to use one of the remaining mosques for worship..."

Now that so many Muslim Albanians live and work in Ioannina and the surrounding villages, some people feel that it would be an appropriate gesture to allow them to use one of the mosques for worship. Perhaps a reciprocal gesture could involve the Christian use of Aghia Sofia in Istanbul, if it could ever be re-sanctified for Christian use?

This is probably all wishful thinking, given the example of what has happened in the northern part of Cyprus since the Turkish invasion of 1974. The "cultural cleansing", the destruction and desecration of Cyprus's cultural heritage, archaeological sites and the illicit trade of antiquities are documented by A. B. Knapp and S. Antoniadou in *Archaeology Under Fire* (1998). The authors state that "Turkish Cypriote archaeologists have...a moral duty to control and protect the cultural heritage in the face of its large-scale destruction and looting".

Was it also the moral duty of Greek archaeologists to protect the Ottoman cultural heritage in Ioannina and other parts of European Turkey? If the Turks converted churches into mosques or used them for other alien purposes, does that mean that the Greeks had the right to remove minarets and mosques from Ioannina?

Kostas Krystallis wrote an appealing short story called "*I Ikona*" ("The Painting", 1894), in which Greeks and Albanians who frequent the same Epirot coffee-shop listen with fascination to the stories told by an old Greek man about the exploits of Scanderbeg against the common enemy, prompted by a portrait of the "King of the Epirots" who some of them think might be King Pyyrhus, but who is in fact George Castriot, i.e. the aforementioned Scanderbeg. The portrait and the story-telling bring the Greeks and Albanians closer together, the Albanians declaring with emotion that "We're brothers, old fellow, even if we're of two different faiths; let our enemies foul-mouth us and say whatever they want..." George Castriot (1405-68), called Georgios Kastriotis by the Greeks, is sometimes claimed as a *Greek-Epirot* Christian prince. He has only played a walk-on part in this book. Albania ("Land of Albania! where Iskander rose", wrote Byron) claims Scanderbeg (Turkish for "Lord Alexander") as its national hero.

Krystallis' message is unifying as far as it goes. Another greater writer is awaited, to finally persuade the Greeks, Albanians *and* Turks that, in spite of the worthy efforts of musicians and forward-thinking curriculum-developers, they should learn to behave as brothers and sisters. In the meantime, let us hope that one day we *will* all find our real or our imagined homes, our "Ithacas" and our *Nostimon Imar*. In the words of Cavafy (the last two lines of "The City"):

Έτσι που τη ζωή σου ρήμαξες εδώ
στην κώχη τούτη την μικρή, σ' όλην την γη την χάλασες.

(As you have destroyed your life here,
in this little corner, you have ruined it in the entire world.)

Bibliography & Further Reading

This listing excludes the classical sources (e.g. Homer's Odyssey) which are available in many editions. Many of the older or rarer titles are reprinted in facsimile editions from time to time; some books can be accessed online. Book titles are shown in italic; articles and poem titles roman in quotes; and foreign language versions of the latter in italic in quotes. We have quoted liberally from historical sources that are out of copyright, but for contemporary titles we have attempted to keep within fair dealing limits. If we have breached those expectations, we will be happy to make amends.

Abbott, G.F., *Songs of Modern Greece*, Cambridge, 1900

Abbott, Jacob, *The History of Pyrrhus*, London, 1853

Agious, Antonios, *I Enosi tis Eptanisoi me tin Ellada*, Corfu 2006

Alevizos, Susan and Ted, *Folk Songs of Greece*, London, 1925 and New York, 1968

Angeli, Anthi, *Orraon*, Ioannina, 2005

Angelopoulos, Theo, *Anaparastasi*, film ("Reconstruction", 1970) and film scenario (Themelio, Athens, 1979)

Anon., *The Ionian Islands under British Protection*, James Ridway, London, 1851

Ansted, D. T., *The Ionian Islands in the Year 1863*, W. H. Allen, 1863

Apostolopoulou-Michaelidou, E., *I Massiga ton Paxon, I Yiatros Maria Mitsiali, 1895-1981 (Massiga of Paxos, The Doctor Maria Mitsiali, 1895-1981)*, Athens, 2008

Aravantinos, P., *Epirotika Tragoudia*, 1880, 1996

Atkinson, Sophie, *An Artist in Corfu*, 1911

Averoff, Tatiana, *To Xefoto*, Kedros, Athens, 2000

Baerlein, Henry, *Southern Albania: Under the Acroceraunian Mountains*, 1968

Baker, Jean, *Old Skala, Memories of the Earthquakes of 1953*, 2007

Baudelaire, Charles, "Un Voyage à Cythère" (tr. Roy Campbell), *Les Fleurs du mal*, 1857

Beaton, Roderick, *Folk Poetry of Modern Greece*, Cambridge, 1980

Beaton, Roderick, *An Introduction to Modern Greek Literature*, Oxford, 1994

Beauchamp, Alphonse, *The Life of Ali Pacha of Janina*, London, 1822

Bernard, Catherine, *Laodamia, Queen of Epirus*, 1689 in *The Lunatic*

Lover, *Plays by French Women of the 17ʰ and 18ᵗʰ Centuries*, ed. Perry Gethner, Heinemann Drama, 1994

Bittlestone, R., Diggle, J. and Underhill, J., *Odysseus Unbound : The Search for Homer's Ithaca*, Cambridge, 2005

Blundell, Sue, *Women in Ancient Greece*, British Museum Press, 1995

Boccaccio, *Landolfo Buffalo*, 1352

Boikos, Nikos, "The Paxiot Workshop in Action", Municipality of Paxos, 2006

Boutos, Vasilis, *I Sikofantia tou aimatos* or *Blood Libel*, Athens, 1997

Bowen, George Ferguson, *The Ionian Islands under British Protection*, London, 1850

Bowen, George Ferguson, *Ithaca in 1850*, 3rd edn, revised, 1854

Bowen, George Ferguson, *Mount Athos, Thessaly and Epirus, A Diary of a Journey from Constantinople to Corfu*, London, 1852

Bradford, Ernle, *The Companion Guide to the Greek Islands*, 6th edn, revised Francis Pagan, 1998

Bradford, Ernle, *Ulysses Found*, 1963, 2004

Bradford, S., *Disraeli*, 1982

Bull, Peter, *It Isn't All Greek To Me*, London, 1967

Byron, Lord, *Byron's Letters and Journals*, ed. Leslie A. Marchand, London, 1973

Byron, Lord, *Childe Harold's Pilgrimage*, 1812

Campbell, J. K., Honour, *Family and Patronage, A Study of Institutions and Moral Values in a Greek Mountain Community*, Oxford, 1964

Capodistrias, John, *Letter to the Tsar Nicholas, Review of My Political Career from 1798 to 1822*, tr. Dorothy Trollope, Doric publications, London/Athens, 1977

Carman, Bliss, *Sappho: One Hundred Lyrics*, 1907

Carver, Robert, *The Accursed Mountains*, 1998

Casanova, Jacques, *The Memoirs of Jacques Casanova di Seingalt*, tr. Arthur Machen, London, 1894

Cavafy, C. P., *The Complete Poems of C. P. Cavafy*, tr. Rae Dalven, 1961

Chandler, Richard, *Travels in Greece*, Oxford, 1776

Chandler, Richard, *Travels in Asia Minor, and Greece; or, An account of a tour made at the expense of the Society of Dilettanti*, 1817

Chatto, James, *The Greek for Love: Life, Love and Loss in Corfu*, 2005

Chesterton, G. K., "Lepanto", 1911

Christomanos, Constantine, *Das Achilles-Schloss auf Corfu*, Vienna, 1896

Christovasilis, Christos, "*O Koutsoyiannis sta Yannina*" or "Koutsoyannis in Ioannina", 1898, reprinted in *Gianniotika Diigmata*, Athens, 2007

Christovasilis, Christos, "*To kaimeno to Tziami mas*" or "Our Poor Mosque", New York, 1929, reprinted in *Gianniotika Diigmata*, Athens, 2007

Chrysostomou, P. and Kefallonitou, F., *Nikopolis*, Athens, 2001

Cicellis, Kay, *Death of a Town*, Harvill Press, London, 1954; Greek translation, *O Thanatos mias Polis*, Athens, 2000

Clark, Bruce, *Twice a Stranger, How Mass Expulsion Forged Modern Greece and Turkey*, Granta Books, London, 2006

Clogg, Richard, *The Movement for Greek Independence, 1770-1821*, Barnes & Noble, 1976

Clogg, Richard, *A Concise History of Greece*, Cambridge, 1992

Clogg, Richard, *Anglo-Greek Attitudes, Studies in History*, Macmillan, Basingstoke, 2000

Clogg, Richard, *Greece 1940-1949, Occupation, Resistance, Civil War*, Palgrave Macmillan, 2002

Cohen, Albert, *Her Lover/Belle du Seigneur*, introduction by David Coward, Penguin, 1995

Comnena, Anna, *The Alexiad of Anna Comnena*, tr. E. R. A. Sewter, Penguin, 1969

Corfield, Justin, *Ionian Islands, a guide to genealogical sources on Corfu and the other Ionian Islands*, Rosanna, Australia, 2000

Corfu Cultural Society, *Corfu: History, Urban Space and Architecture, XIV-XIX* Century, 1994

Corvaja, Santi, *Gli Eroi di Cefalonia Settembre 1943*, Edizioni Horizon, Athens, 1984

Cosmetatos, Helen, *The Roads of Cefalonia*, Argostoli, 1995

Cultural Association of Samarina, *I Samarina*, 2007

Dakaris, Sotirios, *Dodona*, Athens, 1993, 4th edn, 2000

Dakaris, Sotirios, *The Nekyomanteion of the Acheron*, Athens, 1993, 4th edn, 2000

Dakin, D., *The Unification of Greece, 1770-1923*, Palgrave Macmillan, 1972

Dakin, D., *The Greek Struggle for Independence, 1821-1833*, London, 1973

Dalven, Rae, *The Jews of Ioannina*, Athens, 1990

Davenport, R. A., *The Life of Ali Pasha of Tepeleni, Vizier of Epirus*, London, 1823, 1837

Davy, John, *Notes and Observations on the Ionian Islands and Malta*,

London, 1842

de Bernières, Louis, *Captain Corelli's Mandolin*, Secker & Warburg, 1994

de Bosset, Charles-Philippe, *Parga and the Ionian Islands*, 2nd edn, London, 1822

de Jongh, Brian, *Mainland Greece, The Companion Guide*, Collins, 1979

de Saint-Vincent, Jean-Baptiste Bory, « *Histoire et description des Iles Ioniennes, depuis les temps fabuleux et héroïques jusqu'à ce jour; nouvel atlas contenant cartes, plans, etc.* », Paris, Dondey-Dupré, 1823

de Vaudoncourt, Guillaume, *Memoirs on the Ionian Islands*, tr. William Walton, 1816

Dendrinou, Irini, *I Kerkyraiki Scholi*, Corfu, 1971

Dessaix, Robert, *Corfu*, Sydney, 2001

Desyllas, Nikos, *Epirus, An Aesthetic Wander through a Greek Region*, 1994

Devambez, P. et al., *A dictionary of ancient Greek civilisation*, London, 1967

Dicks, Brian, *Corfu*, David & Charles, 1977

Dodwell, Edward, *Classical and Topographical Tour Through Greece*, London, 1819

Durrell, Gerald, *My Family and Other Animals*, London, 1956

Durrell, Gerald, *The Corfu Trilogy*, Penguin, 2006

Durrell, Lawrence, *Prospero's Cell*, 1945

Durrell, Lawrence, *Spirit of Place: Letters and Essays on Travel*, ed. Alan G. Thomas, 1969

Durrell, Lawrence, *The Greek Islands*, 1978

Edmonds, E.M., *Kolokotronis, the klepht and the warrior*, London, 1892

Elizabeth, Empress of Austria (Elisabeth, Kaiserin), *Das poetische Tagebuch*, Vienna, 1984

Ellingham, Mark, *Rough Guide to Greece*, Routledge, 1982

Elsie, Robert (ed.), *An Elusive Eagle Soars, Anthology of Modern Albanian Poetry*, London, 1993

Enessee, Nicholas, *Point and Counterpoint*, Kefalonia, 2005

Eton, William, *A Survey of the Turkish Empire*, London, 1799

Fakiolas, Nikos, *Koinonika Kinimata sta Eptanisa*, Corfu, 2000

Fainlight, Ruth, *Sybils and Others*, 1980

Fauriel, Claude, *Chants Populaires de la Grèce Moderne*, Paris, 1824

Fermor, Patrick Leigh, *Roumeli, Travels in Northern Greece,* John Murray, 1966

Finlay, George, *History of the Byzantine and Greek Empires*, Edinburgh and London, 1854

Fleming, K.E., *The Muslim Bonaparte, Diplomacy and Orientalism in Ali Pasha's Greece*, New Jersey, 1999

Forte, John, *Corfu, Venus of the Isles*, Clacton-On-Sea, 1963

Foss, Arthur, *The Ionian Islands, Zakynthos to Corfu*, London, 1969

Foss, Arthur, *Epirus*, Faber, 1978

Fotheringham, David Ross, *War Songs of the Greeks*, London, 1907

Fowles, John, "Byzantium", in *Poems*, Ecco Press, New York, 1973

Gage, Eleni, *North of Ithaka*, Bantam Press, 2004

Gage, Nicholas, *Eleni*, Collins, 1983

Gage, Nicholas, *Hellas, A Portrait of Greece*, Collins Harvill, 1987

Gallant, Thomas G, *Modern Greece*, London, 2001

Gallant, Thomas G., *Experiencing Dominion, Culture, Identity, and Power in the British Mediterranean*, Indiana, 2002

Gardner, John Dunn, *The Ionian Islands in relation to Greece, with suggestions for advancing our trade with the Turkish countries of the Adriatic and the Danube*, London, 1859

Garoufalias, Petros, *Pyrrhus King of Epirus*, Stacey International, London, 1979

Geisthövel, Wolfgang, *Homer's Mediterranean, From Troy to Ithaca, Homeric Journeys*, tr. Anthea Bell, 2008

Gell, William, *Geography and Antiquities of Ithaca*, 1807

Giannoudi-Avgerinou, Vivian and National Press Bureau, 1953, *La Tragédie des Iles Ioniennes, 9-12/8/1953*, Athens, 2004

Giffard, Edward, *A Short Visit to the Ionian Islands, Athens, and the Morea*, London, 1837

Giles, Frank, ed., *Corfu: The Garden Isle*, London, 1994

Gill, John, *The Stars over Paxos*, London, 1995

Glenny, Misha, *The Balkans, 1804-1999, Nationalism, War and the Great Powers*, London, 1999

Godley, A. D., *Lyra Frivola*, 1899

Goekoop, A. E. H. *Ithaque la Grande*, Athens, 1908

Goethe-Institut, Athens, *Wilhelm Dörpfeld's Lefkada 1891-1913*, Fagotto Books, Athens, 2008

Goldsmith, Oliver, *The History of Greece: From the Earliest State to the Death of Alexander the Great*, London, 1805

Goldsworthy, Vesna, *Inventing Ruritania, the Imperialism of the Imagination*, Yale University Press, New Haven and London, 1998

Goodisson, William, *A Historical and Topographical Essay upon the islands of Corfu, Leucadia, Cephalonia, Ithaca, and Zante*, London,

1822

Goropoulou-Birbilis, *Aphrodite, Greek Traditional Architecture, Corfu/Kerkyra*, Athens, 1984

Gounod, *Sappho*, 1851

Gouzelis, Demetrios, "*O Hasis*", ed. Zisimos Sinodhinos, Athens , 1997

Grasset-Saint-Sauveur, André, *Voyage historique, littéraire et pittoresque dans les isles et possessions ci-devant vénitiennes du Levant; Corfou, Paxo, Bucintro, Parga, Prevesa, Vonizza, Sainte-Maure, Thiaqui, Cephalonie, Zante, Strophades, Cerigo et Cerigotte*, Paris, 1800

Hammond, N. G. L., *Epirus*, Oxford, 1967

Hardy, Thomas, *The Return of the Native*, 1878

Harris, Andy and Harris, Terry, *Captain Corelli's Island, Cephallonia*, London, 2000

Hatzis, Dimitris, "*Drakolimni*" in *Thiteia, agonistika keimena 1940-1950*, Athens 1979, 2000

Haygarth, William, *Greece, A Poem, in Three Parts*, London, 1814

Henderson, G.P., *The Ionian Academy*, Edinburgh, 1988

Henderson, Mary, *Xenia, A Memoir, Greece 1919-1949*, 1988

Hennen, John, *Sketches of the Medical Topography of the Mediterranean; comprising an Account of Gibraltar, the Ionian islands and Malta*, London, 1830

Herodotus, *Histories*, ed. A. D. Godley, 1821

Heurtley, W. A., Darby, H. C., Crawley, C. W, Woodhouse, C. M., *A Short History of Greece, from Early Times to 1964*, Cambridge, 1967

Hobhouse, John Cam, *A Journey Through Albania and other Provinces of Turkey in Europe and Asia, 1809-1810*, 1813

Holland, Henry, *Travels in the Ionian Isles, Albania, Thessaly, Macedonia, &c during the years 1812 and 1813*, London, 1815.

Holland, Robert and Markides, Diana, *The British and the Hellenes: Struggle for Mastery in the Eastern Mediterranean 1850-1960*, Oxford, 2006

Hopkins, Charles, *Pyrrhus, King of Epirus*, 1695

Hounsell, Roy, *The Papas and the Englishman, From Corfu to Zagoria*, Yannis Books, London, 2007

Hughes, David, *Himself and Other Animals, A Portrait of Gerald Durrell*, Hutchinson, 1997

Hughes, Glyn, "Watercolours" in *Dancing on the Dark Side*, Shoestring Press, Nottingham, 2005

Hughes, The Reverend Thomas Smart, *Travels in Sicily, Albania and Greece*, 1820

Hugo, Victor, "The Pasha and the Dervish", in *The Orientals*, 1829; tr.
W. D., *Bentley's Miscellany*, 1839

Jenkins, Romilly, *Dionysius Solomos*, Cambridge, 1940, new edn,
Athens, 1981

Jervis, H. Jervis-White, *History of the Island of Corfu*, London, 1852

Jong, Erica, *Sappho's Leap*, Arcadia, 2003

Kadaré, Ismail, *Chronicle in Stone*, original edn, Tirana, 1971; tr. Al Saqi
Books, London, 1987

Kadaré, Ismail, *Poésies*, Tirana, 1981

Kadaré, Ismail, *The Autobiography of the People in Verse*, Tirana, 1987

Kalaitzoglou, Yiannis, *Kerkyra, mousa kallifonos, Paradosiaka Tragoudia*
("Corfiot Traditional Songs"), Corfu, 2004

Kaldis, William P., *John Capodistrias and the Modern Greek State*,
Wisconsin, Madison, 1963

Kalpaxis, Thanasis, *Archaeologia kai Politiki, I Anaskafi tou Naou tis
Artemidos (Kerkyra 1911)*, Rethymnon, 1993

Kalvos, Andreas, *Apanta Kalvou (Complete Works)*, ed. I. Zervos, Pella,
Athens (n.d.)

Kalvos, Andreas, *Odes*, tr. George Dandoulakis, Shoestring Press, 1998

Karamoutsos, Konstantinos D., *Souliotion genealogies*, Athens, 2008

Karyotakis, Kostas, *Battered Guitars: Poems and Prose*, trans. William
Reader and Keith Taylor, University of Birmingham, 2006

Katsaros, Spiros, *To Souli, O Thrilos kai i Alithea*, 1984

Kavadias, Nikos, *Vardia* ('Watch-Duty'), 1954

Kavadias, Nikos, *The Collected Poems of Nikos Kavadias*, bilingual edn, tr.
Gail Holst-Warhaft, Riverdale, N.J., 2006

Kazantzakis, Helen, *Nikos Kazantzakis: A Biography Based on His Letters*,
tr. Amy Mims, Simon and Schuster, 1968

Keeley, Edmund, *Inventing Paradise, The Greek Journey 1937-47*, New
York, 1999

Kendrick, Tertius T. C., *The Ionian Islands*, 1822

King, Francis, *The Dark Glasses*, Longman, 1954

Kirkwall, Viscount, ed., *Four Years in the Ionian Islands: Their Political
and Social Condition, with a History of the British Protectorate*,
Chapman and Hall, London, 1864

Klimis, K, *The Illustrated History of Corfu*, Corfu, 1994

Klironomos, Martha, "Late Nineteenth-Twentieth Century British
Women Travellers to Greece (1880-1930)", in Kolocotroni, Vassiliki
and Mitsi, Efterpi (eds.), *Women Writing on Greece: Essays on
Hellenism, Orientalism and Travel*, Rodopi, Amsterdam, 2008

Knapp, A. B. and Antoniadou, S., "Archaeology, politics and the cultural heritage of Cyprus" in *Archaeology Under Fire: Nationalism, Politics and Heritage in the Eastern Mediterranean and Middle East*, ed. Lynn Meskell, Routledge, 1998

Kokkalis, Nikolas, "The Tourist", in *Modern Scandinavian Poetry*, ed. and trans. Martin Allwood, Sweden, 1982

Koliopoulos, John and Veremis, Thanos, *Greece, The Modern Sequel, from 1831 to the Present*, New York, 2002

Kolocotroni, Vassiliki and Mitsi, Efterpi (eds.), *Women Writing on Greece: Essays on Hellenism, Orientalism and Travel*, Rodopi, Amsterdam, 2008

Kolokotronis, Theodoros, *Memoirs*, Athens, 1846, tr. by E. M. Edmonds as *The Old Man of the Morea: An Autobiography*, London, 1892

Komnena, Anna, *The Alexiad of Anna Komneno*, tr. E. R. A. Sewter, 1969

Konomos, Dinos, *Zakynthos (Pentakosia Chronia) 1478-1978*, Athens, 1979

Konstantios, Dimitris, *The Kastro of Ioannina*, Athens, 1997

Kontogianni, Theodora, *Kassopi*, Ioannina 2006

Koryialenios Museum, *I palaia Kefalonia, Enas ateleitoos Augoustos*, Argostoli

Kostopoulos, Sotiris, *Paxoi, apo tin adiaforia stin anaptixi*, Athens, 1984

Koulidas, Konstantinos, *Ta mousoulmanika vakoufia tis poleos ton Ioanninon*, Ioannina, 2004

Krystallis, Kostas, *"To Pascha ston Pindo"* ("Easter in the Pindus"), in *Apanta, Echo of Athens*, 1892

Krystallis, Kostas, *"To Panigyri tis Kastritsa"*, in *Pezografimata*, 1894, 1989

Krystallis, Kostas, *Apanta*, Athens, 1959

Krystallis, Kostas, *"I Ikona"*, in *Pezografimita*, Athens, 1894, 1989

Lambley, Dorrian, *The Mythos History of Corfu*, Corfu, 1984

Landon, Letitia Elizabeth, *The Improvisatrice*, 1824

Lane-Poole, S., ed., *Thirty Years of Colonial Government, Sir G.F. Bowen*, Longmans, Green & Co., 1889

Laskaratos, Andreas, *Ta Grammata* ("The Letters and Family Correspondence"), Society of Corfiot Studies, Corfu, 2006

Laskaratos, Andreas, *Ta Mysteria tis Kefallonias, skepses apanou stin oikoyeneia, sti thriskeia kai stin politiki eis tin Kefalonia* ("The Mysteries of Cefalonia, Thoughts on family life, religion, and politics in Cephalonia"), 1856

Leake, William Martin, *Travels in Northern Greece*, 1835

Lear, Edward, *Journal of a Landscape Painter in Greece and Albania*, 1851

Lear, Edward, *Views in the Seven Ionian Islands*, 1863

Leontis, Artemis, *Topographies of Hellenism, Mapping the Homeland*, Ithaca and London, 1995

Leontis, Artemis, ed., *Greece, A Traveller's Literary Companion*, San Francisco, 1997

Levi, Peter, *The Hill of Kronos*, 1980

Liddell, Robert, *Mainland Greece*, Longman, 1965

Lithgow, William, *Rare adventures and painful peregrinations of nineteen years travels through the most eminent places in the habitable world*, 1632

Londo, Bardhyl, "Ithaca", tr. Robert Elsie, in *An Elusive Eagle Soars, Anthology of Modern Albanian Poetry*, Forest Books, London, 1993

Longford, Elizabeth, *Byron's Greece*, HarperCollins, 1975

Louis, Diana Farr, and Marinos, June, *Prospero's Kitchen, Mediterranean Cooking of the Ionian Islands from Corfu to Kythera*, New York, 1995

Lountzis, Nikos, *Zakynthos once upon a time*, Zakynthos, 1990

Makriyannis, General, *Memoirs*, 1907

Mandas, Spiros, *Ta Ipeirotika Gefyria (The Bridges of Epirus)*, Athens, 1984

Manning, Olivia, *Friends and Heroes*, Heinemann, 1965

Manousos, Antonios, *Tragoudia Ethnika*, Corfu, 1850

Marinos, Themistocles, *Me Odigo tin Alithea, Kefalonia, Katochi 1944, Ta Gegonota tis Kefallonias 1944-45*, Athens, 1994

Markoras, Gerasimos, " *Ta Kastra Mas*" (poem)

Marmora, Andrea, *Della historia di Corfu*, 1672

Martin, R. Montgomery, *History of the British Possessions in the Mediterranean: comprising Gibraltar, Malta, Gozo, and the Ionian Islands*, London, 1837

Matesis, Andonios, *O Vassilikos*, ed. Angelos Terzakis, Athens, 2000

Matthews, Kenneth, *Memories of a Mountain War, Greece 1944-1949*, Longman, 1972

Mavilis, Lorentzos, *Apanta*, Athens, 1967

Mavilis, Lorentzos, *Selected Sonnets*, tr. Panos Karagiorgos, The Corfu Reading Society, 2001

Maximus of Tyre, *Orations* (tr. D. Campbell)

Mazower, Mark, *Inside Hitler's Greece, The Experience of Occupation*,

1941-1944, Yale University Press, 1993

Mazower, Mark, *Salonica, City of Ghosts, Christians, Muslims and Jews 1430-1950*, London, HarperCollins, 2004

McNeil, J. R., *The Mountains of the Mediterranean World*, Cambridge, 1992

Merrill, James, *Divine Comedies, Poems by James Merrill*, Oxford, 1977

Meskell, Lynn (ed.), *Archaeology Under Fire: Nationalism, Politics and Heritage in the Eastern Mediterranean and Middle East*, Routledge, 1998

Milionis, Christoforos (ed.), *Ioannina, mia poli sti logotechnio*, Athens, 2002

Milionis, Christoforos, *Kalamas and Acheron*, tr. Marjorie Chambers, Kedros, Athens, 1996.

Miller, Christian, *Greece and the Ionian Islands*, 1821

Miller, Christian, *Travellers of Cefalonia, August 1821*, London, 1822

Miller, Henry, *First Impressions of Greece*, Village Press, London, 1973

Miller, Henry, *The Colossus of Maroussi*, Secker & Warburg, 1941

Miller, William, *Greek Life in Town and Country*, London, 1905

Miller, William, *Greece*, Ernest Benn, 1928

Mitsi, Efterpi, 'Roving Englishwomen': Greece in Women's Travel Writing, Winnipeg, 2002

Moore, Sir Thomas, *Evenings in Greece*, 1826

Moraitis, Erotokritos, *Solomos*, 1999

Morier, David Richard, *Photo the Suliote, A Tale of Modern Greece*, London, 1857

Morier, David Richard, *A Tale of Old Yanina: Photo the Suliote*, edited, adapted and abridged, J. W. Baggally, London, 1951

Morris, Jan, *The Venetian Empire, A Sea Voyage*, Faber, 1980

Moryson, Fynes, *An Itinerary, containing his Ten Years Travel Through the Twelve Dominions of Germany, Bohemia, Switzerland, Netherland, Denmark, Poland, Italy, Turkey, France, England, Scotland and Ireland*, London, 1617

Mousson, Albert, *Ein Besuch auf Korfu und Cefalonien im September 1858*, Zürich, 1859

Moutsan-Martinengou, Elisabeth, *Autobiographia*, Athens, 1997; "My Story", tr. Helen Dendrinou-Kolias, University of Georgia Press, 1989

Murray, John, *A Handbook for Travellers in the Ionian Islands, Greece, Turkey, Asia Minor and Constantinople, 1840*, 5th edn, 1884

Mylona, Zoe, *The Castle of Zakynthos*, Athens, 2006

Nachman, Eftyhia, *Yannina, taxidi sto parelthon*, Talos Press, 1996; "Yannina, A Journey to the Past", Valentine-Mitchell, London (in press)

Nakou, Lilika, *Moscho Tzavella*, Athens, 1995

Napier, Charles James, *Memoir of the Roads of Cefalonia*, 1825

Napier, Charles James, *The Colonies, treating of the Ionian Islands in particular*, 1833

Nicholas, Theresa and Waller, John, *Corfu Sketches, A Thirty Year Journey*, Twickenham, 2008

Nicol, Donald M., *The Despotate of Epiros*, Oxford, 1957

Nicol, Donald M., *The Byzantine Lady, Ten Portraits, 1250-1500*, Cambridge, 1994

Nikolaou, Katerina, *I Thesi tis Gynaikas sti Vyzantini Koinonia* ("The Place of Women in Byzantine Society"), Athens, 1993

Nistazopoulou-Pelikidou, Maria, *Slavikes Engkatastaseis stin Mesaioniki Ellada* ("Slavic Settlements in Medieval Greece"), Athens, 1993

Nucius, Nicander, *The second book of the travels of Nicander Nucius of Corcyra*, ed. and tr. Rev. J. Cramer, 1841

Nugent, Lord, *The Ionian Anthology* (periodical), from 1833

Oakes Smith, Elizabeth, "Ode to Sappho", 1848

Ovid, "Heroic Epistle, XV, Sappho to Phaon", tr. Alexander Pope, 1707

Paizis-Danias, Dimitris I., *Homer's Ithaca on Cephallenia? Facts and fancies in the history of an idea*, Ithacan Friends of Homer, n.d.

Palamas, Kostas, *Poems*, tr. Theodore Stephanides and George Katsimbalis, London, 1925

Papantoniou, Vasileios from Pontic Trebizond; LP, *Avthentika Mikrasiatika*, ACBA Production, Athens, 1980

Papazachos *et al.*, *A Catalogue of Earthquakes in Greece*, University of Thessaloniki, 2000

Partsch, Joseph, *Die Insel Corfu: eine geographische Monographie*, 1887

Partsch, Joseph, *Die Insel Levkas*, 1889

Partsch, Joseph, *Kephallenia und Ithaka, eine geographische Monographie*, 1890

Partsch, Joseph, *Die Insel Zante*, 1891

Payne, John Howard, "Ali Pacha; or, The Signet-Ring: A Melo-Drama, in two acts", London and New York, 1823; also in Cumberland's *British Theatre*, vol. XI, 1826

Percy, William Alexander, *Sappho in Levkas and Other Poems*, New Haven, 1925

Perraivos, Christoforos, *Istoria tou Soulliou kai Pargas* ("History of Suli and Parga"), 1803, 1815, 1857

Pettifer, James, *The Greeks, The Land and People Since the War*, Viking, 1993

Pettifer, James, *Blue Guide to Albania*, London, 1994

Pettifer and Vickers, "The Challenge to Preserve the Cham Heritage", 2002

Philippides, D. (gen. ed.), *Greek Traditional Architecture*, Vol. 1, Eastern Aegean-Sporades-Ionian Islands (includes Corfu and Kythira); Vol. 6, Thessaly-Epirus (includes Metsovo, Ioannina, Zagori), Athens, 1982

Phillips, W. A., *The War of Greek Independence 1821-1833*, London, 1897

Photos, Basil, ed., *Epirus and the Epirotic Muse*, Chicago, 1963

Plaskovitis, Spiros, *The Façade Lady of Corfu*, tr. Amy Mims, Athens, 1995

Plomer, William, *Ali the Lion*, 1936; new ed. as "The Diamond of Janina", 1970

Plutarch, *Lives of the Noble Grecians and Romans Compared Together*, tr. Thomas North, 1579; "Pyrrhus" and "Antony", tr. John Dryden, 1683

Poe, Edgar Allan, "To Zante", 1837

Polylas, Iakovos, *Apanta*, ed. G. Valetas, Athens, 1959

Polylas, Iakovos, "*Ena mikro lathos*", 1891; "The Error", tr. Theodore Sampson, *Modern Greek Short Stories*, Athens, 1980

Potts, Jim, *Corfu Blues*, Ars Interpres, Stockholm, 2006

Poulaki-Katevati, Dionysia, *Cephalonia Before the Earthquake of 1953*, 2003

Pouqueville, F. C. H. L., *Travels in Epirus, Albania, Macedonia and Thessaly*, London, 1820

Pouqueville, F. C. H. L., *Voyage en Grèce*, Paris, 1820-22

Pouqueville, F. C. H. L., *Histoire de la régénération de la Grèce*, Paris, 1824

Pratt, Michael, *Britain's Greek Empire*, Collins,1978

Prineas, Peter, *Katsehamos and the Great Idea*, Sydney, 2006

Psimouli, Vasso, "*Suli kai Suliotes*" ("Suli and Suliots"), Athens, 2006

Puaux, René, *The Sorrows of Epirus*, Hurst and Blackwell, 1918

Pylarinos, Theodosis, *Kerkyra, Mia Poli sti Logotechnia*, Athens, 2003

Ravanis, George D., *Byron in Cephalonia*, tr. Helen Cosmetatos, 2nd edn, Argostoli, 2003

Region of Epirus, *History and Culture of Epirus*, Athens, 2007

Region of the Ionian Islands, *History and Culture of the Ionian Islands*, Athens, 2007

Rennell, J. R., Homer's *Ithaca: A Vindication of Tradition*, Arnold, 1927

Rice, David Talbot, *Byzantine Art*, Oxford, 1935; Penguin, 1962

Richards, Theophilus (?), ed., *The Life of Ali Pacha, of Jannina, Late Vizier of Epirus*, 2nd edn, 1823

Ricks, David, *Modern Greek Writing*, Peter Owen, 2003

Robinson, Mary, *Sappho and Phaon*, 1796

Romas, Dionysios, *Ta Zakynthina*, Athens, 1957

Rosen, Billi, *Andi's War*, Faber, 1988

Runciman, Steven, *Byzantine Civilization*, Edward Arnold, 1933

Runciman, Steven, *The Fall of Constantinople 1453*, Cambridge, 1965

Runciman, Steven, *Byzantine Style and Civilization*, Penguin, 1975

Rusten, Jeffrey, *Four Ways to Hate Corcyra*, www.arts.cornell.edu

Salmon, Tim, *The Unwritten Places*, Lycabettus Press, Athens, 1995

Salmon, Tim, *The Mountains of Greece, Trekking in the Pindhos Mountains*, 2006

Salvator, Archduke Ludwig, *Zante*, Prague, 1904

Salvator, Archduke Ludwig, *Paxos und Antipaxos*, Würzburg and Vienna, 1897; Greek tr. Anastasios Mitsialis, Athens, 1906

Salvator, Archduke Ludwig, *Anmerkungen über Levkas*, Prague, 1908

Sandes, Flora, *An English Woman-Sergeant in the Serbian Army*, 1916

Sandys, George, *A Relation of a Journey begun in An:Dom: 1610*, London, 1670

Santas, Constantine, *Aristotelis Valaoritis*, Boston, 1976

Sarafis, Stefanos, *ELAS: Greek Resistance Army*, Merlin Press, 1980 (original edn, Athens, 1946)

Schmidt, Bernhard, *Die Insel Zakynthos: Erlebtes und Erforschtes*, Freiburg, 1899

Schminck-Gustavus, Christoph U., *Mnimes Katochis*, Vol. 1, Ioannina, 2007; Vol. 2, Ioannina, 2008

Seferis, George, "Kalvos", in *Dokimes*, Vol. 2, 1960

Severin, Tim, *The Ulysses Voyage: Sea Search for the Odyssey*, Hutchinson, 1987

Sherrard, P, ed., *Edward Lear, The Corfu Years*, Athens-Dedham, 1988

Sikelianos, Angelos, *Selected Poems*, tr. Edmund Keeley and Philip Sherrard, Princeton University Press, 1979

Sikelianos, Angelos, *Apanta, Lyrikos Vios, 1-6*, Ikaros, Athens, 1980

Slattery, Luke, *Dating Aphrodite, modern adventures in the ancient world*, ABC Books, Sydney, 2005

Solomos, Dionysius, *Apanta*, ed. Linos Politis, Athens, 1948

Sordinas, Augustinos, "Old Olive Mills and Presses on the Island of Corfu, Greece", Memphis State University Anthropological Research Centre Occasional Papers No. 5, 1971

Sourtzinos, Giorgios, *Toponymia tis Kerkyras*, Corfu, 2006

Spetsieri-Choremi, Alkestis, *Ancient Kerkyra*, 2nd edn, Athens, 1997

Stamatopoulos, Nondas, *Old Corfu, History and Culture*, 2nd edn, 1978

Stamatopoulou, Charoula, *Greek Traditional Architecture, Zagori*, tr. Philip Ramp, Athens, 1988

Stephanides, Theodore, *The Golden Age*, Fortune Press, 1965

Stewart, Mary, *This Rough Magic*, Hodder & Stoughton, 1964

Storace, Patricia, *Dinner with Persephone*, Granta, 1996

Strabo, *The Geography of Strabo*, ed. and tr. H. L. Jones, Loeb Classical Library, 1927

Strani-Potts, Maria, *The Cat of Portovecchio, Corfu Tales*, Brandl & Schlesinger, Blackheath, Sydney, 2007

Strani-Potts, Maria, "*To Poulima tis Panoreas*", CorfuBooks.com, 2008 (abridged version in English, "The Pimping of Panorea", ISLAND magazine, Corfu, August 2008)

Suetonius, *The Lives of the Twelve Caesars*, tr. J. C. Rolfe, Loeb Classical Library, 1913

Swinburne, Algernon Charles, *The Collected Poetical Works*, Heinemann, 1917

Talianis, D., *Vitsa, Zagori*, Topio Publications, 2004

Tennant, Emma, *A House in Corfu*, Jonathan Cape, 2001

Theodossopoulos, Dimitrios, *Trouble with Turtles, Cultural Understandings of the Environment on a Greek Island*, New York and Oxford, 2003

Theotokis, Konstantinos, "*Pistoma!*" and "*Zoi tou Horiou*" in *Diigimata (Korfiatikes Istories)*, Corfu, 1935

Theotokis, Konstantinos, "Face Down!" ("*Pistoma!*"), tr. Theodore Sampson, *Modern Greek Short Stories*, Athens, 1980

Thucydides, *The Peloponnesian War*, tr. Rex Warner, Penguin, 1954

Todorova, Maria, *Imagining the Balkans*, Oxford, 1997

Travlantonis, Andonis, "*Ta Christouyenna tou Amerikanou*" ("The Christmas of the American"), Corfu, 1901

Trelawny, Edward, *Records of Shelley, Byron, and the Author*, London, 1878

Tsigakou, Fani-Maria, *The Rediscovery of Greece*, London and Athens, 1981

Tsimaratos, Evangelos, *Poia I Omiriki Ithaki?* Athens, 1998

Tsonis, Panagiotis A. and Tsonis, Anastasios A., *Kyra-Frosini*, Nostos, 2008

Tziovas, Frixios, " *Ta Magia*" in *Exodos Yia Panta*, Ioannina, 1991

Valaoritis, Aristotle, *Apanta: "Samuel", "Kyra Phrosini", "Thanasis Vaghias", "I Figi", "Athanasios Diakos", "Foteinos", " O Vrachos kai to Kima", "O Lefkatas"*

Vanges, Peter, *Kythera, a History*, Kytherian Brotherhood of Australia, Sydney, 1993

Vasmer, Max, *Die Slaven in Griechenland*, Berlin, 1941

Venezis, Ilias, essay on Lefkas, 1973, tr. A. Cadbury, 1997

Vilaras, Ioannis, *Apanta*, Athens

Vinci, Felice, *The Baltic Origins of Homer's Epic Tales, the Iliad, the Odyssey, and the Migration of Myth*, Rochester, 2006

Vokotopoulos, Panayiotis, *Eikones tis Kerkyras* ("Icons of Corfu"), Athens, 1990

Vokotopoulou, Ioulia, Vitsa, *Ta nekrotafia mias molossikis komis*("Vitsa, the Cemeteries of a Molossian Settlement"), 3 vols., Athens, 1986

Voutepsis, Y., *Synagonistis Akelas* ("Comrade Akelas")

Wace, A. J. and Thompson, M. S., *Nomads of the Balkans, An Account of Life and Customs among the Vlachs of Northern Pindus*, 1914

Waller, John, *Greek Walls, An Odyssey in Corfu*, Yiannis Books, 2004

Waller, John, *Corfu Sunset, Avrio Never Comes*, Yiannis Books, 2005

Ward, Philip, *Albania*, Cambridge, 1983

Warner, Rex, *Men of Athens*, Bodley Head, 1972

Wharton, Edith, *The Cruise of the Vanadis*, Bloomsbury, 2004

Wheeler, William, *The Letters of Private Wheeler, 1809-1828*, ed. B. H. Liddell Hart, Michael Joseph, 1951

Wheler, George, *A Journey into Greece by George Wheler Esq; in company of Dr. Spon of Lyons*, 1682

Whincop, Thomas, *Scanderbeg: or, Love and Liberty*, 1747

Woodhouse, C. M., *The Apple of Discord, a Survey of recent Greek politics in their international setting*, Hutchinson, 1948

Woodhouse, C. M., *The Story of Modern Greece*, Faber, 1968

Woodhouse, C. M., *The Philhellenes*, Hodder & Stoughton, 1969

Woodhouse, C. M., *Something Ventured*, Granada, 1982

Woolf, Virginia, *Travels with Virginia Woolf*, ed. Jan Morris, Hogarth Press, 1993

Wordsworth, Christopher, *Greece, Pictorial, Descriptive and Historical*, 1839

Wright, Waller Rodwell, "Horae Ionicae", 1809

Xenopoulos, Grigorios, *"Nostimon Imar"* and *"O Typos kai i Ousia"*, in *Apanta*, vol. 10

Xyndas, Spiridion, *O Ipopsifios* opera ("The Parliamentary Candidate"), Corfu, 1867

Young, Martin, *The Traveller's Guide to Corfu and the Other Ionian Islands*, Jonathan Cape, 1977

ARTICLES

Alhadeff, Gini, "Paxos/Hero Worship" in "Temptation Islands", Travel + Leisure website

Bowen, George, "Ionian Administration", *Quarterly Review*, vol. 91, Sept. 1852

"Brave Women", *The New York Times*, 8 February 1880

Castlemain, Amanda, *Athens News*, 20 June 2003

Cicellis, Kay, "Cephalonia The First"", in *Descant* XVIII, Contemporary Greek Literature issue, vol. 8, no. 2, 1977 (originally published in *Die griechischen Inseln*, ed. Evi Mylonas, Köln, 1976)

de Bernières, Louis, "How I learned to love Greece again", *The Observer*, 20 March 2005

Durrell, Gerald, "Impressions in the Sand: Corfu", *Sunday Times* Colour Magazine, 1987

Durrell, Lawrence, "Oil for the Saint; Return to Corfu", *Holiday*, Philadelphia, October, 1966; reprinted in Durrell, L., *Spirit of Place, Letters and Essays on Travel*, Faber, 1969

Ellingham, Mark, "Look back in Agni", *The Guardian*, 13 September 2008

Fokas, Nikos, *Mondo Greco*, Fall 2002

Furlong, Edward, "Where did Odysseus Go?" CBC Radio Documentary, 5 & 6 Nov. 1984

Gage, Eleni N., "Corfu/ Siren Song" in "Temptation Islands", Travel + Leisure website, August 2004

Gallant, Thomas W., "Honor, Masculinity, and Ritual Knife Fighting in Nineteenth Century Greece", *The American Historical Association*, 2000

Government *Gazette*, Corfu, no. 575, 29 December 1841

Hoban, Russell, "One Less Octopus at Paxos", Observations, *Granta Magazine*, *c.*1987-8

Ikonomopoulos, Marcia Haddad, "Remembering the Jews of Corfu", www.sefarad.org/publication

Isufi, Hajredin, "Aspects of Islamization in Camëri", *Historical Studies (Studime Historike)*, issue 34, 2004

Kardamis, Kostas, "Nobile Teatro di San Giacomo di Corfù: an overview of its significance for the Greek *ottocento*", paper in the *XI Convegno Annuale di Società Italiana di Musicologia* (Lecce, 22–24/10/ 2004), published in the *Donizetti Society Newsletter* 99 (October 2006)

Kourkoumelis, Nikos, *"To Diazigio tou Protou Gamou tou Markou Botsari"*, Bulletin of the Corfu Reading Society, no. 19, 1982

Krystallis, Kostas, "Easter in the Pindus", *Echo of Athens*, 1892

Martin, Sébastien, "Les vacanciers britanniques, champions de l'incivilité?" *Le Figaro*, 14 August 2008

Montague, B. and Gadher, D., "Boozy Brits—it's the last straw", *Sunday Times*, 17 August 2008

Mullen, William, "The Oddity of Homer: Did Odysseus set sail in Scandinavia?" in Culture + Travel (The Europe Issue, May/June 2008)

Paphitis, N., in *Athens News*, 13-19 June 2008

Selbourne, David, "Club Yob", *Sunday Times* News Review, 19 August 1990

Smith, Helena, *Guardian*, 26 September 2008

Strani-Potts, Maria, "The Pimping of Panorea", ISLAND magazine, Corfu, August 2008

Tomalin, Nicholas, "Mess stops here", *Sunday Times*, 12 December 1972

Venezis, Ilias, essay on Lefkas in Artemis Leontis (ed.), *Greece, A Traveler's Literary Companion*, San Francisco, 1997

Vickers, Miranda "The Cham Issue, Albanian National & Property Claims in Greece", G109, Conflict Studies Research Centre, April 2002

Vickers, Miranda and Pettifer, James, "The Challenge to Preserve the Cham Heritage", websites of the Albanian American Civic League, and PDI (www.pdi-al.com/evidence.html)

Vickers, Miranda, "The Cham Issue: Where to Now?" Balkans Series, Conflict Studies Research Centre, January 2007

Whyles, Paul, "Corfu: An Idyll... or a dump?" in *The Corfiot*, November 2008

Index of Literary & Historical Names

Index of Places & Landmarks